Reckless Devotion

365 Days of Inspiration

ROLLAND & HEIDI BAKER

RIVER

PUBLISHING

River Publishing & Media Ltd
Barham Court
Teston
Maidstone
Kent
ME18 5BZ
United Kingdom

info@river-publishing.co.uk

ISBN 978-1-908393-41-8
Printed in the United Kingdom

Jars of Clay

But we have this treasure in jars of clay to show that this all-surpassing power is from God and not from us.
2 Corinthians 4:7

Simple jars of clay are formed in the dust and the dirt and used in the business of life. They aren't beautiful; they don't stand out as unusual on the outside; it's what they hold inside that is of real value.

In spiritual terms, we are these little jars of clay. All I really am is a little person, sitting in the dirt, just loving my Lord Jesus with reckless devotion. On the outside, I am small and unremarkable, with not much to show for myself. But on the inside, it's a whole other story.

I'm made to carry the all-surpassing power of the One whom I love so deeply, and the good news is, so are you!

The treasure that fills me, making my heart overflow into the world around me, comes from God and not from me. I am nothing; He is everything. He made us to be receptacles for His glory, His love, His compassion, His grace and His mercy. All He wants is a place to inhabit.

"Do not get drunk on wine, which leads to debauchery. Instead, be filled with the Spirit" (Ephesians 5:18). When God fills us with His Holy Spirit, we are filled with love. He desires to pour Himself out through our lives, our jars of clay, into His world, which aches for Him. His all-surpassing power is given to us, not so we can hoard it for ourselves, storing it in a darkened room somewhere, from which it trickles out in small quantities. It is given to us to be splashed out in the light, for the joy of all people everywhere.

We can't love God's way without being filled with Him. If we try it on our own, we end up exhausted and burned out. I've done it; it doesn't work. Only when we let His love pour into us and let it spill out from deep within us will His Kingdom come and His will be done on earth as it is in heaven.

Reshaped Vessels

Then the word of the LORD came to me. He said, "Can I not do with you, Israel, as this potter does?" declares the LORD. "Like clay in the hand of the potter, so are you in my hand."
Jeremiah 18:5–6

God wants to reshape us into vessels that will hold more of His glory. He wants us to understand how different life can be when we are filled and poured out again and again.

For 26 years, we were missionaries, doing our best to serve the people around us. We thought we were doing it right. As we laboured and worked and toiled for the Lord, getting more and more burned out, we honestly thought that was how it would always be. Looking back now, I now know we were bound to a false belief system that said, "If I'm working for God, I have to be cracked and dry, pushed to the edge and always miserable." It's a lie, but it's how we lived for years.

That was, until God broke in, pouring His sweet Holy Spirit into us. He reshaped us on His potter's wheel, lovingly reworking us so our hearts overflowed with life and energy and love and power. We understood for the first time how the love of the Lord completely transforms a life so that it becomes like His own. We began to see miracles and signs and wonders, and our love and compassion increased. It was like someone had switched on a huge light, and we would never be in the dark again!

Now we are compelled to love those we serve through a love for God that never runs dry. Why? It is His Holy Spirit who fills our jars of clay, and all we do comes from Him. We know the love of God lives in us, not because we deserve it, not because we are better than anyone else, but because of His beautiful Holy Spirit. As we have let Him reshape us —moving away from thinking it's all about us to letting it be all about Him—His presence in and around us has multiplied.

Our cry is now, "He must become greater; I must become less" (John 3:30).

Filled With Possibility

For nothing will be impossible with God.
Luke 1:37, NASB

Jesus loves us so much that He will never keep us small. In Him, absolutely nothing is impossible: There are no limits!

Luke 1:37 is part of the angel's announcement to Mary that her old cousin, Elizabeth, who was well past her childbearing days, was six months pregnant with a boy who would become John the Baptist, Jesus' cousin. If that wasn't enough, Mary also had to come to terms with the declaration that she was about to conceive by the Holy Spirit and would give birth nine months later to the Son of God.

That's some news!

God doesn't have a problem with making possible what we think is impossible. He loves to shake us up, out of our small-minded thinking, and free us from doubts about this thing or that thing. He loves to blast through our assumption that, somehow, if it can't be done in earthly terms, it can't be done at all.

Remember, He loves to reshape us. He speaks truth where we've believed lies.

- You think He can't change you? He can.
- You think you have gone too far down to be rescued? You haven't.
- You think you're too old now? You're not.
- You think you have to wait until you're older? You don't.
- Nothing is impossible with Him. It's His love that changes everything.

Here's some news for you: Without Him, you'll never be good enough. I'll never be good enough. We are nothing without our God. He takes our little lives, laid down at His feet in the dirt, and He wrecks us with His love. When we see Him in all His beauty and let Him reshape us and fill us with His Holy Spirit, we no longer look at our failures and faults, because our eyes are drawn to see only Him.

Unless He fills me, everything is impossible.

When He fills me, nothing is impossible!

Good Purpose

*For it is God who works in you to will and to act
in order to fulfill his good purpose.*
Philippians 2:13

Wherever He went, Jesus fulfilled the good purpose of His Father. The gospels are packed with miracles and signs and wonders that show what happens when love breaks in and changes everything.

In Gethsemane, when Jesus prayed, "Not my will, but yours be done" (Luke 22:42), He was giving God permission to work in Him to fulfill His good purpose. It took Him to the cross, into death and out again into glorious resurrection power. Now nothing can separate us from God's love (see Romans 8:38–39).

I have so many stories I could tell you. Miracles I have seen that have blown me away. Beautiful face-to-face encounters between God and His loved ones. I have watched in wonder as the Holy Spirit unblocked deaf ears and opened blind eyes. I have seen the lame walk again and watched food miraculously appear to feed the hungry crowds all around us.

He is so wonderful!

I never want to get in the way of God's glory. I never want to take my eyes off Him—not for one second. He is the one with good purpose. It's all about His love, and all I do is tuck myself under His wings, nestling in as close as I can and offering my life as a jar of clay to be filled.

It's a privilege and a joy to say yes to God and invite Him to come and work in me to fulfill His good purpose. Why does He use me? Is it because I have degrees and can speak different languages? No. All God wants is my laid-down love, my reckless devotion. He wants me to sacrifice my own pride and fall completely in love with Him.

He is asking the same from you. Is it time to reorder your priorities?

"What is more, I consider everything a loss compared to the surpassing greatness of knowing Christ Jesus my Lord, for whose sake I have lost all things. I consider them garbage, that I may gain Christ" (Philippians 3:8).

Undone

And this is my prayer: that your love may abound more and more in
knowledge and depth of insight.
Philippians 1:9

I'm sure people sometimes think, I wish Heidi would get a grip. Why does
she cry so much? What's with the laughing? Can't she just calm down?

When I am talking to a room full of Christians who are more familiar with
the typical preaching style—leaning on a lectern and delivering a three-point
sermon—I know I'm difficult to understand. A lot of churches prefer to have
the preacher stand up, not lie on the floor. I know it can be irritating for
some, and I used to apologize for doing it.

But I don't any more.

Because I really don't want to get a grip! I want to contend to be undone! If I
didn't, I wouldn't be able to handle my schedule or the demands on my time.
I don't want to conform to any expectation of me as a preacher that distracts
me from being totally united with Christ. If that means lying on the floor, I'll
lie on the floor.

What does it mean to contend to be undone?

When Paul wrote his letter to the Philippians, his prayer was that their love
would increase. Read the verse above. It is not just a theological statement; it's
a heart cry. Paul longed for the believers in Philippi to fall deeper and deeper
in love with the Lord so that they would know an increase in knowledge and
depth of insight.

Let's ask ourselves, have we given ourselves so completely to Christ that we
can say we are abounding in love? Do we love Him with reckless devotion?
Are we growing into more and more understanding of Him?

Do we need to go lower? Is it time to risk the judgment of others in the
pursuit of His beautiful face? Are you ready to fall on your knees, your face,
and contend to be undone?

You can do that right now. He's waiting for you.

Going Where He Goes

But Ruth replied, "Don't urge me to leave you or to turn back from you.
Where you go I will go, and where you stay I will stay. Your people will be
my people and your God my God."
Ruth 1:16

When Naomi was left destitute after the deaths of her husband and two sons, she told her two daughters-in-law to go back to their own country so they could each find another husband. One went back, but the other, Ruth, clung to Naomi, determined to remain at her side. This devotion positioned Ruth into the genealogy of Jesus. How's that for a destiny?

At times, it's easier to go for the safe option. We may feel insecure stepping out into unfamiliar places, and we may be tempted to keep our Christian faith as it always has been—not really rocking the boat and living on yesterday's manna. Have you ever felt like that?

But there is so much more!

When you tell the Lord you will go with Him wherever He goes, He takes you at your word. When you devote your life to the pursuit of His presence at the cost of everything else, even family and friends, He will lead you into an adventure beyond your wildest imaginings. When you go where He goes, you position yourself in the line of glory!

I would never go back to being safe, not for one second. I know not everyone will do what we do, but my question to you is this: Will you give yourself wholeheartedly in devotion to the one who is love? Will you let the fragrance of the Holy Spirit so fill you that you deposit Him everywhere you go—even at the gas station and the hotel check-out desk and the baseball game? Will you choose to live your life to honor and glorify the King of kings? Will you lay down your life as an offering to the one who laid down His life for you?

"He made himself nothing by taking the very nature of a servant, being made in human likeness" (Philippians 2:7).

Come Closer

- Are you ready to be filled with more of His love?

- Have you been aching, deep in your heart, for an adventure with Jesus?

- Are you tired of doing the same thing?

- Have you been asking yourself, Is this all there is?

Right now, the Holy Spirit wants to lead you into a fresh encounter with the love of God.

In the Sermon on the Mount, Jesus talked to the multitude about many things related to our relationships with God and other people. About our relationship with God, He said, "Ask and it will be given to you; seek and you will find; knock and the door will be opened to you. For everyone who asks receives; the one who seeks finds; and to the one who knocks, the door will be opened" (Matthew 7:7–8).

He is calling us to trust Him that when we ask for what we want, we will have it.

Sometimes we fear that if we ask God for more, we won't get it. Maybe we think we aren't good enough or don't deserve it. These words of Jesus say the exact opposite. They invite us to approach Him with courage and faith.

God will never say, "Go away!" He will always say, "Come closer."

Will you pray with me?

Lord, I am coming closer to You. I know You accept me for who I am, and I know You know all about me. I am tired of the old religion that keeps me bound to rules and regulations and the fear of judgment from others. I am a simple jar of clay, empty but waiting to be filled now with Your Holy Spirit. I ask You to pour Yourself into me. I am ready to be undone! Thank You, Lord. Amen.

Lower Still

I have found that, just when I think I have surrendered my all to the Lord, He gently, graciously, uncovers a new layer of resistance in me that even I didn't know was there. For a few years now, I have preached a message I call "Lower Still." This sums up the process of Jesus tenderly shaping, patiently reshaping, and then gloriously filling our lives with Himself. Do we think we have humbled ourselves and surrendered everything to Him? We can still go lower; there is still more for us to give up.

Surrendering everything to Jesus sounds risky, like it could be painful, difficult, demanding. Many ask, "If I completely surrender to Him, with reckless devotion, will I still be me?"

Here is what I have found to be true. Yes, it's risky, but the reward vastly outweighs the risk. Yes, it can be painful, difficult and demanding, but the joy and all-surpassing peace that Jesus gives can hardly be compared to such fleeting inconveniences.

Most of all, Jesus doesn't rob you of being you. You don't somehow become less than yourself because Jesus' presence is larger in you. It's just the opposite; the more you surrender to Him, the more you become who Father always intended you to be. This is all part of God's upside economy, which defies the narrow-minded, one-dimensional, limited wisdom of human thinking. In choosing to become nothing, we become everything we were ever meant to be.

As always, Jesus is our model. He made Himself as nothing so His Father might be fully glorified through Him. In Philippians, Paul urges us to imitate Jesus' humility:

If you have any encouragement from being united with Christ, if any comfort from his love, if any common sharing in the Spirit, if any tenderness and compassion, then make my joy complete by being like-minded, having the same love, being one in spirit and of one mind. Do nothing out of selfish ambition or vain conceit. Rather, in humility value others above yourselves, not looking to your own interests but each of you to the interests of the others. Philippians 2:1–4

As we do this, we'll not only find our purpose in Jesus' Kingdom; we'll also truly find ourselves.

Beholding and Becoming

Implicit in Paul's encouragement in Philippians 2 is a question: Have you so surrendered your life to Him that you are united with Christ? He spells out just two of the countless benefits of being united with Jesus: the comfort of His love and His tenderness and compassion. Then he urges us to express those same attributes of Christ to others—to allow what we have been filled with to spill out everywhere and touch the lives of others, to consider the interests of others above our own.

It's reasonable to expect that if we are united with Christ, then we will be Christlike. Sometimes we fail to be as Christ-like as we think we should be, and this disappoints us. We get discouraged; we fail to see how we are becoming more like Jesus. Why is this? Does it mean we're not really Christians? No!

Our disappointment with ourselves is really based on faulty theology. We are disappointed when our expectations for ourselves are not met. We are discouraged when we think we haven't met God's expectations for us. But this is performance-based thinking. At its root lies the belief that we have to earn our way into Father's favor by the things we do. We don't. God's gift to us is all grace, freely given. We can't earn it; we can't work for it.

As I write, I know you know this. But we so easily fall into the trap of performance. Subtly, we slip back into the old habits of self-effort and self-reliance.

Rather than being purpose-driven, I prefer to be presence-centered. All our efforts in God's Kingdom must originate from the place of rest, the place of His presence. They must flow from the realization that even if we did nothing but sit in a cave and pray for the rest of our lives, He would love us no less than He does now.

Graham Cooke calls this process "beholding and becoming." The more time we spend in God's presence, simply beholding His beauty, the more Christ-like we will become and the more we will be motivated to "spill out" all He is pouring into us.

Inside Out

*...In humility value others above yourselves, not looking to your own
interests but each of you to the interests of the others.*
Philippians 2:3–4

Something interesting happens when we begin to place a greater value on the
needs of others than on our own. Something supernatural. As we give out
to others, Father God fills us with more. As we invest ourselves in meeting
the needs of others, Father God meets our needs. As we reach out and touch
someone with love, Father God touches us afresh with His love. It creates a
virtuous circle.

In Romans 15, Paul prays, "I pray that God, the source of hope, will fill
you completely with joy and peace because you trust in him. Then you will
overflow with confident hope through the power of the Holy Spirit" (Romans
15:13, NLT).

I have found that when I focus on me and my needs, my inner spiritual life
begins to shrink. When I look outward, becoming focused on the needs of
others, it begins to grow. Healing happens. Peace increases. Hope overflows.
As we look away from ourselves, the inside-out process of transformation
into greater Christlikeness is accelerated.

We may feel far from complete in our spiritual maturity, but when we dare
to express the love of God to others, regardless of ourselves, miracles can
happen. God takes our sacrifice and multiplies it. He takes the little we can
offer and makes it into something extraordinary. And in the doing, He shapes
us to be a little more like Jesus.

Paul says the outflow of the Spirit in our lives will result in "tenderness and
compassion." Do we allow that tenderness and compassion to be expressed
to others, no matter where we are? Are we tender to others at Walmart? Are
we compassionate at Ruby's? Does the fragrance of Christ flow from us when
we stop to get gas?

As we cooperate with the Holy Spirit inside us, we will notice His influence
flowing out of us into the ordinary situations of life. His love is expressed
in the routine, unremarkable moments—not just on special occasions.
And as we share His love with others, day by day, we are healed, changed,
transformed, grown.

Hunger

One morning I woke up, and I was really hungry. Sometimes my days are so busy that I don't have time to eat breakfast. This day was one of those days. Is it much of a cost to miss breakfast, lunch or dinner when people around me need a touch from God? No, it's not much of a price to pay. But I'm still just a jar of clay, and this day I was a hungry jar!

I felt God say to me, "Lower still." He was asking me to reach out with His love, and yes, it was going to cost me. That week it cost me breakfast—not once, but every day. But guess what? My eyes are set on becoming "like-minded" and "having the same love" (Philippians 2:2). I want to share the love of Jesus with everyone. As I do, He fills me; He satisfies my soul. He feeds me, and the hunger is gone.

My prayer for you is that you will learn how to be like-minded. I pray you will have the same love Jesus has for others, the same tenderness and compassion, the same selflessness and a growing desire to reach out.

Paul encourages us to do nothing out of selfish ambition. We are called to live so deeply inside the heart of Jesus that we feel and move in rhythm with the very heartbeat of the Father. So deeply that we do not just understand how He feels about every person, but we begin to feel how He feels about them. So deeply that our lives are totally given over to Him. So deeply that we become more concerned with the needs He desires to touch than with our own needs and wants.

In Jesus' presence, "I want... I need..." becomes irrelevant. Overtaken with His glory, we begin to say, "What do You want, Lord?" As we turn to meet the needs on His heart, we no longer care whether our own needs are met or not. But our Father is an abundant, generous, overwhelmingly gracious Father. As we understand His heart, He pours more of Himself into us.

I have been hungry, but I want to learn a deeper spiritual hunger yet.

Live Full, Die Empty

When God our Savior revealed his kindness and love, he saved us, not because of the righteous things we had done, but because of his mercy. He washed away our sins, giving us a new birth and new life through the Holy Spirit. He generously poured out the Spirit upon us through Jesus Christ our Savior.
Titus 3:4–6, NLT

Whenever I'm ministering to others on the streets or in the bush, I speak about how Jesus constantly emptied Himself out for others. He modeled so well the life we are to live. He poured His life out so that others might live.

I've heard it said that we are to "live full and die empty." We don't want to pass into glory having held onto what Jesus has put inside us. We must share it. The Bible says the Holy Spirit is placed within us as a deposit, guaranteeing eternal life. Father God has invested a part of Himself in us. He wants to see that investment come to fruition, to multiply and expand.

I want to reach the end of my life having expended every ounce of that which Jesus has poured into me. Not through striving or self-effort. But I want to do it from the place of His presence, having shared His love with others as lavishly as He has shared it with me. I want to be a leaky vessel—always spilling His love everywhere I go so that other thirsty souls can drink.

"For I will pour out water to quench your thirst and to irrigate your parched fields. And I will pour out my Spirit on your descendants, and my blessing on your children" (Isaiah 44:3, NLT).

On our journey, we are learning to imitate Jesus. We are learning to love as He loved. And as we keep loving, He will keep putting in front of us those who desperately need His love. Then we will find the following to be true of us: "The more you grow like this, the more productive and useful you will be in your knowledge of our Lord Jesus Christ" (2 Peter 1:8, NLT).

One

Recently God gave me insight into the depth of His love for each of us as individuals. He showed me a glimpse of what He felt. He broke my heart over just one small child, when we have over two thousand in our care.

This particular kid had behaved very badly, treated others despicably, and then run away from the compound. The world might say, "Forget him; so many other kids need your help, good kids who appreciate it." God doesn't think this way.

Father God filled me with so much compassion for this kid that I couldn't contain it. It was as though a veil was drawn back, and I was exposed to the searing heat of God's passion for this boy. He cared about him intensely—so much that it's impossible to adequately express it in words. For the next six months, His compassion for this boy consumed me, and I could think of nothing else.

Day after day, I literally searched the streets, looking for this one child. This went on for months until, one day, there he was. I was struck again by the kindness and mercy of our Father that causes Him to pour Himself out just to bring one sinner home.

We have been privileged to see meetings where thousands at a time have given their hearts to Jesus. That is amazing, an awesome spectacle. But Father reminds us that He saves one soul at a time. He is always interested in the one. We long to see God's power and glory, the miraculous and supernatural breaking into the temporal. But let's not forget the one. Don't forget the one next to you—the person to whom you can be Jesus' hands of compassion. In God's economy, the person who just reaches out to one and sees that one find grace is just as important as the evangelist who leads thousands to Christ.

"God showed how much he loved us by sending his one and only Son into the world so that we might have eternal life through him. This is real love—not that we loved God, but that he loved us and sent his Son as a sacrifice to take away our sins." (1 John 4:9–10, NLT)

Come Closer

• Are any areas of your life still off-limits to Father God? Allow yourself an honest examination. He is jealous for your love and wants to love you completely!

• Allow Jesus access to your life so He can remove another "layer" of the superficial. Take another step closer to complete transparency with Him

• The more time we spend in God's presence, simply beholding His beauty, the more Christ-like we will become. Set aside regular, special time for doing nothing other than being alone with Him.

God created us for a purpose. That purpose is to love—to lay down our lives for love. He is the primary focus of our love. As we press into Him, day after day, hour by hour, with reckless devotion, He fills our clay jar with His love. Then He places in front of us person after person after person—each needing a touch from Him. All we have to do is love each one with His love. That is our calling, our destiny; it is the cost of love. Let's pray:

Lord Jesus, I see that I have held back parts of me from You for many different reasons. Today, Lord, I open my heart to You fully and surrender. Help me to see, Lord, that I am only fully me when I allow You to be fully You in me! Have Your way in my life, Lord Jesus. Fill me to overflowing with Your love so that it can constantly spill out and touch the lives of others—even as I go about the ordinary, everyday tasks. Amen.

Clean Conscience

Just think how much more the blood of Christ will purify our consciences from sinful deeds so that we can worship the living God.
Hebrews 9:14, NLT

Holiness means never doing or saying anything, even in our most private and intimate times with other people—spouse, parents, siblings, best friends—that could bring reproach to the Gospel. It means never doing anything that could potentially scare away the gentle dove of the Holy Spirit, causing Him to draw back from us.

Holiness is when every act we do holds up to investigation by anyone. Holiness means every thought and conversation we have, every email or text we send, every interaction with others and everything we do when we're alone would stand up to public scrutiny if it were broadcast to everyone in the world.

Imagine the freedom of having such a pure conscience that you didn't mind any aspect of your life being revealed to or discovered by others. Imagine being constantly lighthearted because you had absolutely nothing to hide.

Probably some who have been Christians for years still do not look forward to judgment day! However, when we allow the Holy Spirit access to our inner lives, in full surrender to Him, He purifies our consciences. Jesus has provided full and complete atonement for our sin, but He also wants to cleanse us from guilt, shame, rejection and the many other after-effects of sin.

We can't cleanse ourselves, but we can be supernaturally purified. We can't go back and fix or undo the wrong things we have done in the past—but Jesus can cleanse our consciences and bring His amazing peace to restore and renew us. This is the great prize of the Christian life—more than healing, wealth or any other blessing God can give us. A totally clean conscience makes us totally unafraid to approach a holy God. All you need to do today is come to Him, confess any sin and receive His forgiveness. Now ask Him to cleanse your conscience, and enter a new place of freedom.

Good Day

A few years ago, I finally realized—after many years of missionary work and ten years of studying theology—that in the Kingdom of God there is no such thing as a bad day. Just think about the implications of that for a moment.

Some people think they have the right to have a bad day. Once, after a conference in the U.S., someone emailed me to say, "I don't have to be happy, and you can't make me! I'm going to get to heaven just the way I am!"

For years I was so serious about everything, so concerned about being theologically correct that I would be anxious before speaking a message. I worked really hard to make sure I was delivering a well-researched, biblically sound exegesis.

Surpresa Sithole, IRIS's Ministries National Director, is one of the people who changed my mind. One day we were running a bush outreach meeting in Malawi, and on this day, Surpresa delivered what was, for me, his most memorable sermon.

Malawi had been in famine most of the year. The crops had failed. It was extremely hot, 120 degrees or so. The people hadn't had any proper food in months. A lot of people were sick, and the bubonic plague had just come to this particular village. Surpresa's sermon that day was entitled "How to Have a Good Day"!

No matter where we are or how bleak the circumstances, Surpresa is always having the best day of his life. Irrepressible joy like this culturally clashes with much of the church. I didn't like it myself for a long time.

What I've learned, though, is that we minister to others out of the places in our lives where God has ministered to us. God works in us to produce a miracle, and we minister that miracle to others. God has given Surpresa the gift of joy. When he ministers, the Lord uses this joy, supernaturally, to touch others. Some might think it inappropriate. Actually, it is entirely appropriate. He is bringing an authentic expression of joy to those who have none, and Jesus is producing joy in them. Think about what Jesus has done in your life and how you can express it to others, sharing His blessing.

Being There

My Presence will go with you, and I will give you rest.
Exodus 33:14

We can feel compassion for others and be free to do something about it only to the extent that we ourselves are free and taken care of. When we know we are loved and we know we are secure in Jesus, then we can pour ourselves out into the lives of others, knowing Father God will take care of all our needs and we have nothing to fear.

Out of the place of dwelling in God's presence, we have amazing, powerful, supernatural resources to bring into any situation in which we find ourselves. This means that even on the roughest of days, we can still be a positive answer to someone's need or situation—just by bringing and being ourselves.

Understanding this truth changes the essence of mission. Yes, we warn people that they could perish without Christ. We don't do anyone any favors by dumbing down the reality of hell. We don't help anyone by shielding them from the truth of what's coming around the corner. But we can deliver the "package" of the Gospel message with deep compassion, gentleness, a positive attitude and a hopeful approach.

We do it by simply being ourselves and allowing Jesus to express Himself through us. Wherever we go in the world, we are presence carriers. We carry His light and life into every situation.

We may feel small, weak, incapable, ill-equipped, lacking in articulation. None of this matters. Frequently, all the obedience God requires of us is simply showing up. He does the rest. When we see a need, we go to it, reach out a hand and wait. Father comes into that situation. He expresses Himself through us. All we needed to do was be there, because He has no physical hands or feet on the earth except yours and mine.

So we go, and we allow what's inside us to spill out. The best method of witnessing we have, the best tool for evangelism we can utilize, is an attitude that shows people how much we trust our God.

Choosing to Let Go

In faith, there is no reason why every single day can't be the best day you have ever had in your life. You don't have to wait for Christmas, until the kids come home, until you're healed, until the check arrives in the post, until you're accepted by others. You don't have to wait for anything. You can have the greatest time of your life, right here, right now, any time you choose. Why? Because you can carry heaven around with you, wherever you go, instead of your burdens.

The Bible simply doesn't have anything to say about the "ups and downs" in life. In fact, the most positive, life-affirming, joy-filled words flowed out of the pen of the apostle Paul when he was locked up in a Philippian dungeon, having been whipped to within an inch of his life. He was still having a "good day," singing at midnight, full of inexpressible joy.

How? This is what the Holy Spirit can do in us if we give Him free reign. The world inside us becomes bigger than the world outside. The Spirit of God dwelling in us is overwhelmingly greater than any circumstance or situation in our lives. He overshadows everything.

Control is a big issue for many. We like to be in control; we don't like the feeling of not being able to orchestrate a certain outcome in a given situation. Yet in Christ, we find ourselves functioning in God's upside down economy, where things don't work how we might expect. As we let go of our burdens—difficult situations, unfulfilled needs, dysfunctional relationships—and hand them over to Jesus, He is able to become bigger than all of them for us.

Knowing that He is fully in control—and we don't need to be—is so liberating. We can live as presence carriers rather than burden bearers. As we practice daily the art of relinquishing our burdens to the Lord, we will be carrying heaven around with us, and we will be having a good day.

Centered

God shows his love for us in that while we were still sinners,
Christ died for us.
Romans 5:8, ESV

The longer I walk with God, the more I want to emphasize the basics of the Christian faith. Today, if we want to, we can attend all kinds of special conferences that emphasize particular areas—prophecy, apostolic ministry, spiritual gifts, intercession—all of which are valid expressions. But the more I hear about such things, the more I want to focus my attention on the essence of the basic Gospel.

I keep coming back to the most basic elements of our faith: the message of God's grace, salvation, what makes life life, why we should have joy.

Jesus is the center of our faith. I keep returning to the center because I want to be centered. Here, clinging close to Jesus, we are safe, protected, shielded from the storms of life. The storms will still come; we will still be challenged, stretched, wrung out. But we will be anchored in Him. Secure, unshaken.

Formula 1 racing car drivers are trained to focus their attention on where they want to go, as opposed to where they don't want to go. The premise is simple: They are traveling so fast that if something catches their attention and they look at it, they'll hit it! They learn to tune out the peripheral and focus on the road ahead.

We find ourselves moving in the right direction when we keep our eyes focused on Jesus, our gaze fixed on Him. I don't want to pay too much attention to the peripheral. I don't want to be drawn away to focus on specialty areas on the side. I want to keep my attention on Jesus.

If I take my eyes off Him, I can't follow where He is going. I am less in tune with Him. Less aware of what's on His heart. When I keep my eyes fixed on Him, I stay connected to the simplicity and power of the Gospel. My priorities are the same as His priorities. My heartbeat is in tune with His heartbeat.

I believe when others respond to Jesus, they respond because of the simple Gospel message: from darkness to light, from death to life, from hopelessness to hope, from unbelief to faith. Keep it simple. Keep centered.

Seed of Revival

One of the basics of our Christian faith is repentance. Our journey begins with repentance, and repentance is an ongoing feature of our pilgrimage. All of the world's greatest revivals began with repentance.

Perhaps the most significant revival in all of history, for me, is the one that began with my grandfather in China. It started when the Holy Spirit began to pour out an overwhelming conviction of sin on a group of children. It was so intense that these orphans would lie on the floor sobbing for entire days at a time. They would hide under desks and in closets, because they were so convicted and broken.

What had they done that was so bad? To deserve such conviction? Really, nothing. They had been used as child laborers in the tin mines, which were run by ruthless people who had no intention of paying them. They were abused. Most people would want to care for them, restore them, build them up, love them—not tell them to repent and come to Christ. We would want to show them the love of God! Yet seemingly, before they knew anything about salvation or the love of God, they were made aware of their sin; they ran to Jesus to ask His forgiveness.

This is what Holy Spirit does: He highlights the difference between the nicest, most normal people and our holy God. He reveals the vast difference between our ways and His ways. His ways are higher than our ways like the sky is higher than the sea. There is an impassable gulf between even the most excellent, worthy human being and God.

"For all have sinned and fall short of the glory of God" (Romans 3:23).

We have all missed the mark. Real revival cannot begin until we realize by how much. It cannot happen until we realize how utterly dependent we are, and must be, on Father God. If we long to see His supernatural power poured out, that journey begins with utter humility and sincere repentance, with fully acknowledging His greatness and our need.

"Come close to God, and God will come close to you. Wash your hands, you sinners; purify your hearts... Humble yourselves before the Lord, and he will lift you up in honor" (James 4:8, 10, NLT).

Come Closer

• Thank Father God that when we come to Him in repentance, He forgives our sins fully, completely. Thank Him, too, that He cleanses us from all guilt and shame. If you need to, repent of any unresolved issue in your life and receive God's free gift.

• At times we all feel small and ill-equipped for the tasks before us. This is not a bad thing! It puts into perspective our smallness and God's bigness; our weakness and His power. Remember that we carry God's presence with us. Release every burden to Him. Be a presence carrier rather than a burden bearer.

• Living life centered on Jesus, not focusing on peripheral matters, is one of the most basic and important things we can do. Life works when Jesus is at the center of it.

This week, reflect on some of the truths you've read. Repent if need be, and clear the decks. Now live each day mindful of Jesus' presence with you. Keep Him at the center of every activity, every day.

Lord Jesus, I choose to focus on You and be aware of Your presence with me in everything I do. I want to keep You at the center of my life. Help me to let go of the things I still want to cling to and control. Instead, I ask You to take hold of every burden and carry it for me. Let Your tenderness, mercy and love overwhelm me so I can live with reckless devotion to You.

Dependent

We now have this light shining in our hearts, but we ourselves are like
fragile clay jars containing this great treasure. This makes it clear that our
great power is from God, not from ourselves.
2 Corinthians 4:7, NLT

In the heat and dirt of the bush, under the blazing African sun, we face more
need, challenge, opposition and helpless perplexity than we can bear. But
daily God shows up, and we soldier on. We remain weak and fragile—living
proof that we are nothing more than jars of clay, and it is His all-surpassing
power that enables us to continue, keep moving forward, take one more step.

We often feel as though we are doomed to failure, and that is a pressure. But
even in this, we know it helps us to remain in the place of reliance. We are
not dependent on our own strength, resourcefulness or cleverness. We are
dependent on the God who raises the dead (see 2 Corinthians 1:9).

We exist to demonstrate the all-encompassing love that flows from God's
heart, a love that the unsaved have never seen before. We are here to seek
and save the lost and, in the process, give them a foretaste of heaven and our
unshakeable inheritance that is to come.
We came to Mozambique, one of the world's poorest countries, to "prove" the
Gospel—both in our own hearts and lives and among the neediest people we
could find. And the Gospel is proving itself, spreading out and taking root
wherever we turn. We dare not depend on human initiative and compassion;
that well dries up very quickly. Instead, we want to tap into the infinitely vast
reservoir of Father God's love and compassion. In His grace, we grab onto
and fall exquisitely into a love so deep that it makes us more than conquerors
to the glory of God.

We draw close to God, but not in a utilitarian way. We do not seek intimacy
with Him just to get His power working for us. Our love for Him is our
ultimate joy. Our complete comfort. Our motivating force. Our reason to
love. Our only totally satisfying romance.

Aroma

For me, an airplane is a cathedral of prayer in the sky. My meditations and interactions with Him in the clouds and heights are undisturbed by the tumult and clashing of problems on the ground. Now we are free in our cozy aerial cocoon to contemplate with our God and Lover what is to come in the lives of the incomprehensibly poor in southern Malawi. We delight in our God, but we do not live for bare pleasure. We have come to Africa to face directly the sufferings of this land.

"But thanks be to God, who always leads us as captives in Christ's triumphal procession and uses us to spread the aroma of the knowledge of him everywhere. For we are to God the pleasing aroma of Christ among those who are being saved and those who are perishing. To the one we are an aroma that brings death; to the other, an aroma that brings life. And who is equal to such a task?" (2 Corinthians 2:14–16).

We are here to improve the physical lives of the poor in every way possible and thereby to demonstrate what love looks like. But ultimately, we are here to save souls. We are here to rescue the perishing and bring them eternal life. We bring a Kingdom not made with hands. Not one we can see, but a never-ending Kingdom that is within us, a Kingdom of love, peace and joy in the Holy Spirit. We live for another life, in another place, where Christ is, seated at the right hand of God. We are here to bring Jesus, our perfect Savior, to Africa and to set its sights on Him and eternity!

Even in the midst of chaos, we can find a quiet place where we treasure time alone with Jesus, resting in His presence. Wherever that place is for you, seek it out and covet your time there. This is the place where Father God will fill you with all the resources you need to be the aroma of Him in a hurting world.

Touching Need

The people come for a reason. They are desperate, and they have come to seek the only one who can help them. Their poverty is indescribable. So many are seriously sick. They have been battered by witchcraft, cultic churches, corrupt and immoral leaders, huge frustrations and disappointments, broken homes and a meager economy. Their living conditions and prospects for the future seem hopelessly bleak. But that's why we are here. We preach Good News, a perfect Savior, eternal hope, a Kingdom of love, peace and joy that cannot be taken away.

The people need so much teaching and understanding, as well as an immediate, direct experience with God. We teach them about dwelling in God, connecting with Him, receiving gifts from Him, knowing and relating to Him, being His friend, imparting His love, peace and joy—all predicated on plain and simple repentance and faith in Jesus.

We live for what only God can do, and we thrive on testimonies. We will travel anywhere for the sake of that white hot core of respondents to the Gospel who just want to be close to Him, united with Him in perfect love. Jesus graciously heals people, filling them with His Spirit and loving them as they need to be loved. Outrageously glorious joy descends on some. Young children, deeply touched, sob in His weighty presence.

The spiritually hungry live everywhere, not just in the remote bush. Day by day you may brush shoulders with bankers, businessmen and women, nurses, check-out staff. Appearances can be deceptive. An "I have it all together" façade frequently masks great need. Day by day you carry within you the presence of the Almighty. Allow His presence to touch those you meet. He is no less able to touch, heal and fill the people that only you can reach.

"But my life is worth nothing to me unless I use it for finishing the work assigned me by the Lord Jesus—the work of telling others the Good News about the wonderful grace of God" (Acts 20:24, NLT).

The Little

Thursday afternoon is outreach time. Heidi and I hold one every week, taking any visitors, ready or not, on the IRIS version of an African bush safari—except we are hunting for souls for the glory of God. Most of the day is spent packing and preparing, and by 5 P.M. we are almost ready to go, our Land Rovers swaying precariously with mounds of equipment balanced on top.

On this day, one of our trucks gets stuck in deep mud halfway to the village, and they can't make it. I receive the call. We need an emergency alternate set-up. "Get the church sound system!" I'm told. We've never taken it into the bush before, to get all beat up, but all our spare systems are in for repair—veterans and victims of previous trips.

Some of the boys haul out the large speakers and amp rack, but they are just too big for my truck. "Go home and get the small speakers and video projector from the office." That's fine, but there is no screen, so we are forced to improvise with a sheet and some poles.

Equipment cobbled together, we set off at top speed. It's late, already dark. We're going to show the Jesus film. On the way we realize we have no generator! We stop at a local store and are faced with paying an exorbitant price for one. A visiting photographer buys it for us out of sheer goodness.

Eventually we make the outreach site. The other vehicle makes it in the end. The film is played. Heidi preaches. A deaf-mute lady gets healed and begins speaking, repeating phrases over the mike and then all around the village, speaking, speaking. Many come to Jesus. It has all been worth it.

Out of seeming chaos, God manages to bring order. Sometimes it's hard to see the plan when we are running around, responding to circumstances. But He knows. He has the bigger picture. He is in control. And as we offer up the little we have, He multiplies it into something amazing.

Visions

The meeting started with unusually deep prayer and worship. The Holy Spirit fell on some, and one of the older youth began prophesying spontaneously that our kids would have dreams and visions and encounters with God. Fernando was filled with the Spirit. He got up, walked around with his eyes closed and talked to thin air—but very coherently. He was seeing and hearing things we were not. A vision! We could ask him questions, and he would respond, but at the same time, he was talking to Jesus and to angels, shaking their hands—which we saw him act out—and we heard his responses.

God spoke to him out of Proverbs 7 about following His commandments. He saw angels all around. There were flowers that never decay, houses, a river-fountain and lights with lots of colors—yellow, red, green, blue—lots of blue. He saw fire over people's heads. He saw the hand of God stretched out to help him up a ladder to a higher place where he saw a big gate, and he was given a key. He opened it, and there were many more entryways ahead. He was most moved when he saw Jesus' hands, which had holes from the crucifixion.

He came out of the vision, and we gathered around to hear more. And then he went back into another vision, this time of the healing blood of Jesus and a place full of joy and the Holy Spirit, where all can receive love and knowledge. We enter by a straight path that does not turn, and we cannot leave it. Then Fernando started giving thanks and praising God for His might, His power, His extended hand, all His wonders, and a spontaneous song sprang up from his heart.

Our entire base was deeply stirred after this meeting. We realize we are on course to receive the desire of our hearts, the greatest down payment on heaven we have heard of yet. So are you, as you continue to trust in Him.

"Since, then, you have been raised with Christ, set your hearts on things above, where Christ is seated at the right hand of God. Set your minds on things above, not on earthly things" (Colossians 3:1–2).

Every Bit Counts

We love our joint Harvest/Bible School graduation days—the climax of ten weeks of blending Word and Spirit together in the context of on-the-ground missions. Twice a year we bring in new students and pastors from the remotest bush, along with eager students from all nations of the world who are as zealous for missions and immersed in God as possible.

We love, laugh and worship together, then head for our local village and the deep bush to seek the lost and see them saved. These are some of the most forgotten people on earth.

As much as possible, we bring cultures together—black and white, east and west, rich and poor. We are a cross-section of the Body of Christ. We want to see it function as it should, every person contributing their gifts from God.

It never ceases to amaze me how Jesus' Body works. No one has nothing to bring to the table. No one has no gifts. Everyone has something they can bring. Whether that something is small, unseen and seemingly insignificant or very visible and obvious is neither here nor there. It is irrelevant in God's Kingdom. All that matters is the whole, diverse, glorious Body working together, each part doing its bit to achieve God's greater purposes.

Some have the task of carrying gear, setting up the sound system, making sure everything is working, while others have the privilege of sharing the message of God's grace with the assembled crowd. Some cook or pass out food, while others minister and pray. Various expressions of service to Jesus work together to accomplish His purposes that day.

Never feel that what you have to contribute is too small, not enough, insignificant. It's not. What you have is needed. Without it, other parts of the Body struggle to function. Bring your offering to Jesus and allow Him to multiply it.

"Just as our bodies have many parts and each part has a special function, so it is with Christ's body. We are many parts of one body, and we all belong to each other" (Romans 12:4–5, NLT).

Come Closer

• Reflect on the truth that we are weak when He is strong. Dependence on Jesus is not a sign that we have run out of answers but that we have found the right question: Will You help me, Lord? Draw close to the Father and rely on Him completely.

• This week, seek out time to spend alone with Jesus and ask Him to speak into the situations in your life. Often we are busy, immersed in tasks or problems. Jesus wants to speak. Make time to listen.

• Look for someone who is spiritually hungry around you—at school, home or work. Make a point of giving that person a word of encouragement. Ask Father to speak something to you specifically for that person; then step out and share it.

From a place of rest and dependence in the presence of God, we can reach out to others and help them connect. In the place of intimacy, we hear the heart of God for others. Then we can do something practical for them. Something simple. Something that reminds them they are not forgotten.

Father God, thank You for placing in me gifts and abilities that You want to use to touch the lives of others. Help me to regularly find the place of intimacy with You so I can hear You speaking clearly into my life. Help me, then, to step out and use my gifts to help others find a deeper relationship with You. Help me to do simple acts of kindness that point back to You.

Unexpected

Antonio is twelve years old. He was known to everyone in his village as a deaf-mute from a very young age. Now he is smiling all the time, walking around listening and speaking at every opportunity. Almost every week, the deaf are healed. This time, with Antonio, the result was that three village chiefs gave their lives to Jesus, acknowledging Him as Lord. They opened up the whole area to us and welcomed our desire to bring teaching, ministry and practical help of all kinds.

The Kingdom of God is holistic. We don't just preach heaven; we prove the love of God by drilling wells, building simple churches and schools, supplying teachers, providing for orphans and abandoned women—doing whatever we can with what we have. These villages are primitive almost beyond belief to many Westerners, and they desperately need help and development of every kind.

The Gospel is seen more by what we do than by what we say. As someone once said, "The message of Jesus Christ is a Gospel that can put food in a man's stomach, clothes on his back and shoes on his feet."

The powerful message we carry works in harmony with practical provision. We revel in the spiritual transformation that takes place when people hear the truth of God's words and allows them to sink into their hearts, changing them from the inside out. Equally, we love the material blessings we are able to administer on behalf of our Father. We can feed the hungry, set the lonely in families, teach the unlearned and bring hope and a future to the destitute.

Looked at another way, we are glad to be known as social workers and humanitarians, to have a reputation for doing good. But all that would be in vain if we didn't then bring people to a living faith in Jesus Christ. First and foremost, we want His name to be known.

I encourage you to live by the truth and then to express that truth in actions that matter. Motivated by the love and compassion of Christ, reach out today and meet someone's need. Unheeded. Unexpected.

Passion

Jesus loves us so much that He never leaves us the way He finds us. His love often starts with a question—a question that reaches down from the safety of our minds right into our hearts. Do you love Me? Often we are too quick to answer when God asks a question of us. Usually, our hearts haven't fully grasped what He wants us to understand. God is looking to affect our hearts more than our minds. He wants to wreck our hearts—to change the way our hearts feel about things and react to the situations that exist in a broken world.

The Scripture says, "Love the Lord your God... with all your mind" (Mark 12:30). We are called to love God with every fiber of our beings. All of us, in our entirety, must be wholly given over to the Master—our hearts, our souls, our minds, our emotions. God wants us to be fully yielded to Him with reckless devotion. To "love the Lord your God with all your heart and with all your soul and with all your mind and with all your strength" (Mark 12:30)—this is passion. Let us determine to live lives abandoned to His love, lives made up of passion. Decide to trade the worst for the best, death for life, darkness for light.

But whatever were gains to me I now consider loss for the sake of Christ. What is more, I consider everything a loss because of the surpassing worth of knowing Christ Jesus my Lord, for whose sake I have lost all things. I consider them garbage, that I may gain Christ.
Philippians 3:7–8

In surrender we actually lose nothing. We stand only to gain. We are gaining a life lived in His love. An oak tree starts life as an acorn hidden in the dirt. Nobody would even know it was there. But contained within that tiny, hidden thing are all the makings of beauty, might, splendor and shelter. The little acorn simply takes a lifetime to become all that it was always meant to be.

Before anything else, beloved, we are His, hidden in Him.

Unstoppable

And I pray that you, being rooted and established in love, may have power, together with all the Lord's holy people, to grasp how wide and long and high and deep is the love of Christ, and to know this love that surpasses knowledge—that you may be filled to the measure of all the fullness of God.
Ephesians 3:17–19

When you are in love, you are different. You will do anything, go anywhere. All you want is to be with the one you love. This is passion—being totally committed, not just dipping your toes in the water to see what the temperature is like. If you are not in love, why serve, why minster, why turn up at church, why go to another meeting?

Rolland and I were missionaries for 26 years before we discovered this truth. Rolland was even born on the mission field. But we got really tired and burned out. To say we were missing the point is an understatement. But then God got hold of us and poured His sweet "Holy Spirit love" into us. He transformed us into people who were fully in love, fully committed—and with that love comes unstoppable energy.

When you are in love, you have power; you will do anything and go anywhere your loved one asks. You simply trust the one you love to be there for you. You can run headlong into dark places if you know light is waiting for you. You can jump out of a boat into a stormy sea; you can take extravagant risks; you can live right on the edge. If you fall off or fall over, you fall into grace.

When you start to grasp how wide and long and high and deep is the love of Christ, you start to get full. Full of what? Full of God, full of the understanding that no matter what He asks you to do, you can do it; no matter where He asks you to go, you can go. You can live on the edge, because even in the darkest places, light is waiting for you. His love, His light, in you and me. Passion—it makes us unstoppable.

Quenched

"The water I give them will become in them a spring of water welling up to eternal life." The woman said to him, 'Sir, give me this water so that I won't get thirsty and have to keep coming here to draw water.'"
John 4:14–15

Miracles happen on ordinary days. The Samaritan woman left her house to fetch water from the well on a morning that started like any other. She had been cast out, overlooked, forgotten, passed over. She was not a respectable church member or a pillar of society.

I wonder if, as she walked to the well, she rummaged through the tangle of her broken life. Maybe she was trying to figure out how the tangle started. Maybe she had tried very hard, but things just kept breaking, and all she had now was cracked and dry. She had cried herself out. Hers was a parched life in desperate need of water.

Now she's at the well. A man sits quietly. Unlike any man she had met before, this man is Jesus, Son of the living God. He asks her for a drink; she feels ashamed and inadequate. But He sees beyond her inability. He sees right into her soul, into the breaking and the dryness. Jesus stops to really notice her. He is committed, just to her. He talks gently about her life, but He sees her from a different point of view. This man, Jesus, speaks to her in a kinder voice than shame. His voice is all love.

Already the water is flowing over her parched life. She has nothing to offer, but she is loved—not inadequate, not unprepared or unable. Just loved. The bubbling, living grace water pours in over her cried-out dryness, washes over her shame and the years of stubborn dirt and stained memories. Now all she feels is different, clean, made whole. Even more than that, she feels ready.

Miracles happen on ordinary days. Just like Jesus brought dignity and eternal life to the Samaritan women when He stopped and asked her for a drink of water from the well, He offers the same to you and me—bubbling over life. It is His gift to us, our gift to other parched lives.

Simple

Despite what many would have us believe, the Gospel is not complicated. It is very simple. Jesus has given us everything we need. It is so simple that a child of three can get it: Love God and love the one in front of you. It's not about how to fill a building, build a brand or make sure there is plenty of room to wiggle out of it all. It's just this: Love God and love the one in front of you.

It all starts with one person, just like Jesus, stopping for the one. It's not about looking at ourselves but looking right at Him. He has shown us how to live with passion, to love with compassion. Don't let anyone turn you away from understanding His heart. Do nothing to gain the approval of man. Instead, in humility, consider others better than yourself as you come to understand more and more why His love requires that "the last will be first and the first will be last" (Matthew 20:16).

We are called to love our neighbors as we love ourselves. That means we can't hate ourselves, because we don't want to duplicate that! We need to understand how much God loves each one of us. God loves you as He finds you; He loves both who you are and also who you can become. This is my prayer:

God, open our eyes to Your love and compassion for the man, woman or child in front of us every day. For the one who has been kicked and spat on, who is broken, messed up and alone. For the rich man who is starving on the inside, the young boy who does not know when he will eat again, the girl in the dress that has been ripped to rags. Help us to preach in the street, to preach right in the dirt.

Jesus wants you and me to love Him first and wholly, with reckless devotion, and then to love someone else. This is the Gospel; this is the price; this is our place and our purpose. This, beloved, is where real life and real joy are found!

Christ in You

Jesus wants to live in us, and He wants us to live completely in Him. He loves us so much that He will take a wrecking ball to our tiny hearts, because He wants His love to have room to grow in us. This is Christ in you the hope of glory.

God, who began to work in you before you were even born, before you knew how to say His name or even to pray, will not leave you unfinished. He will complete the work He set out to do in and through you. Never stop short of God's promise. Do not stop short of your destiny. Do not stop short of His glory.

The Holy Spirit will burn in your life and mine with tenacious and holy fire so He can take us over. He wants us to be ready so we can be full of Jesus, full of hope, full of nothing but God's glory being revealed to an empty and hopeless world. If you are empty, if you are broken, He will fill you. If you know what it is like to be desperate, to be utterly needy, He will nourish and sustain you. And when you are full of Jesus, full of His hope and His glory, Christ in you will fill others just like you.

One unforgettable day, Jesus took a wrecking ball to my heart. He stood in front of me, in all the beauty of His presence, and held out a poor man's cup, a half-a-coconut cup. He asked me, "This is the cup of suffering and joy? Will you drink it?"

I drank, and that cup became water for others. Jesus wants us to see as He sees. He looked into hell with heaven's laughing eyes. He suffered, He was tortured and He died. He literally gave Himself away. He drank the cup of suffering and joy; He suffered with joy set before Him.

You are not big enough, strong enough, prepared enough or spiritual enough to do the work God wants you to do. But He is. God is more than big enough. He will complete the work He has set out to do in and through you. Don't stop short of His glory, beloved.

Come Closer

• The powerful message we carry works in harmony with a practical demonstration of God's love. Frequently, meeting a person's need opens that person to hearing the truth. Think about whom you could show God's kindness to this week.

• Jesus wants to fill you and me with His passion. He wants us to share in His compassion and feel His heartbeat more than He wants us to understand truth with our minds.

• Passion makes us unstoppable; with passion we are motivated to do things we otherwise might not do. With passion we will go anywhere, do anything. Lord, fill us with the same passion for others that You have for us.

Remember the story of the woman at the well? Her life felt parched and dry. She went to draw natural water from the well, but Jesus met her in her need and refreshed her soul. If you are feeling dry and thirsty, pray the following:

Lord Jesus, You are one who sustains me and quenches my spiritual thirst. Pour Your refreshment out onto the dryness in my life. Like a stream in the desert, revive me and cause me to thrive. Cause Your life to bubble over in Me. Thank You, Jesus, for Your love for me. Amen.

Partner

In all my prayers for all of you, I always pray with joy because of your
partnership in the gospel from the first day until now, being confident of
this, that He who began a good work in you will carry it on to completion
until the day of Christ Jesus.
Philippians 1:4–6

I want to finish well. I don't want to end up burned out, tired out and dead in
the water. Paul finished well. He carried on doing what God told him to do,
and he was a happy man.

He was happy because he knew he was not alone. God was working on Paul's
behalf, working in Paul. All Paul had to do was work with God. It's a glorious
partnership. God and me. God and you. That's unstoppable love. God is not
going to leave us to figure it out by ourselves. He's not going to leave us out
on a limb.

I live by the ocean in Cabo Delgado, and I enjoy walking the beach. I like to
talk with God there. Quite often I watch a group of men or women casting
a big net into the waters, about twenty men or women, depending on what
kind of net they are using. They sing together as they pull in the fish—sing
and pull, sing and pull.

There is no way any one of them could pull in one of those heavy nets on his or
her own, so they work together. God showed us how to work in partnership
by demonstrating how Father, Son and Holy Spirit work together—never
alone, always preferring each other and esteeming each other.

That's what makes the work a joy—partnership. You can't do God's work
when you are isolated and vulnerable any more than I could cook for fifty
thousand people on my own. We have to both support and release one
other—to worship, to minster, to harvest, to build—each doing the good
work he or she was created to do. If we support and release each other, we
won't end up so exhausted.

Do what God has given you to do. Do it with joy, and do it together. God and
me. God and you.

Stuck

When the worst cyclone to strike Mozambique in many years hit, Rolland and I were on a boat. It was not the little boat we use to reach the villages that cannot be reached any other way. It was a comfortable boat filled with friends, great food and kindness.

I was getting phone calls from my sons; everyone was in trauma. Three hundred and sixty churches had been wiped out by the floodwaters. I was on a nice boat, but I did not want to be on that boat. My people were suffering, and I wanted to go to them so badly I would have flown right there if I had wings.

We did not have wings, but we had techie gadgets, and we were doing our best to find a way home, despite the cyclone; meanwhile, we were stuck. What do you do when you are stuck? You can flail your fists at the wind, cry and get more and more agitated. But all that does is make you like a fly caught on a spider's web: The more you struggle, the worse you get stuck, really fast.

Paul wrote, "This is my prayer: that your love may abound more and more in knowledge and depth of insight, so that you may be able to discern what is best..." (Philippians 1:9-10).

What is best? When you are stuck, the best thing you can do is ask your loving Father, What is best? There is no point trying to get off a boat if you are meant to be on it. Maybe the very thing you are stuck in is His will. Then you find joy in doing what you are meant to do—even if you have a "better" idea!

God told me to finish the assignment He had given me, to stay on the boat. Don't get in the way of God's glory. Don't stop short. Fix your eyes on Him. Trust His love. I pray your love may abound more and more so you will know God and will be able to discern what is best—so you will know in your heart what He wants you to do and will trust Him to do what only He can do.

Letting Go

We have to let go of our pre-conceived ideas, our carefully worked out plans, our way of doing things so God can live in us. We need new life, His life. If we are going to make room to carry His glory, we have to die first. We have to take our place at the cross and say, as Jesus said, "Not my will but yours, God. Your will. I will drink the cup You have called me to drink, whatever the cost."

Paul prayed he would have sufficient courage (see Philippians 1:20). We all need that courage. Sufficient courage to look right into the storm you are facing and see heaven's provision. Enough courage to drink the cup you are called to drink.

When the cyclone hit Mozambique and caused a famine, God asked me, "Do you trust Me, Heidi?" From screaming no I learned to scream, "Yes, Lord! Yes, I believe." In one week, we were given as many containers of food as in the last twelve years combined. We fed twelve thousand people a day, and then we fed more. The trucks rolled out, and the people were fed. God did the impossible.

When we try to fix things in our strength, we become burned out and die of exhaustion. Why not drink your cup and leave your impossible burdens to Jesus? "Not my will, but Yours be done, Lord."

It takes courage to let go—to let go of your way, to let go of being the answer. We are not the answer, my friend; God is.

If we live like this, it will mean fruitful labor. Without fruit, what would be the point of living anyway? But the seed has to be buried deep in the ground before the fruit has a chance to take hold. Before the harvest is ready, the fields look bare. All the life is hidden, ready to be revealed, ready to be released—in His time.

Finish

Whoever dwells in the shelter of the Most High will rest in the shadow of
the Almighty. I will say of the Lord, "He is my refuge and my fortress, my
God, in whom I trust."
Psalm 91:1–2

After the cyclone hit Mozambique, I stayed faithful to the schedule God had
planned for me. I stayed on the boat as God said. I left the boat when God told
me to go preach at Oxford University. Then I was due to speak at a historic
meeting at a cathedral in France. Meanwhile, back in Mozambique, close
to one of our main bases, twenty tons of ammunition started to explode,
triggered by the intense African heat. Two missiles hit the center—at the altar
of the church and the admin block.

I was terrified. "Please change my ticket," I begged the travel agent. "I have to
go home!" But God said, "Finish your assignment."

"Come on, Lord! You cannot mean me to go to a cathedral while bombs are
going off and our children are terrified?"

"Finish your assignment." So I did.

Not one person at the children's center was hurt. The Lord sheltered them
under His wing. None of our missionaries fled for their own safety; they
all stayed to protect the children. Meanwhile, I preached at the cathedral,
and the Holy Spirit met starving monks and nuns with His compassion,
encouragement, mercy, healing and joy.

When we finally got back to Zimpeto, we hugged our children. We had
expected people to scatter, but no one had left. We held the most beautiful
worship service I have ever experienced. God had saved our children's
lives, and we were thanking Him for our very lives. Then we went out and
ministered to the families around the base who had lost their homes. We
took in three orphans who had lost their father to tuberculosis and now their
mother to the missiles. We looked into the eyes of the mother who had lost
her child, and we drank the cup of joy and suffering.

God says to you today, "Finish your assignment." However much you think
you should be somewhere else, and however bad it gets, finish. He who began
a good work in you will be faithful!

Content

I know what it is to be in need, and I know what it is to have plenty. I have learned the secret of being content in any and every situation, whether well fed or hungry, whether living in plenty or in want. I can do all this through him who gives me strength.
Philippians 4:12–13

I have learned a secret! It has taken me thirty years, but now I believe I have it, and of all places, I learned it in a Jacuzzi! I have learned to be content. I am taking hold of that for which Christ took hold of me. I am learning to know Christ and the power of His resurrection, to have fellowship with Him in His suffering.

I am learning to see what He sees, to go where He goes, to feel what He feels—just following the Leader. I am becoming like Him in His death and somehow attaining His resurrection. I am pressing on, and I won't stop. I will continue to take hold of that for which Christ took hold of me. He looks at you and me, and He says, "I want you!" He died to take hold of you. He died on the cross so you could live like He lives. What a Savior!

I will forget what lies behind—all the sin, all my mistakes, every time when I did something stupid—and I will press on, looking forward to the prize, heading toward victory. And while I am doing all this, I will rest because I have learned this secret.

Today, step into His rest. Don't strive. Don't struggle. Don't try to be someone or something you're not. Just be still and allow Father to be Father.

Resting

I was working with some people who had very little, we were out in the dirt ministering to men, women and children who were in great need. But my hosts wanted to bless me, so they put me in a hotel, in a suite with a Jacuzzi. I didn't want the Jacuzzi, because I thought the money should go to helping everyone else, so I asked my hosts to move me to a Motel 6.

But I was actually offending their hospitality, because I thought I should be somewhere else. It can be quite hard when you are coming and going from the mission field—beans and rice then a buffet, food then no food, clean water then no water. But the Lord said, "Stop, Heidi. You need to stay here and get in the Jacuzzi and soak!"

Soak, Lord?

"Yes, receive." So I sat in the Jacuzzi and watched the beautiful, warm, clean bubbles. Water does not just come from a tap where we are, and if it does come out, it is green, and you would not want to soak in it. Often we are out living in a tent in the "bush bush." There are no toilets, not even a hole in the ground, and everybody is watching you do everything.

"...Whether well fed or hungry, whether living in plenty or in want. I can do all this through him who gives me strength" (Philippians 4:12–13).

In all things, we can rejoice. In every situation, He will provide. He will not leave us burned out or discouraged, tired or overcome. His grace is sufficient, and we can do all things—working and resting—through Him, through His strength.

Trust that Your Heavenly Father knows what He is doing when He guides you and directs your life. Be thankful for every provision. Don't forget to rest in the kindnesses He pours out on you—whether you feel deserving or not. You are His child. He loves you.

Come Closer

• Day by day we are learning to live in Christ's sufficiency, learning to rest in Him.

• We have a tendency toward action, doing rather than being. We want to make things happen. There is nothing wrong with action, with getting things done. But when we do them out of a sense of striving, we don't get anywhere. We can't achieve anything worthwhile in the Kingdom through self-effort.

• First we must turn to Jesus and immerse ourselves in His presence. Rest in His love. From that place of rest, we act. We are and then we do. Then, we can act without a hint of performance.

Meditate on the following simple truths:

We do because we are loved—not to be loved.

We do because we are accepted—not to be accepted.

Humble

I was lying on the floor in a church in Brazil as God showed me picture after picture of starving people who were crying out for enough food so they could live and not die in abject hunger. Meanwhile, people around me were receiving from the Holy Spirit and laughing. Are You schizophrenic, Lord? I wondered. But then He released me from the cup of suffering, and I began to laugh, too. Now who looks schizophrenic?

Our Father sees heaven right through hell. He sees freedom beyond the cross. He sees eternal life beyond the grave. He sees laughter through the tears. People often ask me, "How do you cook for all those children, Heidi?" Me, cook? Ask Rolland. I can burn water. If I am cooking in our house, there is always smoke. But God sends help. I don't do everything. I can't do everything.

"Have the same mindset as Christ Jesus: who, being in very nature God, did not consider equality with God something to be used to his own advantage; rather, he made himself nothing..." (Philippians 2:5–7, emphasis added).

Jesus, who is in His very nature God, did not consider equality with God something to be grasped. Here He is, the King of Glory. He can stay anywhere; He can go anywhere and do anything. He knows who He is. Yet what does He do—for us and for our sake? He empties Himself until He becomes nothing. The King of Glory, Jesus, allowed Himself to be born in a borrowed stable with goats and chickens. He had to learn a language. He had to be clothed and fed by someone. He just gave Himself away, always preferring others. He left His Kingdom, left His glory behind to show us how to live.

While we are trying to hold on tight, He is saying, give it away. He is totally equal with God in every way, but He made Himself nothing. He humbled Himself, and He was obedient even to death. What a teacher! All we have to do is follow the leader, be in unity with Him, see what He sees, go where He goes, do what He does, pray what He prays, love like He loves.

Provision

His divine power has given us everything we need for a godly life through
our knowledge of him who called us by his own glory and goodness.
Through these he has given us his very great and precious promises, so that
through them you may participate in the divine nature, having escaped the
corruption in the world caused by evil desires.
2 Peter 1:3–4

His divine power is everything we need! We can have faith in the power of
the living God. We can take that faith into our homes, our workplaces and
our mission field. We can see through the devastation and the suffering to the
opportunity for God to work in every situation we find ourselves in.

His divine power provides everything we need for a life of godliness. He calls
us as His own, by His own glory and goodness. God is calling us, His sons
and daughters, to participate in His divine nature. We get to be like Him! He
is asking us to partake of Jesus, to eat enough to be strengthened and full, to
eat and drink of Him every day so that we are not weak or in despair. And
once we have eaten and drunk, we are to give His body to others, as fresh
bread from heaven. We are called to multiply what we have received, to carry
the glory and divine nature of Christ Jesus.

Let's ask Jesus to open our eyes, to strengthen us and fill us. Let's ask Him to
make us ready by His glory and because of His goodness, so that we can be
with Him and in Him. Christ in you is the hope of glory.

When we live out of this understanding, every situation we find ourselves in
will be touched by God. He prepares the way. His presence goes before us.

First, Last

I have little to give, but I will give the little I have. God loves when we put the little we have into His offering. He doesn't mind that it is only a little. He loves when we give what we have. Even though we have only a little to give, we can give Him everything. Not just a tenth of our lives, not half, not even 99.9 percent, but all of us. Like tiny seeds hidden away in the dirt, hidden deep in the heart of God, waiting for His life, His beauty to shine on and through us so we can bear fruit. Like seeds that fall to the ground—fall from His love and mercy, lower still. Seeds sown with tenderness, grace and compassion. Little lives laid down into fruitfulness.

My heart cries, "Oh, Lord, let me be undone." I don't want to stand up or grow up or get a grip. I want to fall down, lie down. I want my hands and my heart to stay loose, yielded into His heart and His love. It's about being made more like Him, not more like me.

I will contend to be undone. I will ask Him to help me stay undone. Not finished but always ready, always wanting to be more like Him. Always wanting His life and love, poured into my empty life, to fill up and overflow from this little jar of clay.

As we move in this direction, we will understand more and more why His love requires the first to be last and the last to be first (see Mark 10:31). As we look with His heart and eyes to the lost, the broken, the empty, the orphans and start to put them first—doing nothing to promote ourselves but everything out of His love and for His glory—we become more like Jesus, who gave up everything to become like us.

Jesus, the King of glory, made Himself like us; He humbled Himself and became nothing, taking on our form. He gave His last breath for us. He became like us so we might become like Him—transformed, utterly and completely altered, no longer the same. This, my friend, is all we must aspire to be.

United

Therefore if you have any encouragement from being united with Christ, if any comfort from his love, if any common sharing in the Spirit, if any tenderness and compassion, then make my joy complete by being like-minded, having the same love, being one in spirit and of one mind.
Philippians 2:1–2

Are we united with Christ? Does our relationship with Him—the love we have for Jesus and the love He has for us—encourage us? Do we find comfort in His love? Does the Holy Spirit minister to us with tenderness and compassion? Does this love make us more like Jesus? Do we have the same love for others as He has shown to us?

My prayer is that we would become more united and more like-minded with Christ, having the same love that He has. I pray we would encourage like Jesus, comfort like Jesus, have the same tenderness and compassion as Jesus. That way, whoever we are with and wherever we go, we will be like Him.

"Do nothing out of selfish ambition or vain conceit. Rather, in humility value others above yourselves, not looking to your own interests but each of you to the interests of the others" (Philippians 2:3–4).

Sometimes we can look at each other and think, I wish I was more like that person. I wish people would notice me like that. But God values our lives as they are, hidden in Him, and He knows what is best for us. In reality, you may not want to be like the person you think is doing better than you.

You are at your best when you are hidden deeply inside the heart of Jesus. Do nothing out of selfish ambition or because of pride in yourself. Don't do something because you are looking for the approval of people. Your heavenly Father is the only one whose pleasure is worth having.

Never Too Far

Love is patient, love is kind. It does not envy, it does not boast, it is not proud. It does not dishonor others, it is not self-seeking, it is not easily angered, it keeps no record of wrongs. Love does not delight in evil but rejoices with the truth. It always protects, always trusts, always hopes, always perseveres.
1 Corinthians 13:4–7

Love always hopes. God always delights in us. He sees the very best in us and loves us to go for gold. So forgetting what lies behind, we press on to the mark of His high calling. What is the mark of His high calling? Love, love and more love.

His love is big enough to touch any life. His love is able to transform evil, back to front, until it spells love. Don't die in darkness or depression, anger or pain; rather, let Him hold you and speak hope and courage to you until you are ready and able to live in His love.

We heard about a boy in the north of Mozambique who had raped a little girl. When I heard about him, I felt the Holy Spirit reaching out to him. I went looking, but nobody wanted me to find him. They said, "Heidi, we are warning you; this one you cannot have."

But God's love is big enough to touch any life, to make light out of any darkness. Jesus came so that we might have life, so that we would no longer have to die in depression, anger, or pain. He loved people back to life. He would go anywhere and talk to anyone, and wherever He went, He would stop for the one—the forgotten one, the one who was rejected, outcast, sick, even stone dead. Even a thief who was dying for his crimes on the cross next to Him. In the Kingdom of God's love, there is no sinner who cannot come home.

Eventually I found that boy, and we took him in. That boy who did a terrible thing is a picture of God's grace. Oh, that we might be so given over to His loving grace that nothing would come between us and the one in front of us. We are never too far that we cannot be reached by His mercy.

Each Day

My command is this: Love each other as I have loved you. Greater love has
no one than this: to lay down one's life for one's friends.
John 15:12–13

Something about becoming nothing makes for real happiness and peace.
Rolland has found this out so beautifully. He has come to know the joy of not
having to be someone. We do not have all the answers, but God does. We are
not the answer, but God is.

All God wants us to do is lay our lives down into His. Do you know how
much stress disappears when you decide to stop trying to figure everything
out and let Him lead you, day by day?

"Jesus gave them this answer: 'Very truly I tell you, the Son can do nothing by
himself; he can do only what he sees his Father doing, because whatever the
Father does the Son also does'" (John 5:19).

Jesus, the Son of God, told us how to become nothing. Jesus only did what
He saw the Father doing. He only did what God told Him to do. What a
burden that removes from us! We do not have to figure everything out, be
everywhere and do everything. All we have to do is what God is leading us
to do.

What is God leading you to do? Perhaps He wants you to encourage your
spouse or friend, plan something special for your children, go to Columbia,
adopt a child, care for someone who is sick or an invalid. We only have to
give the little we have. He is not expecting more. God takes the little we have
and multiplies it.

Why not start every day by asking Him what He wants you to do? Just one
day at a time. It takes such a load off your shoulders if you don't have to worry
about who you should be, where you should be, and how you are going to
get there. If we decide in our hearts to let God lead and to have no ambitions
of our own, He makes the way. We do not have to make everything happen.
Why not rely on His strength rather than our own? His power is made perfect
in our weakness.

Come Closer

• Jesus humbled Himself and was prepared to give Himself away, time and again. He is our example. All we have to do is follow the Leader. Let's see what He sees, go where He goes, love like He loves.

• In the upside down economy of God, the first will be last and the last, first. All we need to do is to keep on sowing our lives into others as Jesus directs, and He will take care of the rest.

But we don't minister out of our emptiness and need. We minister out of the fullness of His presence that Jesus pours into us, the fullness found in our reckless devotion to Him. Don't walk around starving when Jesus longs to feed you. He so desires to touch your heart with His tenderness, compassion and love. You are at your best when you are hidden deep inside His heart.

There is power and freedom in trusting God for each day, one day at a time. Let's rely on His strength instead of our own. His power is made perfect in our weakness.

Children

When you are a child, you do not expect to plan your own life, find your own nourishment, be wholly responsible for everything. It is the same for children of God. We have a loving Father who wants and expects to take care of us.

We are His children, and here He is, holding His arms wide, asking us to trust Him to lead us and provide for us. I don't lay awake at night worrying how I will feed all the children we care for. Why? Because they belong to our heavenly Father. That means I am free to do anything, go anywhere, as long as I know He is leading me. Before anything else, beloved, we are His children.

Do you know that because you are His child, you are free? Free to love as many or as few as He calls you to love, free to clean toilets or climb on a plane, free to do anything He wants you to do. We are free to serve the One who is worthy, in any way He chooses, even unto death (see Philippians 2:8).

We can give our lives away with great joy and peace, knowing we are losing nothing.

The pressures of modern living are many and varied. While we focus on those pressures and demands, we will never be free. Learn to focus on Jesus. Watch Him. Listen to Him. Gradually, the background noise will subside, and the load will be lifted from your shoulders. Three-year-olds going on a family road trip don't suddenly shout, "Wait, Mom, Dad! Do we have enough fuel? Have you checked the tire pressure?" They just enjoy the ride. You don't have to worry about who you are, where you are going or how you are going to get there. Father has it all in hand.

Fight

Run, speak to this young man, saying: "Jerusalem shall be inhabited as towns without walls, because of the multitude of men and livestock in it. For I," says the LORD, "will be a wall of fire all around her, and I will be the glory in her midst."
Zechariah 2:4–5, NKJV

I was in the hospital, hooked up to an IV drip for eighteen days. While there, I received all sorts of advice. Prophets told me to stand up, so I would try to stand up. Others said God wanted me to lie down, so I would lie down, and so on. Rolland was taught how to make an ionic magnetic thing, and I received herbal remedies and the cousins of herbal remedies. I appreciated everything, but in the end, I thought, Lord, I think these remedies might kill me! I got tired of making plans to get better.

I think this sickness was more than earthly sickness. It was a sign of what God is saying to us. We have flourished in the renewal, in the presence of God and the beautiful work of His Holy Spirit. We have worked like Zechariah and the Jews who rebuilt the Temple. We have labored for years through much opposition. But we are not building walls; we are His temple!

We are to be His resting place, a place utterly given over to Him. We are called to fulfill His plans and purposes, not to be half-filled but fully possessed by Him. We are His temple. "Or do you not know that your body is the temple of the Holy Spirit who is in you, whom you have from God, and you are not your own?" (1 Corinthians 6:19, NKJV).

Satan is trying to destroy your destiny, God's temple. If he can't use sin, he will use sickness or exhaustion. So we have to fight. But the way we fight sounds extremely odd to anyone who likes to plan. The way we fight is not by having it all figured out, planned ahead and sorted. In this case, planning isn't the remedy for sickness or exhaustion. Obedience is. God is calling us to lie down spiritually—to let Him love us until we are full of Him, His love and His life.

The Temple

For twelve years the Jewish people had been re-building the Temple, and they were exhausted. But God gave Zechariah this promise: God Himself would dwell with Zechariah and the people, right there in that place that had no walls, no earthly means of protection. "'For I,' says the LORD, 'will be a wall of fire all around her, and I will be the glory in her midst'" (Zechariah 2:5, NKJV).

God would be the glory in their midst.

He would fill His Temple. His Temple would be a resting place for His glory, and He would be a wall of fire. He would protect it.

We must fight, not to make a temple but to become His temple. To become a resting place for His beautiful, holy habitation. To be fully possessed by the glory of the Lord. He is calling us not to run harder but to lie down.

What is your destiny? Is it to go to a university, be in a hospital, live on a garbage dump or go to the nations? Wherever you end up and whatever you do, your destiny is this: to be fully possessed by God's presence. To carry His glory. To be recklessly devoted. Then, if you are at a university, a hospital or a garbage dump, you are His resting place, and all that can exist there is life and beauty.

Remember, you are a presence carrier. Immerse yourself in Jesus' presence and allow Him to spill into every situation in your life. You are His dwelling place. His temple.

All-Consuming Fire

We cannot fight our battles in the flesh. We have to run into God's holy, all-consuming fire, because that is where we are safe. God's holy fire purifies us; it cleans all the dirt and drives out all the darkness. When we are in the center of that fire, God is a wall of fire around us, and we are safe!

It is an unfair fight. Witch doctors stand outside our base in Pemba, sticking pins in dolls that look like us, but we have no fear. It is an unfair fight. All the witch doctors and demons, all the forces of hell, do not stand a chance. We are burning brands plucked from the fire—His holy, all-consuming fire.

All we are called to do is be in God's presence, to be where He wants us to be. Like Joshua, we stand in His presence, and the Lord rebukes Satan. We have nothing to fear when the Lord rebukes our enemy.

Joshua, standing before the Lord, was not clean:

Now Joshua was clothed with filthy garments, and was standing before the Angel. Then He answered and spoke to those who stood before Him, saying, 'Take away the filthy garments from him.' And to him He said, 'See, I have removed your iniquity from you, and I will clothe you with rich robes.' And I said, 'Let them put a clean turban on his head.' So they put a clean turban on his head, and they put the clothes on him. And the Angel of the LORD stood by" (Zechariah 3:3–5, NKJV).

As with Joshua, all our impurities and sin, all the evil and ugliness, are removed by the blood of Jesus. Will we walk in the rich robes He lovingly gives, robes of righteousness and victory? We have no reason to cower. His love is fearless. Will we take the turban He offers, to transform our minds and our thought lives, so we take on His thoughts, the mind of Christ?

All we have is given. It is all grace. We cannot earn His love. Will you become His resting place? Will you lie down, even appearing not to do anything useful if He asks you to? Just because you love Him?

Fresh Bread

More than the food and drink we need to live, we need fresh bread from heaven. We need the bread of life that only Jesus can provide—His glorious presence. Those who are spiritually hungry will be satisfied as they eat and drink of Jesus. My prayer is constantly that God would give us such hunger for Him, that He would pour out the healing oil of His Holy Spirit on all who are desperate for Him. We need to welcome such hunger. We need to be like helpless little children before our Savior, giving Him full and absolute control of every area of our lives. Then we will know that, truly, Jesus is more than enough.

We don't comprehend how much of God's presence is available to us. Jesus so wants to fill us with His Spirit that there will always be more than enough. Not for us to selfishly consume ourselves, but to give away!

Often, we are so spiritually malnourished that we have nothing to offer anyone. We are weak vessels because we spend all our resources chasing after that which is not satisfying. But we need the presence of God more than we need anything else in life. Only His presence will truly satisfy us. God is looking for people who are hungry enough for Him alone that they will be able to feed a nation with His presence.

Anyone who is desperate enough for Jesus will be satisfied! Thank God we can do nothing in ourselves to earn this provision; it has been paid for already. But we need hungry hearts in order to receive. And when we do, Jesus multiplies whatever He pours into us until we find ourselves feeding others—the spiritually desperate and starving. He wants to place something of Himself in our hands that will be a provision to many.

We live in a broken world. Jesus wants us to notice and help those around us who are so in need of His presence. He wants us to reach out to them. But we can't go to them empty handed. We need the fresh bread of His presence to feed the starving.

Overcome

During a recent outreach in a nearby village, I preached a salvation message in this unreached area, and nearly everyone wanted to receive Jesus as their Lord and Savior. I felt God ask me to challenge the people to bring the blind, deaf and crippled to be healed.

I held a deaf and mute man in my arms and prayed for him to hear and speak in the name of Jesus. His tongue was immediately loosed, and his ears opened. For the first time in fifteen years, he spoke and heard! It was beyond beautiful.

The next lady had not heard anything in twelve years. I put my fingers in her ears and commanded her ears to be opened in the name of Jesus. Her smile lit up my world as Jesus opened her ears.

Next was a little boy around twelve years of age. He had been completely blind since birth and was sent away from his village by his parents to beg in the city. His guide, who led him around the streets of Pemba, was with me on the truck. I spit on my fingers and put them on his eyelids. I held him in my arms and rocked him back and forth as I felt the deep love the Father has for this boy. When I asked him to open his eyes, he saw light for the first time! He looked around in amazement as his eyes were opened by the glorious love and grace of Jesus. I held him close and began to weep at the beauty of what Jesus had just done.

After such a fabulous miracle, others pressed forward to receive healing. A lady with a crippled foot for ten years leapt for joy as her foot was made whole by the Lamb of God. Drunks came weeping to the front, declaring their desire to be saved.

Most of us won't face the challenge of such need on a daily basis. But we still have challenges to overcome; still obstacles stand in our way, insurmountable to the natural eye. No matter what we go through in life, we will get through because we are in love with the one who is altogether lovely.

Come Closer

• Small children don't plan or worry about their lives. They are content to allow their parents to do things for them. Let's exhibit the same kind of trust for our Father, who only wants the best for us all the time. Trust Him to guide, lead and provide.

• Sometimes, when we go through life's trials, we are surrounded by well-meaning, loving people—who give us conflicting advice! In these times, what we need is Father's advice—His word on our situation. So go and find a quiet place, shut the door, and enter His resting place. Be still. Listen. Wait. He will speak His words of life into your situation.

• This week, remember that you are a presence carrier. Immerse yourself in Jesus' presence and be mindful of His presence wherever you go and whatever you do.

• Take time to feast on the Bread of Life. If we walk around spiritually malnourished, we won't be able to survive, let alone feed anyone else.

The Hungry Always Get Fed

Something we have learned by feeding the poor is that the hungry always get fed. The hungry eat; the thirsty drink. They are so concerned with being fed that they dispense with all apathy. The hungriest people will always push and shove their way to the front of the line to receive the bread. There is no "Well, if we get it, we get it; if we don't, we don't."

Sometimes the Church is like that. "Whatever God wants to do is okay with me," we say. "I'm here if He wants to show up." Yet, something about the person with an all-consuming desperation for Jesus touches His heart.

I freely admit I am a glutton for God. I am so desperate for whatever God has to offer me that I will let people from any stream of Church life pray for me. It makes no difference to me who they are, where they are from or what they look like. If they have an anointing from God, then I want it, too!

Once, a minister prayed for me and God really touched me. Our backgrounds and experiences were so different it made my head spin. I had been living in the slums for years, working with the poor, walking in the dirt. My friend wore an $8,000 suit and spoke about the $15 million house he owned. To say that the worlds we lived in were a little different would be a gross understatement.

But he had an anointing. So I didn't give a rip about his $15 million house. I thought, Whatever that guy has, I'm getting it. I did this because I am a glutton for God. I didn't want his house, but I did want his anointing. I didn't care about the package. The package can upset you. But who cares about the package? We must go for whatever God has for us, because we know it will always be good.

Junk Food

Spiritually speaking, so many believers attempt to live on spiritual junk food—the equivalent of cotton candy, diet coke and Twinkies. This is all they ever eat, yet they complain they are tired. Why are they tired? Because they are trying to live on junk food!

Why do people try to survive on spiritual junk when God has laid out a feast for us to eat? Instead of consuming stuff that makes us sick, we need to eat food that will make us strong and well. We need to constantly eat of Jesus. We need to drink of Him.

My prayer for you is that God will provoke you to a holy hunger.

Isaiah 55:1 says, "Come, all you who are thirsty, come to the waters; and you who have no money..."

Sometimes the Western Church feels disqualified by its wealth. In Africa, it is impossible to feel that way because of the poverty. When it is time for church in Africa, we never have any parking problems when the people turn up. If we have even one car in the parking lot, when four thousand people gather to worship, it is a big deal: "Wow! Who has a car? It must be somebody really important!"

In Africa, we cannot come to God any other way than with our poverty. But in the West, we often have the mentality that we must pay for the free gifts God wants to give us. The greatest trap is thinking we have to pay for God's blessings with our spiritual discipline. I teach on spiritual discipline all the time, but here is a fact: You cannot pay someone for food that has already been given freely. You cannot pay for something that has already been purchased by the blood of the Lamb. It is free!

If you are thirsty, God invites you to come and drink. He wants you to come without your money. Leave your wallet at home, because you cannot buy this food and drink. It is not for sale.

Seeing

We arrived at the rubbish dump as night set in. We drove down a bumpy dirt lane, then turned right. Towering off and up to our right were 100-meter-high piles of rubbish, stretching out for a kilometer back up the hill to the main road. Every fifty meters or so, fires burned to reduce the volume of waste. Smoke wafted overhead, the stench a combination of the fires and the refuse. Silhouettes of men, here and there, rummaged for food or re-sellable scraps. The scene was apocalyptic.

We could hear the singing as we parked the car immediately outside the front of the church. We walked into a dimly lit room. Two kerosene lanterns hung from the supporting branch poles. A narrow five-foot concrete platform formed the front of the room. On the platform were seven kids ranging from a couple of sixteen-year-old girls down to five-year-olds. They were leading worship. All we could see of their faces was their smiles, it was so dark! They sang passionately, nasally, and in tune. In front of them on the dirt floor was the local pastor. The singing finished, and the pastor began to pray. He poured his heart out in a desperate prayer, his voice rising and falling with the anguish and desire in his heart.

The pastor then asked all the visitors to line up at the front, as the church wanted to bless us. Many people stepped forward to lay hands on us and pray. One of the young ladies from the worship team, along with an older lady, stood before me. In my spirit, it occurred to me that I was in one of the richest places on earth, because they loved and knew Jesus so passionately. This was the Body of Christ, standing before me, ministering to me. It was even more special than that: I recognized in their eyes the characteristics of Jesus, just as you can often see the likeness of a mother when looking at her daughter. Jesus Himself drew near to me; He was that recognizable in their faces!

If we have eyes to see, it's amazing where Jesus will reveal Himself to us. Remain open.

Love, Not Victory

People tend to want to read about only the glory stories coming out of this revival Jesus is leading, but there are gutsy stories, too. Unless you have the wider perspective of life here, you will have a lopsided understanding of what God is doing. Often, He teaches us about His glory presence through suffering.

Once, we had a meeting in which we were praying for four of our kids who were really sick. They had measles and malaria, and in the end, two of them died. It happened just before we were due to go away for our annual staff retreat. That year, we had a visiting speaker who had come to minister to our one hundred and sixty staff. Bear in mind that the children who had died were our babies, our precious children. I was not at all impressed, then, when the speaker told us, "You all just need to laugh more!"

I thought to myself, I don't think the Lord is laughing at the moment. In fact, I wanted to say, "I think your head is a little tilted my friend!" But I had to make a choice. Was I going to get angry with this person, or was I going to bless this person? I ended up blessing the person, of course, but it shook my world.

The very next Monday, I found myself lying face down on a grass mat with the mother of one of the little girls who had died. I lay down with this woman and wept with her, holding her in my arms. It was then God said to me, "Heidi, it's about love. It's not always about victory." Our whole life cannot be about victory and glory, but it must be about love. Love is patient and kind and long-suffering. God's love is the kind of love that is extravagant, bottomless, ceaseless and endless. That's what you need when you are on the floor holding a grieving mother.

Won Over by Love

We all need a download of holy love that so motivates us that it doesn't matter what anyone does to us. We just love them, regardless. If people offend you, like I was offended, you love them. If people spit in your face, you love them. If people falsely arrest you, you love them. When they put you in jail, you love them. When they beat you, you love them. We won over the garbage dump by love.

The first time I walked into the garbage dump, a guy named Vidal, who had a broken bottle in his hand, stuck it against my neck and said, "I'm going to slit your throat. What are you doing in my dump you idiot white woman? I'm going to kill you now."

I said to him, "Wait a minute. I'm so sorry. Just wait a second." And then I told him about Jesus dancing on the dump and putting clothes of beautiful gold and silver and blue and purple on the people in the dump. I told him I was walking with Jesus and said, "We put our hands upon your big bellies, and they sink in. We put our hands upon your bullet wounds, and they are healed. We put our hands upon your bleeding sores, and they disappear, and the lice die." I said to him, "I want to tell you about a feast that is ready and prepared, and God wants you to be there. Vidal, you are very beautiful, and you are invited to the head table."

After about half an hour of him grabbing me and threatening me, listening in between, he knelt in the garbage and began weeping. He said to me, "Could you please bring this man Jesus here because I want to meet Him." Vidal was the first person to receive Christ on the rubbish dump, and now his entire village is saved. They were hungry, physically and spiritually, and we were offering them free food, physically and spiritually. They were very hungry. Are you? Jesus wants to give you more of Himself. He wants you to be immersed in His love so you can love others recklessly, completely, full of God's outrageous grace.

Do This...

God is not interested in using the mighty, but the willing. He is not into using amazing people, just ones who are prepared to lay their lives down before Him. God is not looking for extraordinary, exceptionally gifted people, just laid-down lovers of Jesus who will carry His glory with transparency and not take it for themselves.

In Luke 10:25, we read about a wise man, a well educated expert on the Law who stood up and challenged Jesus. He wanted to test Jesus, so he asked Him, "Excuse me, teacher. What must I do to inherit eternal life?" The question, in and of itself, was a good one. But Jesus, being predisposed to answer a question with another question, shot straight back at him with: "What is written in the Law? How do you read it?"

The Law expert already knew the answer. He replied, "'Love the Lord your God with all your heart and with all your soul and with all your strength and with all your mind'; and 'love your neighbor as yourself'" (Luke 10:27). This man knew how to answer Jesus' question, but he did not know what he ought to do about it. He was unable to comprehend what it meant in practical terms.

This man who spoke to Jesus did not get it. He spoke out the words, but he missed the point. Jesus responded to him, saying, "Yes, you've answered correctly," but then He added one more little statement: "Do this and you will live" (Luke 10:28). This is what the Law expert really needed to understand. And this is the part we need to get if we want to see revival. If we love God with all our beings, with reckless devotion, we will live! If we do this, we will see revival. If we do this, the Gospel will go forth. This is the simplicity of Jesus' message.

Come Closer

• The hungriest people always find a way to get fed. Let's nurture that kind of spiritual hunger in our lives so we become passionate about His presence.

• Jesus' call to us is, "Come, all you who are thirsty. . ." (Isaiah 55:1). We may try all kinds of things to fill our lives, but in the end, only Jesus can satisfy us. And His invitation is always before us. We are always welcome to come to Him. Nothing can disqualify us.

• Life is not all about victory, but it is all about love. God's ceaseless, bottomless, endless, extravagant love. People are not won to Christ by words but by a demonstration of real love.

Pray this prayer:

Father God, You are not interested in using the cleverest, wisest, most resourceful people, but You are interested in the willing and freely available. I want to make myself available to You, to be useful to You in whatever ways You see fit. Pour Your love into me afresh today so I can share it with whomever You put in front of me. Amen.

Nothing More

I get into some wild spots at times, but nothing I do is difficult. It's not difficult because I am driven by love. I am compelled and motivated by love. My passion for Jesus causes me to pour compassion into others. That's the Gospel—a passion that births compassion.

All fruitfulness flows from intimacy, and it is intimacy unto a harvest. Intimacy has to be for a purpose. If we want to embrace our Father's heart, we must know that our Father's desire is for His house to be full. The Father looks out at all the orphans of the world and wants them to be loved, accepted, welcomed home. When I stop to pick up an orphan off the street, it is a prophetic act that reflects the Father's heart.

The King of Glory is looking for servant-lovers who will bring in the poor, the crippled, the blind and the lame and fill up His house. He is looking for servant-lovers who know who they are and are not afraid—who are so full of love that fear is not a word in their vocabulary. Radical lovers of God move in radical compassion!

The expert of the Law who questioned Jesus couldn't accept the simplicity and directness of His words. "No, no," he said, "surely you don't mean that. There must be something else. It can't possibly be that simple." He was unable to comprehend the simplicity of the truth that the whole of life flows out of a reckless love for and devotion to the Father—that such a love spills out of us and touches everyone we meet.

Actually, it is that simple. Love God and love the person in front of you. Keep doing it over and over. That's all it takes. Then we will be fruitful. But it begins with intimacy, nothing more.

Herb Tea

The power of God, the presence of God, the multiplication of the Gospel is as simple as this: a physical demonstration of the love of God. We have overcomplicated our message, thinking we were being wise. We have analyzed the Gospel to death until it doesn't work any more! We have made it so intensely difficult to understand that we have theologized, theorized and strategized ourselves into a corner. We have not understood that the Gospel is as simple as this: love, love, love, love, love!

The Gospel is about passion. Do you understand that when you are a passionate lover of God, He will do anything for you? When you are madly in love with someone, you will do anything for that person, won't you? Rolland hates herb tea. He thinks it's disgusting. But when he came to see me when we were dating, I would often say to him, "Would you like some herb tea?"

And he would say, "Oh, yes, thank you!"

The day after we got married, he told me, "I hate herb tea. It's horrible! I can't believe you would ever drink that!"

Amazed, I said to him, "But, you drank it for months when you came over to visit me!"

Rolland replied, "Yes, but I was just so in love!"

People who are in love do things like that. They don't care. They don't care when they get shot at or when their heads gets banged against a wall. They don't care when people put knives to their throats. They don't care when the Marxists are firing their machine guns in the air. They don't care because they are in love! Love is what drives us forward. We are not driven through slavery or a desire to be somebody, because we already know we are children of the Most High God. It doesn't matter what anyone thinks of us. It doesn't matter what we look like or what the world says. We are adopted sons and daughters of God, so in love that we will do anything for Him!

Good Samaritan

The Law expert tried another line of questioning with Jesus. "Who is my neighbor?" (Luke 10:29). Another good question. Is it the famine victim in Malawi? The person in prison in Afghanistan? The person who lives under a bridge in Mozambique? The person who lives down the street from you and works at K-mart? The answer is: all of these people. But because Jesus knew the man would not understand the depth and reach of a simple word like everyone, He began to tell a story.

The story of the Good Samaritan is one that has so impacted my life, because I am challenged to live it every day. I'm not saying that to make any grand claim, but for me, this story illustrates the simplicity of the Gospel, and it has come alive inside me. I believe it is as simple as Jesus says it is.

I've walked the road from Jerusalem to Jericho, where Jesus set His story. It is a descending road that is dusty and not very wide. It is impossible, naturally speaking, to miss someone lying at the side of the road. You would almost have to step over the person. You could not pretend you didn't see a dying man there.

Sometimes we cannot see and don't want to see because we are blinded. We need eye salve to put on our eyes. We cry out for revival, and yet God says, "I want to open your eyes so you can see what is before you. Revival has a face and a name. It lies bleeding on the roadside."

If we want to see revival, we need to begin with the one in front of us.

Gito

When God let the Good Samaritan message burn in my heart, He told me, "Heidi, I want you to stop for them all." It was a prophetic statement. When I first arrived in Mozambique, I was on my own. Rolland was finishing writing his doctoral thesis. I went out with a one-way ticket and no possessions. After two days I ran out of money. I was sitting alone on the curb side, wondering what to do, and God met with me there and told me, "This is where I have sent you. You are going to see revival here, and all I want you to do is stop for the one."

So that is all I did. I didn't have some strategic plan for how to reach the city by 20XX. I didn't have it all figured out in my mind. All I knew was God had told me to stop for the one. He told me, "Heidi, I want you to see. I want the passion I put inside you to be so full that compassion flows out of you." So I began to sit with the poor and pick up little children and love them.

One day I picked up Gito. Gito had been beaten and raped and was dying there on the street. He was a skinny little kid who had been violated, abused and left for dead. He was dying on the road under a flyby, and I sat with him and held him in my arms and loved him. He had AIDS. I held him in my arms and said, "Come home with me, Gito."

His was the face of revival.

There was no snazzy plan, no slick brochures. Later, God totally healed Gito of AIDS. We received the negative tests back from the doctor. There are thousands more orphans like Gito. They are the face of revival. Jesus said, "Whatever you do to the least of these you do to me" (see Matthew 25:40). I have seen the face of Jesus in the faces of the street children. I have seen His eyes looking at me through their eyes.

When you stop for one person like Gito and pour the compassion of God into him and tell him he is adopted, it has a dramatic effect on him. Many others on the road are bleeding, desperate and dying, yet they are well-dressed. They work in banks and offices; they attend universities. They do not look poor. They look affluent, but they are wretched, naked and dying. Can you see them?

Miracle of Suffering

Early on in our ministry we lost our buildings (all 55 of them) and were left homeless. We were at the most desperate place we've ever been. We had nothing at all. Yet it was at that moment I suddenly thought, Who cares! In fact, who cares if we literally starve to death—us and all our children? I had come to a place where I realized God's presence was worth more to me than life itself. This is not a joke or an exaggeration. I am seriously saying Jesus' presence is worth more to me than anything; His love and precious blood are worth more to me than life. I don't see the point of prosperity and wellbeing in life if all it does is distract you from Jesus.

What was surprising was that here, when we had reached the lowest place ever, all heaven started to break open for us. When we were suffering, God manifested Himself in a very real way. In the West, we don't like the idea of suffering. We would prefer that no one had to suffer—especially not those who are in Christ. But the fact is, when we began suffering and when hundreds of children fell on their faces worshiping God and crying out to Him—then the miracles began to flow. What food we had was miraculously multiplied; power came from heaven that supernaturally sustained us, and many other miracles occurred. The miracles that happened when we had lost everything and had no backup plan and nothing to eat or drink were amazing. When we literally had no ability to live, no way to function in the natural, God came like a cloud and took care of us.

Sometimes suffering can be a wonderful thing. Maybe you need to hear that? Suffering can bring you closer to God. Of course, it's never our first choice, but when it happens it can birth either bitterness or compassion in us. Through suffering a great compassion has been birthed in me—compassion for anyone who is hurting.

Don't be afraid of suffering. The immense love of Jesus is far bigger than anything you will face in life. Surrender yourself to Him completely, and the challenges life throws you will never look the same again.

Rejoicing

God hates the injustice of sickness and wants it to be destroyed. Having watched what God does, now I hate sickness with a passion, too, just as He does. But so often, the battles we win against sickness here are won for others more than ourselves. Several times in my life, I have been very sick, and I have asked God, "Why is it that I have to fight against sickness?"

God said to me, "You are fighting for the Church." In many ways God is mirroring in my life what He wants to do in the Church. I don't understand why, but He is using me as a kind of prophetic symbol.

I was in South Africa with a friend. I was meant to be looking after her, but I ended up being hospitalized and fed antibiotics through an IV drip. I didn't like being there, so one day I said to her, "Let's just rip the IV out and go and get some Chinese food!" So we did. The hospital was not at all happy about this, but we paid my medical bill on the way out, so what could they say?

In South Africa, I learned an important principle for all who want to move in a healing anointing and all who want to experience God's healing in their own lives—thankfulness and rejoicing. Often, when we are prayed for, we feel a little better, but maybe we are aware we are not fully healed. We tend to look for instantaneous, complete healing instead of rejoicing in the fact that God has touched us. In that hospital, I learned to give thanks for every little bit of healing God gave as He gave it.

I became grateful for every little step I could take until I was able to run and jump. With every step I took, I rejoiced in what Jesus was doing. I didn't moan and say, "But, I can only take a few little steps." Rejoicing is so important.

Come Closer

• Intimacy with our Father is wonderful. But intimacy is for a purpose. We immerse ourselves in His love so we are equipped to share that love with others. We can't impart anything of eternal value to others out of our own natural resources, but we can draw on the riches of heaven and change a person's life.

• When we stop for a person and pour out the compassion of Jesus, it is life changing. It can and will have dramatic effects. But we must learn to see—to see the needs of those around us, even if they do a good job disguising them.

• In life we go through bumpy patches. It's inevitable. But does not need to be unfruitful. Suffering connects us to the heart of God like nothing else. Instead of becoming bitter about our circumstances, we can ask Father to birth a deeper compassion in us. Suffering is a season. Seasons come and go. When you move into the next season of your life, take compassion, not bitterness, with you.

• Remember to rejoice!

Running Shoes

God made us to run our course and finish our race. We must never take our eyes off the finish line or give in. Even when I was sick, I was determined to run—both physically and spiritually.

On my first day in the hospital, I told Rolland, "Oh no, I forgot my running shoes." It seemed like a stupid statement. Just walking a few paces was agonizing. Nevertheless, I told Rolland, "Go and get some!"

Rolland didn't argue with me. He just said okay, went off to a shopping mall and found me some running shoes. He didn't come back with a bunch of flowers and say, "Look, you really won't be running, so I brought these." He knew I was determined not to die. Rather, I was determined to run!

While I was in the hospital, Jesus reached out to the spiritually malnourished around me. One doctor came to me and told me I'd better think about writing my epitaph. I bought him a Bible. He was a Russian doctor who had never read or even seen one before. I talked to him about Jesus, and the presence of God filled my room.

As time went on, God's presence got thicker and thicker in my room until, eventually, the ladies who came in to change my sheets wouldn't leave. They wanted to stay in my room, and they just kept weeping. They would say, "There's so much life in this room!"

After 32 days of battling, tired and weary, I prayed, "God, I know your presence can kill this infection. Your presence can kill what antibiotics cannot. You are a powerful God who destroys the work of the enemy." Rolland and I decided we would leave the hospital and visit another "Specialist." We would, after all, attend a conference in Toronto I was due to speak at. While I was there preaching, hardly able to stand, our sovereign Lord healed me completely, and I danced in His presence once again!

Never reduce your theology to your experience. Believe every word God says. Be thankful for everything. And know that it is time to get out your running shoes and finish your race. Run with perseverance and never, ever give up!

How Deep?

God loves us so much He wants to destroy our preconceptions about Him so His Holy Spirit can move freely among us. God likes to shatter the boxes we create in order to contain Him and His work among us. The fact is, God does not like being put in a box! God is sovereign and holy. He likes to be God! He wants us to participate in His divine nature, follow in His footsteps. But He makes all the decisions. We just follow. God likes to be in control. He wants to take over because that is just God doing His thing. Our job is to be yielded lovers, willing to cooperate with Him.

A few years ago, I determined I didn't care how God used me; I just wanted to be fully possessed by His Holy Spirit. That is my prayer every day. Consequently, I often don't know what day it is, what time it is, what country I'm in or what time my flight is leaving! My only desire is to be led by the Spirit wherever and whenever. I just hope somebody puts me on my plane when I'm due to be on it. I often don't know where I am going, but I do know I'm in love. That's all that matters to me.

In Ezekiel 47, Ezekiel is given a prophetic vision by God. The angel of the Lord leads him deeper and deeper into the river that flows from the temple of God. What is this river of God that is talked about so much? When we speak of the river of God, we are talking about Jesus, about His manifest glory. The river is not an it but a Him. God draws us into the river so we can be immersed in Him. He desires to swallow us up until we are not seen any more. We must allow ourselves to be so immersed in His presence that He has total control over us. Then His glory-presence enfolds us in such a way that we start thinking His thoughts, and His heart begins to beat inside us, and we feel its rhythm.

Deeper Still

The angel of the Lord asked Ezekiel, in effect, "How deep do you want to get?" (see Ezekiel 47). How deep into the heart of God are you willing to go? How deep into His presence do you want to be? God wants to saturate you in His presence—to literally drown you! Yes, God wants you dead! But then He will kiss you to life, as a new creation, to be the fragrance of Christ to a dying world.

At first Ezekiel only went into the water up to his ankles. Most of us like the thought of that. When we are ankle deep in God, it feels good, because we can still do our thing. We have something of God, but we can walk and talk and, more importantly, be in control.

The angel of the Lord said to Ezekiel, as God says to us today, "I want you to come in deeper than that." God wants us to lose ourselves in Him, to be out of our depth in His presence, carried away by the irresistible currents of His love. God is wooing us, persuading us to go deeper and deeper into Him, to pursue Him with reckless devotion. He is leading us into the glory presence of the Most High, leading us into a place where we will no longer be in control but rather out of control and fully yielded to His Spirit.

Perhaps God has spoken to you about what He sees for your life, yet you are still only knee deep in the water, at best. You will never come into the fullness of your destiny until you allow God to draw you in and drag you under. You have to die first! Then you will see God's purpose for your life come to pass. He will resurrect you. You need not be afraid; only surrender completely to Him.

How deep will you go into Him? Wade out into the waters of His presence, and whatever you do, don't stop until you are completely submerged in His love, mercy and grace.

Going Under

When Ezekiel was drawn by the angel of the Lord deeper and deeper into the river of God, eventually the water came up to his waist, and it was a river he could not cross. The water was deep enough to swim in. Ezekiel had come to the place of immersion. I am continually contending to be in this place in my life. I pray a holy hunger rises up in you, too, so you will begin contending for a life of full submersion and enter the place where your will is totally subject to His will, your spirit to His Spirit. This is the place where the miracles can begin to happen.

The more immersed in God you become, the less of a grip "normal" life has on you. Circumstances throw themselves against you, but you remain unmoved. When you are deep in God's river, even the tragedies of life that inevitably come only force you deeper into Him.

When all hell breaks loose, you have a choice. You can either go deeper into the river of God's presence, or you can retreat from the water and try to figure out what to do in your own strength. For a long while, I was in the twilight zone between these two places, yet the Spirit of God was continually calling me deeper.

At times of great need—even though I was not full of faith—I have cried out to God and expressed my dependency on Him. He has answered, time and again, with miracles. Each time it happened, I went a little deeper into Him. Eventually, I began to plunge into His river with little hesitation.

The deeper you get into the river of God's glory, the more you discover how good He really is. He turns out to be so much more beautiful than you can imagine. Don't worry today if you feel you are in over your head. Something fresh and powerful can begin to flow through your life when you allow yourself to soak in the river of God. Surrender to Him and let the river flow! Go deeper still.

Sustained

We are sustained by beholding Jesus' beauty. We are confident in His cross. We are satisfied by what He has done. His Gospel is all-sufficient. We will immerse ourselves forever in the river that flows from His throne. We are more than conquerors through Him who loved us!

We choose His perspective. From another perspective, we are assaulted relentlessly. Often we are exhausted, overextended and overrun by needs, crises, corruption, disappointment and the desperate cry for relief that rises up constantly from the poor of the world. We cannot keep up with the demand for spiritual relief that calls for our attention from all over the world.

But His mercy and compassion never fail. They are new every morning.

We are never discouraged, for:

"We have this treasure in jars of clay to show that this all-surpassing power is from God and not from us. We are hard pressed on every side, but not crushed; perplexed, but not in despair; persecuted, but not abandoned; struck down, but not destroyed. We always carry around in our body the death of Jesus, so that the life of Jesus may also be revealed in our body." (2 Corinthians 4:7–10)

Here in Africa, among the poorest of the poor, we are seeing revival fuelled and sustained by the power of God, in spite of all our weaknesses. Onlookers react in many different ways, and there is always so much to criticize, but at the core of this movement is a white-hot, total abandonment to Jesus and His Kingdom.

We will not be led astray from the simplicity and purity of devotion to Him. We are advancing. Our weapons are a firm faith, gentleness, peace, patience and love that cannot be resisted. In Him we cannot lose!

In God I Trust

For an entire year and a half, we did not lose one child to sickness or accident—until Maria. For a few days, I had no peace. I could not understand why God had given us Maria only to take her away so quickly. In painful sincerity, I expressed my confusion, questions and doubts to God, not so much in words as in tears.

"Record my misery; list my tears on your scroll—are they not on your record? Then my enemies will turn back when I call for help. By this I will know that God is for me. In God, whose word I praise, in the LORD, whose word I praise—in God I trust..." (Psalm 56:8–11).

"Trust in the LORD with all your heart, and lean not on your own understanding; in all your ways acknowledge Him, and He shall direct your paths." (Proverbs 3:5–6, NKJV)

"When I tried to understand all this, it troubled me deeply till I entered the sanctuary of God; then I understood their final destiny." (Psalm 73:17)

When the challenges, hardships and tragedies of life come—and they will come—where do we turn? To our own logic? To what we think is best? Or will we turn to Him?

Only in the refuge of His presence can we find true peace, healing and strength for this life. Jesus knows and cares. Will we trust Him? Perhaps one of His greatest (and hardest) love lessons is to live out Psalm 56:11: "In God I trust..."

"My soul, wait silently for God alone, for my expectation is from Him. He only is my rock and my salvation; He is my defense; I shall not be moved. In God is my salvation and my glory; the rock of my strength, and my refuge, is in God. Trust in Him at all times, you people; pour out your heart before Him; God is a refuge for us. Selah." (Psalm 62:5–8, NKJV)

Come Closer

• God always finishes what He has started. No matter where you are in your "race" today, know that He is committed to finishing what He has begun in you. You may feel like you have tripped and fallen, failed. Perhaps you feel like you've lost the path and don't know how to get back on track. Maybe you feel like others have cut in front of you and are frustrating your progress. No matter. God started this race of yours; He will finish it. Hold on. Keep going. Trust.

• We tend to be experts at putting things in boxes. We like to know how things work; we like things that are predictable, because it makes us feel safe. God is not predictable or safe or definable. We can't put Him in a box. We'll never get to the bottom of Him. The sooner we stop trying, the happier we'll be.

• Instead, we can immerse ourselves in Him and allow Him to be fully in control of our lives. He's not content with ankle-deep devotion; He wants us to lose ourselves in Him, to be swept under, knowing full well that as we lose ourselves in Him we will truly find ourselves.

Father, my simple prayer today is: Help me to lose myself in reckless devotion to You. Let me be submerged so that You alone are fully in control. Thank You that in losing myself, I truly find You. And in finding You, I find everything. Amen.

Are You Blind?

I went through a season when I longed to see God heal the blind. Everywhere I went, I looked for blind people so I could pray for them. If I was driving my truck and spotted a blind person, I would slam on the brakes, leap out and pray for that person. It was okay because they never saw me coming!

One day, in a mud hut church, I noticed a blind lady and got excited, thinking, Here is another opportunity. Maybe God will heal this lady! I took hold of her and began to pray. A wave of supernatural compassion engulfed me, and I began sobbing my heart out until God touched this lady and—bang—she fell backward onto the floor.

I could see her totally white, unseeing eyes. As I stared, her eyes turned from white to grey to brown, and she blinked as God restored her sight. When she realized she could see, she began screaming in excitement. I managed to ask her, "What's your name?"

To my surprise she answered, "Mama Ida [Heidi]."

"Oh," I said, "That's my name, too!"

A couple days later, I was in the next village and prayed for another lady. The same thing happened. She was healed, and when I asked her name, she replied, "Mama Ida." Two Heidi's in two days! I thought. That's amazing!

A day later, I prayed for another blind lady. When she was healed, her church began shouting, "Mama Ida can see!"

I couldn't believe my ears. I asked God what it meant. He said, "You're blind!"

I was shocked. I argued, but eventually I gave in. "If I am blind God, I want to see."

He said, "I am giving you eye salve, and I'm causing your eyes to open. I am giving you eye salve for the Church. My Church's eyes have been blurred. They have been slow to see. But I am opening the eyes of the Church."

The Lord used these strange healings to show me how blind I was and how much the Church also needs to see—to see what He is doing and join in with Him. Let's not resist Him. We need to see!

Pure Religion

Pure and undefiled religion before God the Father is this: to visit orphans and widows in their trouble, and to keep oneself unspotted from the world. James 1:27, NKJV, emphasis added

What is pure religion? What is pure Christianity? What is pure love? What is this life all about? Is it about how many people we lead to Jesus or how many churches we plant or how good we are as people? Or is it about being so hidden in the heart of our awesome, eternal God of love that we are swallowed up in Him until it is no longer we who live, but Christ lives in us?

"And the King will answer and say to them, "Assuredly, I say to you, inasmuch as you did it to one of the least of these My brethren, you did it to Me" (Matthew 25:40, NKJV, emphasis added).

The reason I am in Africa, the reason I have come to serve here, the reason I am alive, is for this purpose and this purpose alone: to learn how to love like Jesus loved.

Every day Jesus meets me in unexpected ways. Sometimes He is an orphan looking for love and unconditional acceptance. Sometimes He is a widow desperately begging for a simple job in order to provide the basic necessities of life for her hungry children. Sometimes He is another lost and broken person who just needs a hug and someone to listen. But every day I see Him in a new way.

What matters most is love. Jesus living inside us is happy to use our hands to heal the sick, our arms to hug the lost, our feet and our mouths to go and speak about the Kingdom to all who need to hear it.

This is "faith working through love" (Galatians 5:6, NKJV).

Multiplication

Once, a little boy who had a packed lunch—some bread and fish—gave it up to God and saw a great miracle (see John 6:2). Jesus was surrounded by a group of hungry people, and He needed to feed them. This little kid had a meager offering of food, but Jesus received the gift he offered, and God extravagantly multiplied it.

Here is a multitude of need, and Jesus has a problem—a huge crowd of people who are hungry and want to be fed. I can easily visualize the scene. Recently, we had a conference where twelve thousand people gathered in the bush. They were ravenously hungry, spiritually as well as naturally. Many people had walked three days without food to get to the meeting. They had waded through crocodile infested water with bare feet. They had slept outside on the dirt with no grass mats and no cover for four or five days because they were so desperate to get a touch from God. And He would not let them down.

No doubt Jesus looked around, spotted this little kid with his lunch, and thought, I can use him. We are a lot like that kid. We are nothing special, naturally speaking, yet in God's eyes we are totally awesome. He can do great things with us if we will cooperate with Him. Your little lunch in the hands of God can feed a multitude!

But hear this: We have to stop looking at our lunches (because they are kind of pitiful) and look at God! Stop looking at your limited resources and start looking at the one who can multiply them. Stop looking at your life and thinking how insignificant it looks! Yield it to God—fully, totally, completely—and allow Him to multiply it.

Look at Me

Most people look at their own inadequacies and protest—"But, look at me!"—whenever anyone suggests God could use them in incredible ways. They think God couldn't do a miracle through them, that somehow they are a special case.

Whenever we say, "But look at me, Lord," He responds, "No, look at Me!"

As God has worked in my life, eventually I have stopped looking at me all the time. I don't want to look at me any more. I know me! Instead, I want to live in the secret place and look at Him. When we focus totally on Him, we stop worrying about me altogether.

My purpose became to keep my vision fixed on the beauty of Him, the glory of Him, the holiness of Him, the all-sufficiency of Him. In effect, I said to God, like the little boy, "You want my lunch? Well, here, take it! It's small and insignificant, so I don't know what You can do with it, but You're welcome!"

I think if that little boy had held anything back from Jesus, he may have prevented a miracle. I'm theorizing, of course. In the same way, we cannot hold back from God. You cannot divide up your life, giving a bit to God and holding some back for yourself, just in case He doesn't show up. It's all or nothing! God doesn't do half-measures. You have to throw yourself into Him completely, holding nothing back. Then, He is able to do the miraculous with your life. Then, He can do what only He can do.

Please give Him your "lunch"—your life! What do you want to hold on to it for? Remember, God can do anything with anybody.

Perfect

Though you have not seen Him, you love Him, and though you do not see Him now, but believe in Him, you greatly rejoice with joy inexpressible and full of glory.
1 Peter 1:8, NASB

Faith and joy are rare commodities among us, but they are valuable and precious beyond words. How extraordinary that we chase after other things at the expense of these. Our salvation is complete in Him, and we honor our God by not detracting from the all-sufficiency of the Gospel. In faith our desperation gives way to righteousness, peace and joy in the Holy Spirit—without measure. Our total trust in our Savior is the substance of our intimacy with Him, and no self-condemnation or weakness can diminish our fiery love affair with our God.

We trust Jesus to save us from ourselves. We trust Him to take initiative in and through us. All bright ideas come from Him, and He has no lack of them! We are set completely free from all pressure. There is no compulsion in His Kingdom.

But if we are so totally helpless without Him, how does He still enjoy our company?

In Jesus we are the crowning achievement of all His creative power. We find our greatest liberty at the point of His most complete control, where we are set free by His Spirit to do what is most spectacularly, ravishingly perfect. We and our lives are the field of the activity of His mind, which we must never underestimate. We are the outcome and substance of His joy. By His Spirit we partake of His pleasure, tasting the perfection of relationship that could rise only from His infinite imagination. He delights in His own handiwork, which is our delight in Him.

How perfect is our God!

Wonder

Missions work has often been portrayed as unromantic—a tough, disciplined response to the Great Commission. Prayer is sometimes viewed as hard work—something to be maintained, regardless of our feelings. In fact, feelings have no place in the Christian life; it's getting the job done that counts. Surely we don't need a spiritual experience to proclaim the Gospel.

We believe the opposite. We've been through enough fire and hardship to know that without experiencing God's manifest presence we cannot do what we do. We cannot love others without supernatural, unstoppable love first being poured into us. Trying to function without it is a recipe for burnout and failure.

Jesus is the radiance, the exact image of the invisible God. He is our perfect, our ultimate companion. Our first priority is to know Him in an intimate, passionate relationship, to experience firsthand His love that is stronger than death (see Song of Solomon 8:6).

We are involved in missions work. But our first priority is not strategy, fundraising methods or project management. It is having the life that the world needs and craves. This is not mindless mysticism; it is passion and truth as the basis for life; our motivation for being and doing. When we find Him, we can do anything. Without Him, we can do nothing of real value. We need to set our hearts and minds on Him and hold our gaze in wonder.

Come Closer

• Often we are quick to rely on our own wisdom and resources and slow to see what God is doing. Jesus wants to open our eyes, to help us see Him in every situation in our lives. He is not absent from a single circumstance in your life. Therefore, though the situations before you may perplex and trouble you, you can ask Jesus:

Lord, what do You want to speak into this situation?

Lord, what represents Your will in this situation?

What would You have me do, Lord?

• Wait on Him. He will speak. The answers He gives will be the key to unlocking that thing that currently perplexes and troubles you.

• It is tempting to think that what we have to offer is of no use to God. Nothing could be farther from the truth. God delights in taking the little we have and performing a miracle with it. All we have to do is surrender and obey, to offer the little we have into God's hand and stand back. God can do anything with anybody.

Ask and Trust

When facing great human need with our human frailties, we rapidly reach the limits of our resources, wisdom and love. We face overwhelming poverty, sickness, demonic attacks and every kind of evil. But with excitement and joy we aim beyond what we can imagine doing in our own strength. We run into the darkness looking for bad news, because the power of God gives the world hope. We don't apologize for seeking and valuing power, because without it love is incomplete and ineffectual.

Heidi and I began our life of missions with the dream of living out the Sermon on the Mount, taking Jesus at His word that we do not have to worry about tomorrow. We imagined addressing extreme human need by example— living without anxiety, free to bless always with pure motives, looking to God alone for what our hearts and bodies need. We turn neither to the left nor to the right to gain support. At every obstacle our only confidence is in the cross of Christ and the conviction that God is thrilled to be trusted for miracles all along our way.

We believe we experience miracles because we value them and ask for them, understanding that He will give them to us only if they will not take us farther from Him. For His sake we will lose our lives daily, knowing that by His power we cannot lose, but we will be sustained and become more than conquerors.

Today you can know He is sufficient for whatever challenges you face. You only have to ask and trust.

Opposite

We are not experts. We haven't learned how to do church and revival; we only know to humble ourselves under the mighty hand of God (see 1 Peter 5:6). We gravitate to the low things of the world. Competition and comparison with others don't suit our DNA. We feel no pressure to succeed and excel, but we find joy in doing things well by the power of the Spirit.

God's ways are the reverse of the world's. We waste our time on the uninfluential and the few, stopping for the one. We show that God cares when no one else does. We go to the neglected, the forgotten, the lonely. We will go anywhere, if possible, to minister to the meek and desperate, the poor in spirit who truly understand their need of God.

The truth is, we are doing what Jesus has told us to do where He has placed us. You must do what God has told you to do wherever He has placed you. But these values we have learned are transferable. If you can learn to humble yourself and depend fully on Jesus, in reckless devotion, you will see miracles. You will see fruit. You will see broken lives restored. It might be at the office, in the supermarket, at the tennis club—anywhere. But as you determine to empty yourself and be filled with His presence, you will begin to see His life spilling out all over.

"But the Helper, the Holy Spirit, whom the Father will send in My name, He will teach you all things..." (John 14:26, NASB).

Joy

Perhaps the most controversial of our IRIS core values is joy. Joy doesn't appear on many people's job descriptions as a non-negotiable item. But for us, it is. Our aim is to impart so much of the Holy Spirit that people cannot stop bubbling over with love and joy.

Why?

The characteristics of God's Kingdom are righteousness, peace and joy in the Holy Spirit (see Romans 14:17). When we have this joy, we are unfettered by our own sorrows and all the more capable of compassion for others.

Heidi and I could never have endured this long without a river of life and joy flowing out of our innermost beings. We are not cynical and downcast about the world or the Church, but we are thrilled with our perfect Savior, who is able to finish what He began in us. We gain nothing by being negative, but we overcome the world with faith that we can cast our cares on Him.

Joy, laughter and a light heart are not disrespectful of God and incongruous in this world. Instead, they are evidence of the life of heaven. We are not referring to cheap and foolish levity that ends in grief but to exultation in the truth and reality of our salvation, a powerful work of the Spirit.

"Our mouths were filled with laughter, our tongues with songs of joy... The LORD has done great things for us, and we are filled with joy... Those who sow in tears will reap with songs of joy. He who goes out weeping, carrying seed to sow, will return with songs of joy, carrying sheaves with him." (Psalm 126:2–6)

Joy is not an abstract concept but a tangible reality. It is birthed in His presence and can fill us, empower us. If you currently struggle to find joy, ask Jesus to fill you afresh.

Imbalance

We trust and love Jesus because He died for us and rose again on our behalf. He is the one who suffered for us. He paid the penalty for our sins. He purchased our lives with His blood. He showed us what love is. So we are loyal to Him alone. We belong to Him and not ourselves. We make it our ambition to please Him. He is our greatest pleasure, our ultimate companion.

We stay on track in life, navigating the many challenges by maintaining a pure and simple faith—eyes fixed on Jesus, the author and perfecter of our faith. When hard pressed, He is the one we focus on.

It is impossible to be devoted to Jesus and not share Him, pure and simple. We cannot see Him now, but God has ordained that we love Him by loving each other, by loving the ones we can see. He is love, so we cannot separate the first commandment from the second. There are many callings, but none is higher than giving water to the thirsty and food to the hungry. The intercessors at home and the troops in the trenches are equals in the Kingdom. We learn to love just as we are gifted and called by God.

Reaching out to others is the logical conclusion of knowing Jesus, because we become like Him and do what He did. We have life and hope; others don't. We have love in our hearts; others don't. All believers are called to spend their lives correcting this imbalance. This may take us around the world or just across the street. Either way, we have to make ourselves available to Jesus and go at His prompting.

Balance

God is so amazing that we cannot adequately describe Him with mere words. When we try to define Him by talking about one particular spiritual issue or one aspect of His character, we soon create a distorted image of Him. It is the same when we examine our own spiritual experience.

For example, Paul counseled Timothy to be dignified, sober, self-controlled. He told him to keep his head in all situations. On the other hand, he tells us to be filled to overflowing with the Holy Spirit and overtaken with joy. Elsewhere we are encouraged to dance before the Lord with all our might and express our love for Him in extravagant displays of affection.

The fact is, if we were confined to one expression or the other, it would be terrible. The choice between a grey, colorless existence or one only marked by displays of emotion is out of balance. Instead, Father God calls us to experience the full spectrum of life in the Spirit—just as Jesus did—which will include tears, sorrow and deep grief married with lightness, mirth, deep peace and inexpressible joy.

In laying down our lives to Jesus, we can know He does not desire to rob us of our personality. Rather, He wants to make us fully, truly human, but touched by the glory of heaven. In Him we become complete. Balanced. Truly ourselves, truly who we are destined to be in Christ. Fully alive for the first time.

Adopted

I grew up in a well-to-do family in Laguna Beach, California. We had a house overlooking the ocean with a private beach. Our neighbors were generally very wealthy. Some were Hollywood actors and actresses. Yet the many millionaires around us were often the poorest people on the beach. God called me to give up my Laguna Beach existence to become a missionary, and I set off penniless to pursue Him on a missionary adventure to some of the most crowded, noisy, smelly, dirty cities in Asia, initially, and then beyond to the heat, dirt and dust of Africa. I was challenged to give up my natural inheritance in pursuit of a spiritual one.

When we give our lives over to the Father, we discover that He adopts us. We're not orphans. He takes us in, because He loves us and we are His kids. It's not because of anything we can do or have done, not because we're better than anyone else, not because we succeeded through hard work where others have failed. Before the foundations of the world He picked us out to receive His grace and mercy, and He just loves us because we are His kids. Period.

Today you are totally accepted. Loved unconditionally. You don't have to worry when you mess up; God still thinks you are awesome.

Whatever effort we put into doing things for Him—like children scribbling pictures for their parents—He thinks we are great. As parents we put those scribbled picture on our fridges, and we're proud of them. While God probably doesn't have a fridge, He does keep and treasure every prayer, every action, every tear, every sacrifice, every heartfelt expression of praise and worship. He simply loves you because you are His. Adopted. Part of His family forever. Destined to live in joy with Him for eternity.

Come Closer

• Remember, your Heavenly Father is sufficient for all your needs. Whatever problems, difficulties or challenges you face today, remember to ask and trust.

• Ask and trust. He is aware of your needs; He just wants to capture your heart.

• Joy is our greatest weapon. The characteristics of God's Kingdom are righteousness, peace and joy in the Holy Spirit (see Romans 14:17). Joy, laughter and levity are not offensive to the Father. On the contrary, they are the evidence of heaven's presence.

• Ask Jesus to fill you again with His joy today.

Paradox

As adopted children of our Father, we don't have anything to prove. Our Father loves us, and He has a future mapped out for us that will fulfill the desires of our hearts. He knows what is embedded deep within us, even before we see it ourselves, even before we have dared to express those hopes and desires to Him. He knows how to bless us and, as one author put it, "subjects us to His relentless kindness." One of the great messages of the recent worldwide renewal has been a fresh discovery of the Father heart of God and His incredible love for His children.

This is a great thing, but it's good this is not the only side of our God. The flip side of this position of unmerited favor is that great joy comes from being rewarded for doing something. So we have the dichotomy of not having to perform for God to earn His grace—and performing works for God to be rewarded with His joy, peace and favor!

It is one of the many apparent scriptural paradoxes. It is amazing that God lavishly pours His love and grace upon us. Yet, it would feel empty if everything was simply handed to us and we did not respond to it by doing something.

Such is the paradox of the life of grace. We are undeserving recipients of unearned grace from our Father. But that grace does not leave us unmoved. Rather, we respond gratefully to His love, and it motivates us to action. This is the grace equation working the correct way around. He initiates; we respond. This is the message of the Gospel. While we were still helpless, Christ died for us.

Counted Worthy

An interesting phrase often crops up in the New Testament: counted worthy. In the book of Acts we first read of the disciples being persecuted for preaching the Gospel. The Pharisees told them to be quiet, but they continued to preach the truth, regardless. So they were persecuted. But they reason: "Is it better to obey God or men?" (See Acts 5:29.)

They were beaten and thrown in jail, but this didn't blunt their joy. Rather, it made them rejoice all the more. Why? They rejoiced because they were counted worthy.

They considered it an honor to suffer for the sake of the name of Jesus. Somehow, this sacrifice supernaturally increased their joy. They were rejoicing more than if they had not been beaten and thrown into prison!

I met a Chinese pastor who had recently been released from prison. He was telling his congregation how he had been mistreated and tortured for his faith. The whole congregation was weeping. I admired their tender hearts. But then someone told me why they were weeping—not out of compassion but because they as individuals had not yet been counted worthy to suffer for Christ!

We are told by Paul to live in such a way as to be counted worthy of the Gospel. Today you may not be called to suffer persecution for your allegiance to the name of Jesus, but maybe you will be tempted to compromise your integrity, to cheat, to tell lies, or to do any one of a number of things that would mean living below the standards of Christ.

Let's remember today the honor of our calling, the privilege we have of serving our Lord.

May we be counted worthy.

Doing

We are called to live lives that are worthy.

In heaven we are going to be rewarded for what we have done while on earth. Doing good works, proving our faith and living a life that is worthy of our calling—these are the things we should pursue.

So often in the renewal we have heard that we don't need to do anything; we can just be still in God's presence, just enjoy and receive. This was a message the Church needed to hear in a specific season. Too many believers, for too many years, had lived a driven lifestyle. They had been obsessed with performance, so focused on serving and pleasing God that they had forgotten how to be children.

That message was perfect for its time. And we are still called to dwell in God's presence, to soak in His love, to be still. If that is all we ever do, however, we are living out of balance. Because we are called to do as well as be.

Jesus is our model. Before His ministry began, He must have spent a vast amount of time simply being in His Father's presence. He came to the public part of His ministry supremely confident in His identity as His Father's Son. Then, as His ministry began, He set aside periods of time to be alone with Father, to dwell, to just be. This was balanced with a very active ministry program, lots of travel, lots of meeting people's needs as the Father brought them across Jesus' path.

So in our quest to follow Jesus, let's not be so busy that we have no time to dwell. But let's also not spend so much time simply being that we forget doing.

Works of Righteousness

We can rest assured that our lives are covered by the grace of God—our sins forgiven, our past mistakes and failures wiped out. We can move forward, certain in the knowledge that our Father accepts us completely and affirms our identity in Christ. We can enjoy God's amazing, unmerited favor on our lives.

But the wonder of His grace becomes all the more wonderful when on top of that blessing, He rewards us for what we have done.

God is not impressed with our righteousness; the righteousness we have is given to us by Him anyway. But He does something amazing with it: He blesses us for exercising the righteousness He has given us!

It's wonderful to hear Father say to us, "I love you just as you are, no matter what." And often we need to hear that message and absorb it into our souls. But it is even more wonderful when He says, "I love you for what you are doing for Me."

God notices and loves us for the sacrifices we make.

He loves us for the faithfulness we prove in our lives.

He loves us for the strength of spirit we display.

He loves us for the quality of character we demonstrate.

To know that God is pleased with us—and not just because we are His kids—spurs us on to greater works of service.

"For God is working in you, giving you the desire and the power to do what pleases him." (Philippians 2:13)

Quality

What God is really after in our lives is to produce quality—quality of character that compels Him to bless us all the more. Quality of life that sees us increasingly transformed into the Bride of Christ. For that reason, we are not content just to be; we also want to do things for our Lord.

We are not called to sit back and enter God's Kingdom after doing nothing. We are called to develop lives of quality so that Jesus Himself is blessed, proud and honored to be the Bridegroom of the Church. So that on the Day of Judgment He can look around at the powers and principalities and say, "Look at My Bride! Look at the quality of My people."

Then He will take immense pleasure in rewarding His faithful, blessing us with His rich inheritance. Rewarding us for every tear we've shed, every sacrifice we've made, every hardship we've endured in the pursuit of reaching others with His love.

We live in the paradox of grace and works. We get out of bed each day, assured we live in His grace today. We need do nothing more. But equally, we get out of bed and realize we are called to prove ourselves worthy of our calling today, called to prove ourselves worthy of our Lord Jesus.

We need do nothing more. But we want to do so much more!

Even More

The Westminster Shorter Catechism, written in the 1640s by English and Scottish divines to educate lay persons in matters of belief, is one of the grandest doctrinal statements to come out of the English Reformation. It is composed of 107 questions and answers, and the most famous is the first:

Q. What is the chief end of man?
A. Man's chief end is to glorify God, and to enjoy him forever.

After thirty years of missionary work, Heidi and I understand more than ever that God wants to be our greatest pleasure. He is most pleased with us when we are most pleased with Him! And when He is pleased with us, He grants us the desires of our hearts (see Psalm 37:4).

But there is more. We do this through the grace of God and the power of the Holy Spirit. And here begins the controversy. There is an attitude among some that sees fiery revival and a life of miracles as the rare exception, not to be expected in normal Christian living. According to them, we should learn to live most of the time without the miraculous, overpowering intervention of God and simply prove our love for God by our quality of character.

We understand that our foundation is the righteousness of God, freely given to us in Christ. But then we learn that to love God and appreciate Him is to long for His presence. Here we make a decision. As in any love affair, we love everything about God, and we choose to treasure any way in which He manifests Himself. We continually desire more of God and will never settle for distance from Him. The great outpourings of the Holy Spirit in history are beacons to us, always giving us hope for an even more abundant life in Him. They are not meant to be hopelessly out of reach for the rest of us but to spur us on to all that is possible in God.

Today, enjoy the full spectrum of all God's grace to you, and press forward to what lies ahead: even more of Him!

Come Closer

• You are adopted by Father God. He loves you perfectly and completely. This means you have absolutely nothing to prove. Isn't that liberating? You are the object of God's "relentless kindness"—a recipient of His boundless grace.

• We are called to live lives that are worthy of our calling in Christ.

• You can do this from your position of absolute acceptance in Christ, by the Father. Don't get confused and think you have to start performing for God or else. Nothing you can do can make Him love you any more or any less.

Jesus is our role model. He was supremely confident in His identity as the beloved Son. Therefore, He was able to function in life, doing whatever Father told Him, securely grounded in that truth. He could just be who He was meant to be.

So can you.

Made for Encounter

All the good work we have been able to accomplish in Africa has been sparked, fueled and sustained by the fire of revival and the supernatural. We never could have gotten to this point—more than ten thousand churches and over ten thousand children—without miracles all the way. Life is more than food and the body more than clothes (see Luke 12:23). The Holy Spirit gives us rivers of living water that flow out of our innermost being. We love and enjoy all the manifestations of God's presence and find that as we take more and more pleasure in God, we are filled with all the more strength and motivation to do His will through good works.

We do what we do because of visitations, visions and heavy doses of His Spirit. We are excited and keep going because the dead are being raised and the blind and deaf are being healed. The poor come to Jesus whole villages at a time because they see the power of God's love. We are financed because God grants supernatural generosity to thousands of people without appeals from us. We are awed and thrilled that God would tangibly enter our meetings, touch our bodies and fill us to overflowing with love and joy—inexpressible and full of glory. We are on fire because He does more than we ask or think.

It's very simple. We desperately need revival, all the time. Heidi and I would both be dead now without miraculous healing. Every day we face need, pain and suffering that cry out for more than any human can give. Our own hearts pant for the living God like the deer pants for streams of water (see Psalm 42:1). We are made for God. We are made for revival. We are made for the glory of His presence. We must encounter Him.

While we live in extraordinary circumstances, in so many ways our situation is not different from yours. You will find true freedom from self-effort and striving when you live each day dependent on His Spirit to meet every need and sustain you through every hour. You are made for encounter.

Word and Spirit

How much more of Jesus do we want? He is willing and able to pour out His Spirit without measure. May we never lose our appetite for more righteousness, peace and joy in the Holy Spirit. All these are found only in our magnificent Savior, with all the intensity and fire of the author of life Himself.

This is not the time to be hindered by doubts, divisions and politics in the Church. We don't have room for worrying about titles, positions, credit or recognition. We don't know how to engineer a program of revival. We are simply dependent on our God like little children. What we have already seen, heard and experienced here in Africa has raised our expectations to new heights. We know He is able to keep us, complete us, finish what He began in us. We can trust Him with our hearts, our spirits, our health, our well-being.

Today it is important to realize that God's power to act and work in your life knows no limits. By the power of His Spirit, all things are possible. Are you in need of guidance? Help? Healing? Words of knowledge? Wisdom? He can and will supply it all.

When we surrender with reckless devotion to His Holy Spirit, all things become possible—supernatural power, peace, refreshment, revelation, healing, an insatiable longing for more of His presence, a new sense of wonder and awe.

All these demonstrations of God's love propel us toward the ineffable goal written of by Christian mystics for centuries: union with God. "But the one who joins himself to the Lord is one spirit with Him" (1 Corinthians 6:17, NASB).

When fruits of character are joined by gifts of power, truly our lives reflect His glory and presence. We need His love in our hearts. We also need His anointing to accomplish anything. We need both Word and Spirit.

Receiving Power

We are still learning to go even lower, which is the only way forward. And we are still learning to stop for the one in the middle of a sea of need. We are still learning what it means to be a friend of God and to value fellowship with Him and each other above all else. We are not professional, high-power, efficient missionary machines. We measure the quality of our lives by the depth of our relationships. We are still learning to love.

We cannot function in this world without the power of our God. Some of us haven't yet been brought to our extremity, so we aren't fully and forcibly aware of our dependence. But our time will come. We need Him to stay alive. We need Him for our health. We need Him for our healing. We need Him for righteousness, peace and joy in the Holy Spirit.

We need more than any human being can do for us. We need sheer, raw power in the goodness and love of God. We need power to appreciate our God, to make Him the greatest pleasure in our lives. We need power to rejoice with joy inexpressible and full of glory. We need power to experience His Kingdom, to move in His environment.

How do we get power? It is the grace and gift of God. He plants in us a hunger that will not be denied. He opens our eyes to our poverty without His powerful presence. He grants faith where there was none. In His power we can rest, even while under demonic attack. His power fixes our eyes on Him. In His power we are able to discipline ourselves in everything. We can cast our cares on Him, because He is willing to use His power on our behalf.

How can we be sure He cares for us? The cross. We go to the cross always to find confidence to approach Him. We will not empty the cross of its power. There and only there do we find salvation of every kind. At the cross we come to know our God and His heart toward us. At the cross we learn to become utterly dependent on His power.

Walk

Our outreach last night was a perfectly normal outreach, which is to say, practically the entire village gave their lives to the Lord on the first night, and one young boy who had been deaf received his hearing. We fell asleep happy in our little circle of tents. The next day started for us at 3 A.M., when the children sleeping in the nearest mud-walled hut scrambled to sweep the dirt around the tents and peer through our netting. They were ecstatic to have visitors. I looked up to see stars shooting across the most incredible African sky—our own billion-star hotel! I came out to precious, smiling faces all around me and thanked Jesus for the privilege of being in such a hungry place. I started boiling water for our most happy and comforting bush drink—Starbucks coffee.

We came across a five-year-old girl, Joanna. She had never walked in her life, and her knees were crusted over with calluses from years of crawling in the dirt. I felt the Father's compassion for her, so I picked her up by her two hands and called her to walk. I steadied her spindly legs and blessed her to come. Many of us cried when she did come, walking for the first time. There was also a lot of clapping and rejoicing. What a joy! How incredible that we get to be alive for such a time as this!

Today you may feel like this little girl—crushed, broken, forgotten. But the greatest thing I can tell you is, Jesus has not forgotten. You are not unseen. You are incredibly important to Him! Whether anyone else has noticed your situation or not, open your arms and lift up your head to Him today. Because He is calling you to rise up and walk!

Saved!

It's great to be saved. Let's pause for a moment and think about some of the many implications of salvation.

1. Total forgiveness of sin. If we reflected on nothing else for the remainder of our lives, we could immerse ourselves in thankfulness and pour out our gratitude for this incredible truth alone.

2. A clean conscience. Not only can Jesus wipe the slate clean and remove all our sin—past, present and future—but He also removes the guilt and shame we feel, too. We can stand before God with a clean conscience. What a remarkable thing!

3. No fear. God's Word says perfect love casts out fear. When we are full of God's love, God's presence, He fills our beings so we have no space left for fear or anxiety to occupy. If you are afraid, the answer is more of God's presence. His love will banish all fear.

4. Total security. We know God's salvation is secure. Our Father is not a capricious God who takes back His gifts when we fall or fail or even willfully disobey Him. Where we ebb and flow, He remains constant. Where we are weak and fickle, He remains faithful.

5. Access to the resources of heaven. The truth is, with God as our Father— committed to providing for and caring for His children—we have all the power of heaven at our disposal.

6. Eternal life. Through Christ we have been transported into a new realm. We've moved from the kingdom of darkness to the Kingdom of light, from death to life. And we are promised eternal joy in the company of our Savior.

7. Peace and joy. Though the earth may quake, the mountains crash into the sea, and flood, fire and disaster come upon us—still God's peace can dwell in us supernaturally and remain unmoved.

Paul wrote, in a Philippian jail, that the slight, momentary afflictions we suffer are nothing compared with the glory that is to be revealed. We need to hold on to that perspective!

Boasting in Weakness

In 2 Corinthians 12:9–10, we see Paul boasting in his lack of strength:

"But he [Jesus] said to me, 'My grace is sufficient for you, for my power is made perfect in weakness.' Therefore I will boast all the more gladly about my weaknesses, so that Christ's power may rest on me. That is why, for Christ's sake, I delight in weaknesses, in insults, in hardships, in persecutions, in difficulties. For when I am weak, then I am strong."

Incredibly, we see Paul, the ultimate missionary of all time, boasting and delighting in his weaknesses. But he understood what doing so would mean.

When we talk about Jesus, or the Holy Spirit dwelling in us, we are not just talking about His character and His gifts but also His unlimited, creative, wonderful power. The fact that we have the power of God living inside us is truly mind-blowing. It is good to be reminded that tremendous and infinite power is at our fingertips. That is why Paul was willing to put up with weaknesses and thorns in his flesh.

He actually boasts about his inability and delights in it because it makes him humble and dependent on God. This lowering of himself opens the way for the power of God. God's upside-down ways mean His power is perfected in weakness.

This is counter to an awful lot of teaching today. We never boast in our weaknesses. We do the opposite. Our leaders say, "Come to my life-changing conference. Buy my book! It will give you a totally new way of thinking!" We boast in our strengths, but that is the wrong way round.

The serious power of God is attracted to extreme humility and empty-handedness.

It is helpful to remember that someone with the skill, wisdom, theology, holiness, encouragement and teaching ability of Paul was aware of his shortcomings and infinitely more aware of God's strength and power.

Come Closer

• The apostle Paul was a capable man. He was well trained, well educated and highly motivated. But God had to bring Paul to the place where he understood the concept of power in weakness—God's magnificent strength working through our human frailty.

• Once he'd had this revelation, Paul got excited about it and went on to boast about his inability, exulting in the power of Holy Spirit working through him.

• We have to take the same journey. It's more difficult for those who are naturally capable and have many natural gifts and talents. They are more inclined to take action, to make things happen. But each of us has to learn to surrender to God's power working through our lives, to submit to His ways with reckless devotion.

• The more we lay down our own ability or cleverness, the more Christ is made visible in us. This is the beautiful paradox of the Gospel.

Happy

Recently I was reflecting on what kind of character or personality we need to develop in order to truly honor God. What is the main thing we could focus on that would really please our Father's heart?

Here is the conclusion I have reached: Suppose you were God and you had created a bunch of people—your children. How would you want them to behave? How would you want them to react to you? Would you most like them to be happy, thrilled to be in your presence? Or would you prefer them to take things very seriously, to be conservative and considered, not impulsive?

Parents, when are you most pleased with your kids? Is it when they do household chores without having to be asked? When they do their homework on time without being prompted? When they begin to mature and become responsible? When they act like good people?

All these are good, acceptable things. But I think parents are most pleased with their kids when they see them truly happy. Full of joy. Over-the-top happy. All good parents want their kids to feel accepted, safe, secure and, above all, happy—joyful.

Our heavenly Father is no different. We may think of many different things we could do to please Him, many different attitudes we could cultivate that we think will bring Him joy. But what brings Him the most joy of all is our joy! He is happiest when we are happy with Him.

Inexpressible

When children are happy they don't even know how to express it. They can't find the words to describe what they are feeling; they just are. This is the kind of joy the Bible speaks about in 1 Peter 1:8: "You love him even though you have never seen him. Though you do not see him now, you trust him; and you rejoice with a glorious, inexpressible joy" (NLT).

The Voice translation renders the second part, "celebrate with a joy that is glorious beyond words."

Sometimes childlike Christians who brim over with joy are criticized for their attitude of abandon; they are frowned upon because their behavior can't be explained in theological or doctrinal terms. But I think these are the people God finds the most pleasure in.

Inexpressible joy means I can't sit you down and explain it to you in mere words. By definition, it defies explanation. It is the type of joy so glorious, so far above any earthly comparison, that it is simply other-worldly. We'll never understand it.

And that is the point. We are called to be full of the joy of the Lord. We are not called to measure it, analyze it, critique it. We do not need to find empirical evidence to underpin its existence. God's joy just is, and our job is simply to allow Him to fill our beings with it and enjoy it.

We return to the first premise of the Westminster Shorter Catechism: "Man's chief end is to glorify God, and to enjoy him forever." His joy is inexpressible, unexplainable, indefinable, without measure, totally glorious and completely fulfilling!

Seriously

The reason the whole world is not in the Church is because they looked inside one once! They'd rather go to a baseball game, where they know they will at least find some measure of joy! But seriously, over the centuries an attitude of sobriety and solemnity toward the things of God has developed in the Church. We have come to associate all that is grave, solemn, reserved and heavy with the fear of God, thinking seriousness correlates with a respect for His presence.

At times, stillness is called for. At times, we need to be quiet in the presence of God, showing our love and respect for Him by not speaking and simply listening to His heartbeat. But if seriousness, stillness and gravity are our predominant attitudes before our Father, then we are seriously out of balance. Throughout Scripture we read of emotional and physical reactions to the presence of God. When God shows up, people are totally overwhelmed. They don't know how to react. Often they fall flat on their faces.

"As Jesus said 'I AM he,' they all drew back and fell to the ground!" (John 18:6, NLT)

"When I saw him, I fell at his feet as if I were dead. But he laid his right hand on me and said, 'Don't be afraid! I am the First and the Last.'" (Revelation 1:17, NLT)

At other times, the reaction to God's presence is one of reckless abandon and devotion, which is something others frequently find hard to process:

"Others in the crowd ridiculed them, saying, 'They're just drunk, that's all!'" (Acts 2:13, NLT)

"David danced before the LORD with all his might. . . . Michal, the daughter of Saul... said in disgust, 'How distinguished the king of Israel looked today, shamelessly exposing himself to the servant girls like any vulgar person might do!'" (2 Samuel 6:14–20, NLT)

The truth is, God wants us to experience the full spectrum of human emotions and express ourselves appropriately to Him. One person's appropriate reaction today might be stillness. The next day, joyful abandon. But I believe our attitude should mainly be one of joy—because our Father delights in it and finds joy in our happiness.

Authentic

Have you noticed today that the Christian world is divided over many issues it considers controversial? Different church streams have differing opinions on many things. Some think we should all be rich. Others think we should all be poor. Some say God heals today. Others say He doesn't. Some people focus on getting everyone into heaven, while others say we should be building heaven on earth.

A huge amount of controversy ensues whenever God shows up and does anything!

But I'll tell you what really upsets people—when they see others are not practicing what they preach.

It upsets people to hear others talking constantly about God's miracle-working power, while nobody seems to get healed.

It upsets people when others talk so much about manifestations of God's power and spiritual experiences, but Jesus is never mentioned.

It upsets people to hear churches talking about prosperity and taking over the world, but hardly anyone gets saved, and evangelism is rarely mentioned.

Instead of immersing ourselves in the controversial debates surrounding what we think God will and will not do, we need to connect with the fundamental power and simplicity of the true Gospel. God will always defy our definitions of Him. He will always break out of our imagined boundaries for Him.

Let's seek to be authentic.

Valleys and Mountains

Often we get upset when God doesn't act in the way we expect.

Maybe you have seen a friend of yours miraculously healed, while you have been praying for years for your own healing and have not received it.

Maybe you've prayed for family or friends to be saved, yet nothing seems to happen.

Maybe you've been believing God for something He's promised you will come to pass in the future, yet the promise is a long time coming.

Some relatives of mine, who were all children of missionaries, gave up on the Lord because their father died of malaria in the jungle. They couldn't understand the plan of God in this tragic event and became bitter against Him. God didn't behave the way they expected.

Each of us will face challenges and difficulties in our lives. Each of us will know valley as well as mountaintop experiences. Often we don't anticipate the approaching valleys—hoping to remain on the heights; we just stumble into them, and there we are. It doesn't seem to be part of God's plan for us, yet we are going through it.

What has happened? Is God judging us? Have we lost sight of Him?

First, we can be sure God will never, ever desert us. His presence accompanies us always.

Second, the challenges and difficulties of life refine our character. Sometimes God allows these things to shape and mold us. It doesn't diminish His exceedingly great love for us in any way. He is never punishing us. He has a bigger plan in mind. Frequently we don't perceive this bigger picture. But God is still working intentionally in our lives—both visibly and behind the scenes—to shape us into the likeness of His Son. Even if we don't understand certain things, we can understand that He is a good God all the time.

Journey of Joy

Dear brothers and sisters, when troubles come your way, consider it an opportunity for great joy. For you know that when your faith is tested, your endurance has a chance to grow. So let it grow, for when your endurance is fully developed, you will be perfect and complete, needing nothing.
James 1:2–4, NLT

How many of us would like to possess pure joy that nobody and nothing could take away from us? All of us, of course. But how do we get there from here? It's easy to experience a kind of emotional, transient joy—being happy for a short time—but we return all too swiftly to our former state, with all its anxieties and cares. How do we receive and maintain the kind of biblical joy that remains constant, transcending the cares of life?

In the verses above, James points to a process that has to take place in our lives.

Inevitably, the trials of life come upon us. How we react is very important. If we hold an eternal perspective, then we can respond to a trial with joy. Are we in denial? Being unrealistic or super-spiritual? No, because James says when our faith is tested it is stretched and it grows. It builds into our faith the glue of endurance. Over time, trials toughen up our faith. They cause our faith to mature. This leads to completion—the essence of the joy that cannot be overcome by trouble.

We would learn very little if everything in life fell into place without challenge or difficulty. In terms of faith, we would be spiritual weaklings. Just as athletes "test" their bodies over and over again in order to build endurance and, therefore, be able to perform at their best, our faith must be tested so we can become mature soldiers for Jesus who are able to endure and continue to persevere, with reckless devotion, in all He sets before us.

Come Closer

• Along the road of life, we will always find mountain top experiences tempered by dark valley experiences. Highs and lows, good times and bad. This is the reality. As Christians, sometimes we don't understand why God doesn't just deliver us from the valleys and make everything soar.

• This side of eternity we will never fathom why some of our harder experiences were necessary. But one thing we can be assured of in life is the constancy of the Father's presence.

• Life may be tough right now, but He has not deserted you. Though you may be experiencing a valley time, God is not punishing you for something. We accept that often, in challenging times, God is working in ways we cannot see or easily discern. But His love for us never, ever diminishes, and He continues to lovingly shape us into the image of Jesus.

Though we may not always understand, we can at least pray, Father, I thank You that You are with me and Your love for me never fails.

Need and Perseverance

For when your endurance is fully developed, you will be perfect and
complete, needing nothing.
James 1:4, NLT

Heidi and I have lived and served in one of the poorest nations on earth for
many years. Daily we have been confronted by the most appalling, devastating
poverty and need. Hunger is a constant threat. Sickness abounds. If anyone
needs to be "perfect and complete, needing nothing" it is these people. But
like anyone in immediate need, trusting God to meet that need is an issue.

Every Sunday after church, Heidi, having poured out everything she has, will
go to her truck ready to drive home. And every single time, a crowd of people
surrounds her as she attempts to get into the truck and drive. This isn't a little
gathering of well-wishers, come to wave her off.

This is a clamoring crowd of angry, shouting people! A mob of youth who
are really upset because Mama Ida won't provide them with a house right
away. Or whatever else they want. Typically, they will yell something like,
"You don't love me anymore!" Or, "You don't care. You took me off the street,
and now you've forgotten me." They beat on the car and slap the windshield.
Eventually, Heidi manages to pull away and escape.

This is perhaps an extreme example, but the principle translates into every
person's life. When we don't get what we want immediately, it is all too easy to
interpret that as a lack of God's care for us. Where has He gone? Why doesn't
He answer? Can't He see I'm in need?

At times like these, we have to trust. We trust in the consistency of God's
character, because while we ebb and flow, He remains constant, reliable,
faithful. We trust He will give us what we need, when we need it. We trust He
knows us better than we know ourselves, and He will care for us accordingly.

Persevere. As you do, your trust in Father God will be proven true. And your
needs will be met.

Frustration

Everyone gets frustrated in life. Others don't treat them right. Bad things happen. It makes them mad. Anger and frustration occur when something is standing in the way, keeping us from achieving our goals.

Your goal may be to get a promotion at work, but your boss won't consider it. Or your goal may be to make the team, but the coach keeps saying you're too old. Perhaps your goal is simply to eat to survive, but a lack of money or help from others means you're not achieving that most basic of goals. All of these things can frustrate and make us angry.

Typically, we vent our frustration on others. How come that person got a promotion when she has only been with the firm a few months? How come that person made the team when he is much less talented than I am? How come those people have plenty of food and waste so much of it when I'm starving? It's not fair!

So often we fall into the trap of comparison. We experience frustration because we're not reaching our goals, and immediately we question why others are in a better position than we are.

One of the greatest lessons we can learn is this: My journey is my journey. Other people's journeys are not my journey. Whatever their lives look like on the surface, they will face challenges, unseen and unheard—just like me, just like you. Only the Lord knows each person deep down. He knows you. He knows your frustrations. He understands your journey, and He knows the destination, the beginning and all points in between.

God has a glorious plan and purpose for the lives of each of His children. He has a glorious future planned for you! In the meantime, we live in the tension of the now and the not yet. We walk along our journey, daily knowing His plan will be brought to fruition in due course. It can be frustrating, but we cling onto His promise: "Never will I leave you; never will I forsake you" (Hebrews 13:5).

Relevant

In our efforts to make contemporary church more "relevant," we are in danger of becoming more concerned with what people want than with what God wants. The concept of "relevant church" is borne out of good intentions: If we give people what they want, then they'll come to church, right?

Let's provide for people's needs, and then we'll have more people in church, and they'll hear the Gospel. It's a logical argument.

A friend, who comes from an area near some very large, seeker-sensitive churches, shared with me recently. He said his experience was that people who were in the most need—who really wanted to encounter God and find His supernatural help—would go to a humble little church, farther away, on the wrong side of the tracks, where it was reputed a person could meet with God, simply and powerfully.

I'm not trying to make an argument for small churches over large ones. I'm not saying it's wrong to be sensitive toward those seeking God, though I think compassion is a better quality to possess than sensitivity.

What I am arguing for—what we at IRIS contend for, day after day, with all our might—is the simple, fundamental, undiluted Gospel. This is what I believe to be truly relevant. The Gospel is relevant because what people lack more than anything else is power. They lack the power to change, to break enslaving habits, to live better, to save their own souls. And what the simple, undiluted Gospel has in abundance is power. The power to transform. The power to change lives and break habits, the power that enables people to live better, fruitful lives that transcend their own needs.

"My message and my preaching were not with wise and persuasive words, but with a demonstration of the Spirit's power." (1 Corinthians 2:4)

Popular

To be successful in the world's eyes, all the Church needs to do is preach what people want to hear. If we speak to where people are at, expressing a popular opinion, then they will love us. But this can reduce the potency of our message to mere pop psychology and motivational speaking. It dilutes the Gospel.

If that approach actually brought the power of God, it would be worth considering. If it glorified God, it would be worthy of our attention. If it resulted in conviction, repentance and a change of heart, then it would be an effective method of spreading the Gospel.

The fact is, the Gospel of Christ is highly offensive.

It is tempting to shy away from delivering the unvarnished truth to others, because it will upset them. It's not "politically correct" to point out to people that they are desperate sinners, greatly in need of repentance and salvation, yet it is the truth.

We need wisdom to share the Gospel message with others, wisdom that will enable us to speak the truth with love (see Ephesians 4:15) and always act with the love and compassion of our God. But we mustn't dumb down the message of truth. The Gospel speaks for itself. And Jesus will meet with those in need in the powerful way that only He can.

In our own day-to-day lives, we also face the temptation of taking the "safe" route—saying and doing what we think will make us popular with others. Instead, we need to embrace the difference Jesus has made in our lives and live authentically. Live for truth rather than popularity.

Embrace the pure power of the fundamental Gospel, both for your life and for the lives of those around you.

Heart

What do we need most in life?

It's not a trick question. There is no doubt we need stuff. We need food; we need clothes; we need a place to live; we need basic provisions for life.

But beyond the basic necessities for life, what do we need most? What do we need, even if we have nothing else?

When I get into tense situations and am tested, I realize my limitations, and I understand that what I need most of all is a good heart.

We need good hearts more than we need to be healed. We need good hearts more than we need money. We need good hearts more than we need success and influence. We need good hearts more than we need to be loved and treated rightly by other people.

It is so easy to be caught up with the process of getting our needs met that we forget we are immersed in a love affair with our Savior. He is only too willing to meet our needs. But what He is really after is our hearts. He desires to captivate us with His love—to capture us and delight us so we delight in Him. He wants to shape us so we have good hearts and we come to resemble Him more and more.

People who are hopelessly in love are always mindful of the needs of the one they love. They are eager to ensure their loved one is fulfilled and happy. Today, let Jesus captivate your heart with His love. Choose to be recklessly devoted to Him. As you welcome Him to fill you with His presence, your needs will be met. And you will also understand His heart, His desires. Then you will want to see the desires of His heart fulfilled. Then you will live, heart to heart.

Hungry Heart

In our African church services, we're not afraid to shout and dance and laugh and get excited about Jesus. Some find that difficult to connect with at first. Some find it a little offensive. They think we should be more reverent in church.

But plenty of people are extremely interested in, attracted by, and drawn to such joy and the visible manifestation of God's presence. Many are compelled to find out more when they see God doing something supernatural. For every story I hear about people who are disturbed by manifestations of God's power, I hear many more about those who are drawn to Him because of the manifestations.

"Wow, God is in this place," they say. "Tell me more!" They are so hungry for a touch from Him that they overcome any reservations they may have. All they are interested in is connecting with Him.

Do you have a hungry heart?

A hungry heart will seek out God's presence.

A hungry heart will express its delight in Jesus and overcome the embarrassment some might feel.

A hungry heart cares most about connecting with the one who can truly satisfy us.

We chase after many things in life—money, food, clothes, success, influence. But what good can we do with these things if we don't have a good heart? A heart recklessly devoted to Jesus? Without a good heart, these things become a meaningless pursuit. With a good heart, they add to the richness of life, and we can hold them lightly—possessing them without allowing them to possess us.

Keep your heart hungry for Him!

Come Closer

• Holy Spirit is working diligently in your life to produce a good heart—a heart that is hopelessly in love with Jesus.

• We can easily get side-tracked by the cares of life, the many needs we have, the needs and problems of others, but we mustn't lose sight of the fact that central to our lives is our great love affair with our Savior. Life is all about Jesus, Jesus, Jesus.

• Holy Spirit is also working to give you a hungry heart—a heart that is restless until it finds rest in the presence of God. A heart that is relentless in its pursuit of and delight in Jesus.

Allow Holy Spirit to stir your heart, to warm your heart whenever your passion begins to wane, to excite your heart with the all the possibilities of the adventure that is following Jesus.

Wrong Person

Once I was invited to speak at a pastors' conference. I was given a particular topic to speak on, and I wasn't happy. I felt like they had invited the wrong person! All the other great speakers seemed, to me, to be far more suitably qualified to speak on the topic at hand. I felt out of place, uncomfortable. "Why am I here, God?" I wanted to know.

"Just share whatever I put on your heart," Father said to me. So that's what I did. And somehow, God took my faltering words and stumbling delivery and touched people's hearts with it. He took my meager offering and made it into something beautiful. Unwilling as I was, when I finally swallowed my pride and showed the tiniest bit of obedience to God, He was able to step in.

Do you ever feel inadequate? Do you feel like you're the wrong person—at the wrong place, at the wrong time, with the wrong set of gifts and abilities to confront the task ahead of you?

Today I believe God is saying this to you:

Allow Me to work with you. All I need is your willingness. Overcome your pride and come to Me. Let go of your preconceptions. Let go of every reason why something miraculous should not happen in your situation. Be obedient to Me. Allow Me to step into your situation and show you what I can do with the smallest amount of trust. Trust in Me.

Though you may feel out of your depth, stretched to the limit, extended beyond your comfort zone, you have an incredible Father. If you begin to trust Him with every situation in your life, every challenge, every mountain that has to be climbed, He will come to your aid, and you will experience miracles.

Better Late Than Never

I had a great father. He was an amazing dad. He was Jewish by race but Catholic by religion. Then he became an atheist during his time at Stanford University. Later he became an agnostic. That was my dad: a Jewish Catholic Atheist Agnostic!

He didn't like it when I became a Pentecostal Christian. It freaked him out. In fact, it freaked him out so much he took me to see a psychologist in an effort to "deprogram" me. Needless to say, it didn't work!

However, our Father in heaven is so gracious to us, so kind and loving. Years later, He gave me the incredible privilege of leading my dad to Jesus. Then Dad was ordained as a Christian minister at the age of 72. I felt so humbled when he said to me, "Heidi, I am going to follow you. It's better late than never." He was a wonderful minister of the Gospel until Jesus took him home.

No matter what journey people go on in life, they never reach a point where they are beyond the grace of God. No one is too far gone. There are no hopeless cases, no matter how entrenched people are in their own sin and selfishness. The Father's grace is unfathomable in its depth and immeasurable in its length.

Though it would be better to come to the Lord as a young person and look forward to a life spent in His service, it is never too late to come. Better late than never. If you are praying for someone to come to Jesus today, be encouraged. Not one person alive on the earth today has passed the point of no return. Don't give up. Keep praying. It's never too late.

Standing on Daddy's Feet

When I was a little girl, I would do that funny thing that many kids do with their dads. I would walk around with my feet planted on top of his feet. He would hold my hands to steady me while he took his big steps, and wherever he went, I went.

For me, this captures perfectly how our Father wants us to be with Him. He wants us to stand on His feet. As we do, allowing Him to move us, we go where He goes. He takes us places, and we do things. He is solid and secure, and He can take bigger steps than we can, but we are safe in His embrace.

Once, when I was facing a particular challenge and feeling vulnerable and a little helpless, not knowing what to do, I just lay down on the floor on my face and said to God, "Lord, help! Help!"

Guess what? He did. He came to my aid. He said to me, "Heidi, stand on My feet. Let me carry you."

I felt such a relief. It took me straight back to my childhood. I was just a little girl standing on my Dad's feet. Having fun. Being carried.

My burden was lifted away. I knew Father God was willing to "walk into" the situation I was facing while I stood on His feet. I was perfectly safe, perfectly secure, perfectly able to contend with whatever was ahead because, in fact, my Father was in control. He was the one handling things. I was just hitching a ride!

Today, don't worry about what you are facing. Instead, hand your burden over to Father. Stand on His feet. Do what a child does, and allow Father to do what a Dad does.

Wrong Shoes

Once, while at a conference, I sat listening to one of the other speakers. This man was the most amazing teacher—so eloquent, so well researched. I noticed he had pages of beautifully written, well organized notes and quotes. His delivery of the message was just amazing. I lapped up everything he had to say and got busy jotting down notes.

Then, all of a sudden, I realized, Wait a minute! I'm up next! A wave of fear hit me. Heidi, you're going to be up there speaking next, and you have to follow that! I was seriously worried.

Then something else happened. An awful wave of arrogance rose up inside me. Wait, I thought. I can use notes and quotes. I can wow people. I have a Ph.D. in theology. I can do this!

I used to be severely dyslexic until God healed me (that's a whole other story). But when He healed me, He gave me the ability to speed read. So I decided I would go to the bookstore, skim some books, and find some impressive quotes to use in my talk. My little arrogant self wanted to be as coherent and amazing as the previous speaker.

Just as I was approaching the bookstore, my legs turned to jelly, and I felt myself falling. I went bam straight into the bookstore's door and then lay there, literally blocking the entrance! I remonstrated with God, "Lord, surely it's okay for me to go into this bookstore and get some good notes and quotes for my talk." Apparently not. He had a simple message for me.

"Heidi, don't try to walk in someone else's anointing."

Here's what I learned that day. Each one of us must wear the shoes God has given us to wear.

He has made each of us unique. God has made you to be awesome. You don't need to try to be anyone other than yourself. Your Father is thrilled with who He made you to be. Walk in His acceptance and love.

Effortless

In the art world, originals are priceless. Copies, though they may look nice hanging on your wall, are worthless.

In the same way, we don't need to try to be like anyone else. You don't want to be me; you want to be you, fully filled with the power of the living God!

Whenever we try to copy others, it's like putting on a suit that was tailor made for them and not us. It is ill-fitting. We end up never being comfortable with it. It doesn't suit us. It looks great on them; it doesn't look great on us.

After I fell flat on my face in front of the bookstore, a number of well-meaning people passed by and prayed for me. I lay there for a long time. Then, when it was time for me to speak, a group of them decided to haul me onto the stage and dump me in front of the pulpit! It was my turn to speak—no notes, no quotes. God was very clear with me: I had to be me and walk in the shoes He had given me, not trying to impress anyone else.

I asked God to help me do just that, and He gave me a beautiful message to share. It was amazing. I could take no credit for it whatsoever. Once I stopped trying to be somebody else, trying to make a name for myself—once I was content just to be me and allow Father God to do His thing through me—it was effortless. His words flowed through me, and He accomplished what He wanted to do.

God is in the business of creating originals, not copies. Embrace the fact that He made you to be you, and then cooperate with Him. When you stop striving and struggling and give Him space, that's when His power can truly flow through you. His ways are so much higher than ours.

Stop and Go

The story of the Bible can be summed up by this simple phrase: God initiates and we respond.

"Just at the right time, when we were still powerless, Christ died for the ungodly" (Romans 5:6).

So often we like to run off and do our own thing. We like to initiate things and then pray for God to bless them, pray for Him to stamp them with His rubber seal of approval. Then we wonder why our efforts bear little fruit.

We have the equation mixed up. God initiates; we respond. If we want to learn how to bear much fruit and know His power infusing all we do, then we need to learn this simple principle: Stop and then go.

What do I mean?

Stop: Stop running around trying to make things happen, and enter the secret place—His presence. Spend time there. Abide there. Dwell in the secret place and listen. Hear Father's heart; listen to what He is telling you.

Go: Now, go! Go and do what He has told you to do. God will empower you to do what He has instructed you to do. He will make the necessary resources available to you. He will equip you to carry out His will. He will empower you and sustain you.

Stop and go. Every day, go into His presence before you go out onto the streets. Live out of the secret place.

Stop and then go.

Come Closer

• Remember today that Daddy God wants you to stand on His feet, hold His hands and go where He goes. In Him you are secure, and as you allow Him to move you, you can take bigger steps and go in directions you never thought possible.

• Remember, God made you to be uniquely you, and not anyone else. When we stop wishing to be like others or to walk in their gifts rather than our own, we will finally discover how amazingly unique and special God has made each one of us. We will finally be fully ourselves—and fully His.

• Practice Stop and Go this week—taking time to dwell in the secret place and listen to Father's heart, then going to do the work He has put before you. What a difference you will find as you live from the secret place of His presence.

• Reflect on the following Scriptures:

"He guides the humble in what is right and teaches them his way." (Psalm 25:9)

"For the LORD gives wisdom; from his mouth come knowledge and understanding. He holds success in store for the upright, he is a shield to those whose walk is blameless, for he guards the course of the just and protects the way of his faithful ones. Then you will understand what is right and just and fair—every good path." (Proverbs 2:6–9)

Childlike Faith

It's very important to stay low and remember to stand on Daddy's feet—so we don't keep on trying to do things in our own strength.

Some of us are strong and resourceful, tenacious and resilient. We can do a lot of stuff. Despite that, our abilities are not the way forward in His Kingdom. Life in God's Kingdom demands childlike faith.

It demands radical dependency on Him.

Wherever I travel in the world, I often invite children to pray—for people, situations, healing, anything. I especially do this when I'm travelling in first world nations like the U.S. and the European nations. I especially do it when I'm in a place where adults have outgrown the sense that God still moves in the miraculous, where they find childlike faith hard to grasp.

I find that the younger children are, the more they believe, the more they are prepared to trust God implicitly. They have not yet learned to rationalize Him! They have not learned to put Him in a box or place imagined limits on His abilities. They just believe.

And Father responds to their faith. I always make sure we have children as part of our prayer and ministry teams in Mozambique. My Land Rover is constantly jammed full of kids. They are the ministry team on all our bush outreaches. They see God do miracles in answer to their prayers.

Amazing things happen when kids pray. The power of God comes. Father hears and responds.

It's hard to let go when we are capable. But we need to learn radical dependency. We need to acknowledge that He is so much stronger than we are in every possible way. As we lay down our abilities and surrender to Jesus, He responds to our faith. As we depend on Him, like little kids, He delights in answering our prayers, constantly surprising us with His love and grace.

Knowledge

The apostle Paul, so full of God's presence, wrote one of the most amazing books in the New Testament—Colossians. He wrote to the church in Colossae, but also to us today. His prayer was that God would fill us with the knowledge of His will.

"For this reason, since the day we heard about you, we have not stopped praying for you. We continually ask God to fill you with the knowledge of his will through all the wisdom and understanding that the Spirit gives, so that you may live a life worthy of the Lord and please him in every way: bearing fruit in every good work, growing in the knowledge of God." (Colossians 1:9–10)

This is one of my favorite passages in the Bible. I so long for us to be filled with the knowledge of His will. We need to know how to live, how to fight, how to love like Him!

But we don't understand the full picture of God's will for our lives on day one. It comes as an unfolding revelation. This is something that frequently annoys and frustrates us. "Lord, why can't you just tell me everything now? I don't like surprises!" Wouldn't that be great—if we could see the rest of our lives all mapped out in tune with God's perfect will for us? But it's not going to happen.

Why?

First, if we knew beforehand all the experiences God would take us through in the future, in order to shape in us the likeness of His Son Jesus, we might run away from them.

Second, if God gave us the full picture, perfect knowledge of the future, we would not be required to trust Him.

Third, if we had the full picture, it would leave no room for faith.

We are to grow in the knowledge of God—not have it all downloaded into us at once like programming a robot. God delights in revealing His will to us, but He will reveal to us what we need to live and serve Him today. One day at a time—we discover the unfolding pattern of His grace.

Qualified

Paul continues his amazing, revelatory writing with the following:

"...growing in the knowledge of God, being strengthened with all power according to his glorious might so that you may have great endurance and patience, and giving joyful thanks to the Father, who has qualified you to share in the inheritance of his holy people in the kingdom of light. For he has rescued us from the dominion of darkness and brought us into the kingdom of the Son he loves, in whom we have redemption, the forgiveness of sins." (Colossians 1:10–14)

What amazes me about these verses is that they are just Paul's preamble—his opening remarks and greeting. He's not even warmed up yet, but his words are steeped in truth; they are weighty with incredible revelation.

We could draw so much from these words to focus our attention on. They hold so many important themes: being strengthened by God's glory in us, endurance and patience being built into our characters, being translated from the kingdom of darkness to light, redemption, forgiveness. Let's just pick just one thing for today.

Your Father has qualified you. He has included you in the inheritance of the saints. You belong.

Do you feel ill-equipped for the challenges ahead of you? Father has qualified you.

Do you feel under-resourced? He has qualified you.

Do you feel unprepared? He has qualified you.

Do you feel you're not talented enough? No, you are qualified.

Do you feel like you're always second best? Not to Father. You are qualified.

From before the foundations of the earth, our Father saw you and wanted you to belong. He called you. He saved you. He made you one of His own. He qualified you. That makes all the difference.

Inheritance

Naturally speaking, we are not "qualified." We can't do much. We can't produce anything of eternal worth on our own—not one thing.

Whenever I think about this, in my mind I always have this picture of a tree—a tree that is trying to produce fruit. How absurd! A tree cannot decide to produce fruit. It doesn't work. If a tree is not a fruit tree, it can't bear fruit. If it is a fruit tree, it will bear fruit. It's as simple as that.

In the same way, we can't strive our way into our inheritance. It's not possible. It doesn't work like that. Our inheritance is given to us; it cannot be earned. God qualifies us to share in His inheritance. If we could "earn" it, we could hardly call it an inheritance. Rather, Father gives it to us as a gift, because we are His sons and daughters.

Once we were empty, non-fruit-bearing trees. Now God has transformed us into fruit trees. He has infused us with His divine power and fundamentally changed our spiritual DNA, giving us His fruitful characteristics.

Now that He has qualified us, we can be truly fruitful in Him. We can produce something of eternal worth as we cooperate with Holy Spirit who lives inside us.

This is the miracle of inheritance, the miracle of fruitfulness. Your life is incredibly precious, of magnificent worth, because He has bestowed worth upon you. Today we can live fully assured of Jesus' love for us and know we are a part of His glorious inheritance.

Translated

Because Jesus was crucified for us, died for our sins on the cross, was buried, rose to life again and ascended into heaven, we—having confessed our faith in Him—belong to the Father.

Through His actions, Jesus reconnected us to the Father. We were far away from Him in our sin, but because of Jesus, we now have an inheritance. We are now sons and daughters, part of God's family.

In Colossians 1:13–14, Paul writes, "He has rescued us from the dominion of darkness and brought us into the kingdom of the Son he loves, in whom we have redemption, the forgiveness of sins."

This means we have been translated from one thing to another. We have changed citizenship. We used to belong to the kingdom of darkness; now we belong to the Kingdom of His Son. We were lost; now we are found. Like orphans who are taken off the streets and given a home, a new identity, we now belong.

It means all the junk from our past is taken care. The orphan spirit that plagued us and caused us to believe so many lies about ourselves is no longer in force. Jesus has done away with it. Now we are marked by the spirit of sonship. We no longer need to have an identity crisis, because we can be sure of who we are. We are royalty!

What does this mean for us?

Having stepped into this new place of sonship, we are free to be like Jesus. We're free to lower ourselves, like He did. We know we are princes and princesses of the Kingdom, but we choose to humble ourselves.

Those who are secure in their identity don't worry about giving their lives away to others. When you know that what you have cannot be diminished, you won't care about giving it away.

Abiding

We are connected into the vine, grafted into Jesus. John the apostle wrote the beautiful passage about abiding in Jesus. It explains so clearly how we ought to function. We stay connected to Jesus, and He causes us to be fruitful. We can't be fruitful if we chop ourselves away from the vine and try to function on our own. We wouldn't last more than a few hours before we withered and died from lack of spiritual sustenance.

"Remain in me, as I also remain in you," Jesus says. "No branch can bear fruit by itself; it must remain in the vine. Neither can you bear fruit unless you remain in me" (John 15:4).

However, if we remain connected, abiding in Jesus, we are greatly fruitful: "...If you remain in me and I in you, you will bear much fruit..." (John 15:5, emphasis added). He is our source of life, strength and fruit.

Abiding is a discipline we need to learn and practice more. It means "to stay with, to remain, to rest, to dwell, to be firm and immovable".

The demands of modern life mean we are always in a rush. We rush over everything, even our words! Abiding is somewhat counter-cultural to the Western mind. We don't tend to stay still for very long. But most of the workings of God's Kingdom are counter-cultural.

In the Creation account of Genesis 1, we read that God created the heavens and earth in six days, forming man on the last day before having a day off. The implication of this is that man's first day on earth was a day of rest.

Most people work all week and then rest. The Kingdom equation is the other way around: We begin in the place of rest; then we work. We are not to rest from our work, but work from a place of rest.

First we abide and then, secure in our identity and calling, we do. This is the way to bear real fruit.

Come Closer

• This coming week, reflect on your connectedness to Jesus and the fact that all your fruitfulness in life results from abiding in Him, remaining in Him.

• Use the following verses in your prayers or devotional times, and let them soak into you:

"So then, just as you received Christ Jesus as Lord, continue to live your lives in him." (Colossians 2:6)

"And now, little children, abide in Him, that when He appears, we may have confidence and not be ashamed before Him at His coming." (1 John 2:28, NKJV)

"That Christ may dwell in your hearts through faith; that you, being rooted and grounded in love, may be able to comprehend with all the saints what is the width and length and depth and height—to know the love of Christ which passes knowledge; that you may be filled with all the fullness of God." (Ephesians 3:17–19, NKJV)

Prepared

When we work from a place of rest—rather than frantically running around trying to make stuff happen—it is amazing what God can do. Abiding with Him in the secret place unlocks so many seemingly impenetrable situations.

More can happen during one minute under the anointing than can be achieved by hours, days or weeks of striving. When we wait on Holy Spirit and we connect with Him, hearing the Father's heart, then we know how we should pray, what to do and how we should do it.

Another meaning of abiding is "to be prepared." As we abide in Jesus, resting in Him, He prepares us to go out and touch the lives of others, to be His hands and feet in the situations of life we encounter.

Time spent abiding is time spent being equipped. Our human minds argue that time spent abiding is time doing "nothing." This is not true. It's actually the most valuable time we will ever spend. It's a sound investment. Abiding in the vine means we are "plugged in" to the resources of heaven.

How do we approach this practically?

Make space in your life for time spent alone with the Lord—with no distractions. For some people, this is early in the morning; for others, it is late at night. It can be during your lunch break, if you work in an office. Or whenever. But find time to be alone with Jesus, with no agenda other than listening to Him.

Find a special place where you can be alone with Him. It may be a quiet room in your house. Or you may find it easier to listen to Him as you walk outside. But finding a "special" place is good; it reminds us why we're there and helps us tune out the background noise and give Jesus all our attention.

Practice abiding in Him.

Unscrambled

When I was a young girl, my parents discovered I suffered from severe dyslexia. It was so bad I couldn't read a single page of a book properly—not even as freshman in high school. Everything was jumbled and back-to-front. The letters D and B were transposed. My mother would write letters on sandpaper, so I could feel them with my fingers and figure out which way they should go.

I only did well in school and graduated through memorization. I memorized entire text books and plays. But I couldn't spell at all, which really embarrassed me.

I asked my parents if I could study overseas. Since they'd already sent me to Switzerland previously, they said I could live on an Indian Reservation instead. There I first discovered the poor and found myself living among them. There I also became a Christian, at the age of sixteen, on March 14, 1976.

I was invited to a meeting and told, "If you come, God will do a miracle." I needed a miracle—I needed my parents to get saved. I arrived at the meeting and discovered the preacher was a "Word" guy. Great, I thought. Lots of reading, and I can't read. But something amazing began to happen. The preacher called out Deuteronomy, and I flipped my Bible open at Deuteronomy. He mentioned Lamentations, and I opened my Bible to it. It was strange—supernatural.

Later we all lined up for prayer. Someone prayed for me—for my miracle—and I fell to the floor. Holy Spirit touched me. When I returned to my seat, I picked up my Bible. When I looked at the pages, I could hardly believe my eyes. I could read! I could understand the words; they were no longer mixed up. God had healed me!

I share my story, hoping it will encourage you with two truths. First, God knows everything about your situation, about the miracle you need—even if it's not the one you think you need! Second, He still heals today. Keep pressing into His presence. He will meet with you, and something supernatural can happen.

Larger Vision

Naturally speaking, I was not "qualified" to go to college and graduate with a degree. How could I make up for sixteen years of dyslexia? Everything was stacked against me. But God changed things. He stepped in and brought a miracle. Suddenly, impossibilities became possibilities. The odds against me were overwhelming, but God overruled and overturned the odds.

If your vision of your future can be accomplished by you alone, it probably is not the real vision God has put inside you. God fills us with visions that are impossible for us—utterly impossible for us to accomplish in our own strength or by our own resources. He wants us to come to the place of complete dependency on Him. When we are dependent, then He can do a miracle.

God's method of working in our world is always through willing sons and daughters. God's method is a man or a woman. But He can only work effectively through people who refuse to strive with His will; who are recklessly devoted, laid down and surrendered to Him; who are transparent and unwilling to take His glory for themselves. God chooses people whom He can fill; He chooses those who are ready to contain His life and love and let it spill out of them.

Today, set aside some time to seek Jesus and talk to Him about what He has placed in your heart—the things He has spoken over your life or told you to do. Reflect on these things and, if needed, ask Jesus to enlarge your vision, to give you a bigger picture of what He wants to accomplish through you. Grasp hold of the vision that can only be achieved with His miracle help.

Now empty yourself and ask Jesus to fill you—completely, totally, to overflowing. Surrender to Him and ask Him to work supernaturally in your life to fulfill everything He intends, all that is pleasing to Him. Now enter the rest of the secret place of His presence and trust Him for everything.

Persevering Faith

Some of us have awesome encounters with Jesus, in which we are filled with His power, touched by His glory. And for a time, we bask in this and see how our futures could change. But then we back away. We return to how we were before. In effect, we abort the promises of God in our lives.

Why?

Sometimes it's because we don't want to pay the price. The cost of laying everything down, the cost of complete submission to His will, seems too great to bear. Yes, we want to surrender to Jesus, but we also still want to hang on to a little bit of independence, to just hold back a little piece of ourselves.

Sometimes it's because we don't want to carry something uncomfortable. Deep down we know that reaching out to the poor—for instance—will be painful, discomforting and emotionally costly. So we draw back and hesitate.

The apostle Paul lays the challenge before us, speaking about paying his own price:

"But whatever were gains to me I now consider loss for the sake of Christ. What is more, I consider everything a loss because of the surpassing worth of knowing Christ Jesus my Lord, for whose sake I have lost all things. I consider them garbage, that I may gain Christ and be found in him...." (Philippians 3:7–9)

But look how Paul speaks about loss and gain. He may have lost everything, but what he had gained outstripped his loss. In fact, Paul was saying the two things can't really be compared—they are so radically far apart. His gain towers over his loss; it dwarfs it.

I implore you to consider sacrificing everything for Jesus. Take the risk; take the leap of faith. I promise, you will never, ever regret. What you will gain by losing everything will overwhelm you for eternity.

Full Access

Now all of us can come to the Father through the same Holy Spirit because
of what Christ has done for us.
Ephesians 2:18, NLT

We have full access to everything for which Jesus died, to touch the poor with His love and grace and bring wholeness and freedom. To touch those who are sick and see them healed and restored. To bring hope to the hopeless and freedom to those in bondage, to find the lost and bring salvation. To cause His Kingdom to break into our world, bringing light where darkness presently reigns.

Every time we go on a bush outreach and encounter a village where the people know nothing about Jesus, we are confident Jesus will come, by the presence of His Holy Spirit, and make Himself known. We boldly ask the villagers to bring forward all who are deaf or blind or sick. We do so trusting the Father's promise of full access to His Son's inheritance.

Once again, we ask our faith-filled children to pray. We let them lead the way with their prayers. As they do, many healings happen, and frequently the whole village comes to Christ.

Jesus longs for His Father's Kingdom to burst out everywhere—whenever, wherever. I don't want you to read this and think there is something special about us. There isn't. I don't want you to think Jesus has specially anointed us for a "special job" that somehow qualifies us to see more miracles than others. He hasn't.

What we are privileged to be partakers in is the normal Christian life. You have the same full, unfettered access to all the resources of heaven that we do. Miracles can happen where you are—no matter where that is or what you do.

If we begin to understand the Kingdom in these terms, we will begin taking risks. We don't have to wonder if God will show up. Neither do we have to beg Him to do something. Those who understand they are sons and daughters of the King can walk with confidence. We know we are co-heirs with Jesus. We have inherited all that Jesus Himself has access to.

Walk in your true identity. You have full access to all the power of heaven!

Influence

Some of the world's most influential people are those who never sought to gain influence through their lives in the first place. Those who are among the most admired in the world, those who have most shaped global opinion on certain issues, are typically people who aren't trying to do that. They are just consumed with a cause they deeply believe in and are passionate about.

Mother Teresa is perhaps the perfect example—a lady who was admired the world over and was deeply influential, but who had no personal ambition. All she cared about was reaching out to those in need, being the hands and feet of Jesus to the poor and suffering.

She was influential simply by being and doing what Father had called her to be and do.

This principle is important for us to understand. We need to be clear about our identity in Christ and understand all the blessings, rights and privileges conferred on us because of Jesus. But then we need to rest in that identity, knowing we are loved, accepted and called, and cooperate with Holy Spirit to do what He wants us to do. There need be no striving.

When we simply love people and do what's good, we please our God. When we humble ourselves under His mighty hand and persevere in good works, He will exalt us at the proper time, if He so desires.

We don't need to seek influence in order to make a name for ourselves or achieve God's will for our lives. Rather than influence, we pursue humility.

Whenever we face a challenge in life, the answer is not to use our influence to try to change things; the answer is to go lower, to humble ourselves more and allow Christ in us to become greater than the problem.

Be who you are. Don't try to be who you're not. Simply act out God's love every day, and you will grow in influence.

Come Closer

• Life can be frantic. In this online, 24-7 connected world, it can be hard to find quiet, peace and rest. Yet, the Father wants us to abide with Him in the secret place and work from a place of rest—rather than resting from our work.

• Finding rest and peace is not unattainable; we just need to be more intentional about seeking them out.

• This week, meditate on the following verses. This is a great way to start to enter His rest.

"And He said to them, 'Come aside by yourselves to a deserted place and rest a while.' For there were many coming and going, and they did not even have time to eat." (Mark 6:31, NKJV)

"My Presence will go with you, and I will give you rest." (Exodus 33:14)

"Peace I leave with you, My peace I give to you; not as the world gives do I give to you. Let not your heart be troubled, neither let it be afraid." (John 14:27, NKJV)

Actions and Words

Matthew 5–7 records Jesus' famous Sermon on the Mount. In it Jesus identifies the character traits and qualities of Kingdom people. They are humble in spirit, acquainted with sorrow, meek, hungry for righteousness, merciful, pure in heart, peacemakers, prepared to be persecuted for the cause of Christ.

Jesus goes on to identify, mid-way through His message, a list of the most common areas of conflict and challenge that we struggle with in life:

- Anger
- Lust
- Broken relationships
- Breaking our promises
- Retaliating when others hurt or offend us
- Dealing with our enemies
- Our attitude toward the poor

Taken out of context, Jesus' guidance could sound like harsh rules and regulations: "Do this... don't do that..." But what did Jesus do before He delivered this iconic message?

He demonstrated it. He lived out the message.

During the silent years of Jesus' preparation, before He was thrust onto the world stage to begin His public ministry, Jesus learned the discipline of surrender. He grew in grace, obeyed His heavenly Father, obeying his earthly parents. He listened to His Father's voice and persevered in what the Father had given Him to do. Out of this wellspring of relationship came forth the power ministry—the miracles, healing, changed lives, God's Kingdom breaking out all over.

Later Jesus was qualified to speak about these things because He had lived them. He instructed His followers to go out and minister to those who were sick, in pain or in bondage with great compassion—because He had already done it and had demonstrated how it should be done. He preached the Gospel. He was the Gospel.

If our ministry is not born out of the wellspring of relationship, if it is not birthed in compassion, let it die.

Good to Be Here

Have you ever, when life was going along nicely, suddenly had a wham! experience? Suddenly, you are somewhere you don't want to be, and you ask yourself, "Why am I here? How did I get here?"

It could be an unexpected health issue or a sudden relationship crisis. Maybe you were moving along in your career, thinking everything was fine, when boom!—you're let go. "Why did that happened?" you ask, invariably following with, "What now?"

When we find ourselves facing circumstances beyond our control and are floundering, feeling misplaced, asking questions that don't seem to have answers, it is tempting to think God has lost the plot, is not paying attention to our plight, has stopped caring for us. None of these are true, of course, but that's how we feel.

How should we react when life's problems seem to conspire against us and circumstances threaten to overwhelm us? I'd like to suggest two things.

First, look up, not down. Often our first reaction is to look down, into ourselves, to scrutinize ourselves and wonder what we did wrong. Instead, we need to look up, toward Father. Life has its ups and downs, but Father doesn't. He is constant. So we can take the advice of Paul, "Don't worry about anything; instead, pray about everything. Tell God what you need, and thank him for all he has done" (Philippians 4:6, NLT).

This is not a trite statement. Rather, it tells us how to intentionally position ourselves, calling on our Father to assist us in our need. We must take all things to Him in prayer.

Second, in Mozambique we have a simple saying: It's good to be here! Whatever is happening, we say, "It's good to be here." Why? Because it is good to be wherever God is, wherever He has placed us. Even in a crisis, it is good to be here, because we are perfectly positioned to receive His supernatural help, to His glory.

Though you may not have chosen to be here in life right now, know that He is with you; call on Him in prayer. Count it an opportunity for Him to be glorified.

Keep Worshipping

Life in Mozambique is characterized by frequent power cuts. Our lights go off all the time—unless we happen to be in a village somewhere, of course, in which case we don't have any lights to begin with!

Generally, we have a power cut on Sundays, when the local authorities figure people aren't working. So they cut the power for our whole area. Often, as we are holding a meeting in the evening, right in the middle of it, we are plunged into darkness.

When this happens, we just start singing. We may have lost the use of our sound system temporarily, but we can still use our voices! We sing and praise God and sing some more until the lights come back on—or don't. No one freaks out about it or cries, "Oh no! Things aren't going as planned!" We just keep on worshipping.

Kingdom life is characterized by praise and worship. We can praise God when things aren't going according to plan. We can worship Him, even when the unexpected happens. We can find things to be thankful for, even when we don't have what we consider a basic necessity.

First Thessalonians 5:18 says, "Be thankful in all circumstances, for this is God's will for you who belong to Christ Jesus."

I like The Message version: "Be cheerful no matter what; pray all the time; thank God no matter what happens. This is the way God wants you who belong to Christ Jesus to live."

A spirit of gratitude touches our Father's heart. A thankful heart acknowledges all He has done for us and trusts He will give us what we need, when we need it.

If you feel like the lights have suddenly gone out for you, and you've been plunged into darkness—confused and disorientated—stay focused and praise God. Worship Him. You might want to pray out loud, "Father, I don't know what's happening right now, but I choose to worship You anyway." Cultivate an attitude of thankfulness. Trust Him in all things.

"O LORD, you alone are my hope. I've trusted you, O LORD, from childhood ... No wonder I am always praising you." (Psalm 71: 5–6, NLT)

Help!

I am like a little kid. If God doesn't show up and take care of me, I'm in trouble. Rolland often wonders how I manage to get around an airport when I'm travelling alone! Most of the time, I am wandering around praying, "Help, Lord!" People see me looking lost and often ask if they can help. Do I need help? What an understatement!

Here's what I've realized: We are supposed to work together and help each other. We are not all meant to be capable of doing everything. We are gifted to do some things, while others are completely beyond us. That's okay. That's how God made us. He made us to need each other—and to need Him.

Sometimes, when people hear we have over ten thousand children in our full-time care, they ask me, "How do you cook for them all?" I certainly don't cook for ten thousand kids! I can barely cook successfully for my immediate family, let alone all the kids, and then it's never without producing much smoke. But that doesn't matter; we have a bunch of people who love cooking and are really good at it.

The Body of Christ is such an amazing thing. In it God brings together diverse people with diverse gifts who can work together to accomplish His purposes. It is a sign and a wonder to our world when the Body functions and the seemingly impossible is achieved through cooperation and commitment to a common goal.

It is also beautiful to see. Where potential weaknesses exist in the Body, God supplies people with the gifts needed to strengthen those areas. Paul summed it up simply in 1 Corinthians 12:7, "A spiritual gift is given to each of us so we can help each other" (NLT). We should celebrate that!

Remember, as a part of Christ's Body, you have a vital role to play. Father God has given you specific gifts to use to help others. And they have been given gifts to help you. Working together, we can help each other and carry out the Father's will. Be glad you have a part to play, and don't be afraid to shout Help! when you need it.

Need

The wife of a man from the company of the prophets cried out to Elisha,
"Your servant my husband is dead, and you know that he revered the
LORD. But now his creditor is coming to take my two boys as his slaves."
2 Kings 4:1

This widow found herself in dire circumstances. She was broken and broke—
in a terrible situation. Her life was falling apart around her.

Her words to Elisha reveal anger and bitterness. It's like she was saying, "He
feared God, and look where it got him!" The verses imply her husband died
prematurely, and she was ticked off at God. Now the creditors were coming
to take away her two boys as slaves.

In the West it might be hard to imagine such circumstances. In Mozambique
we understand. I have picked up little girls from garbage dumps who were
sold in exchange for a piece of bread or a shot of alcohol. Why do such things
happen? Great sin and, therefore, great destruction exist in this world we live
in.

This woman experienced similar anguish as darkness closed in on her. Elisha
responded by saying, "How can I help you? Tell me, what do you have in your
house?" (verse 2). Doesn't that seem strange? She was poor and desperate in
the midst of a national famine, yet the prophet asked, "What do you have?"
Why did he ask instead of just giving her something?

Instinctively she replied, "Nothing." Then she remembered; she had a little
oil.

God uses this tiny amount of oil to bring about a miracle in this woman's life.
But she had to be willing to place it in God's hands and trust Him to come
through. You may be in a similar place; so much of what you had has been
stripped away, and you are clinging on to the last bits and pieces of your life,
afraid to let go.

Today, Father says to you, "Come to Me. Bring that little amount of oil and
surrender it to Me. Then I will provide for you." God knows and cares about
your situation more than you do. Trust that, in surrendering all to Him, you
will actually gain everything. Trust Him, and don't be afraid to let go.

Practical Passion

Every Monday I spend a few hours walking around the local village and surrounding area. Many of the children attend our schools, so the people recognize me. I stop and chat with many friends and especially the local widows.

One Monday recently, I was chatting to one such widow. She called out to me as I walked by and invited me into her house. I went inside and sat down in the dirt with her. She was caring for her child who was severely disabled after suffering from cerebral malaria. I asked how she was.

"I want to say good," she told me, "but I'm not really doing so well." When I asked her why, she told me she was raped most nights. The reason? "Because I don't have a door," she informed me. I was shocked, angry, upset. I wanted to do something about this situation that was so wrong.

When God fills us with Himself, He fills us with compassion. But compassion isn't real unless it is moved to respond. Unresponsive compassion is just pity. Could I just pray for this lady and say, I'm so sorry? No. First of all, I would get her a door! Then I would take her to our medical clinic and for some antibiotics for the STDs she had no doubt picked up. Then I would pray God will heals her wounded spirit and restores her with His love.

The Gospel looks like something. Love expresses itself in action. Passion has to find physical expression, or it dies and is meaningless. God has called us to carry His passion in the world, and that means being His hands and feet.

We can't do it in our own power. It's too hard. The need is too overwhelming. But when we are filled to overflowing with the oil of Holy Spirit, we can respond with Father's compassion and do something. Without the presence of Holy Spirit, we are just weak and miserable. But Holy Spirit brings joy—supernatural joy. And supernatural joy brings supernatural strength.

The Kingdom of God spills out through joy-filled people, and lives are changed. Simply getting this lady a door with a lock changed her life for the better.

Come Closer

"Abide in Me, and I in you. As the branch cannot bear fruit of itself, unless it abides in the vine, neither can you, unless you abide in Me. I am the vine, you are the branches. He who abides in Me, and I in him, bears much fruit; for without Me you can do nothing." (John 15:4–5, NKJV)

• Frequently in Mozambique we experience power cuts. They come randomly, plunging us into darkness. Whatever we happen to be doing at the time, we have no choice but to stop and wait. We are powerless—literally!

• If we learn how to abide in Jesus in our Christian lives, however, we will never be without spiritual power. We need not fear being plunged into sudden darkness. We need not fear becoming suddenly helpless and powerless. Holy Spirit is the one power supplier who is always on and never fails!

• Abiding in Jesus is simply remaining plugged into the power source.

Little Oil

People often ask me, "Why do you do what you do?"

Generally I say, "Because I'm in love." It's true. What I do is not hard. It's not some terrible sacrifice I have to make because God is forcing me to do something against my will. I don't spend every day weeping about how hard my life is.

No. I want to be here. I want to do this. I'm joyful about what I'm doing because I'm in love. I do it because He is worthy. I do it because I have glimpsed His heart. What else would I want to do with my life?

I may feel totally unqualified to do what I do, but that doesn't matter. He is eminently qualified. All I need to contribute is my willingness.

Remember the widow who cried out to Elisha for help? Elisha asked her what she already had in her possession. Instinctively she replied, "Nothing!" Then she remembered: "Oh yes, I have a little oil—that's all."

So often we are dismissive of ourselves. We say we have nothing—nothing God would want to use, anyhow. But no, we have a little oil. And that is all God needs to take us and do a miracle. We come up with all kinds of good reasons for why God can't do anything notable or meaningful through us.

I have done it myself numerous times. "God, what can you do with my life?" I would ask. "I have no special gifting, no special talent, no outstanding abilities."

One time God stopped me mid-flow and said, "Stop it! I like your little offering. Bring it to Me and let Me use it." Eventually I realized all He really wanted was my willingness, and He would do the rest. He wanted me to stop telling Him why He couldn't use me and just say yes. I didn't need to be special, talented or outstanding in any way. I just needed to be willing to come to Him and offer up the little reserve of oil I had.

Come to Him today. Offer up the little you have in reckless devotion.

Pour it out willingly. He will do the rest.

Confronting Darkness

So much darkness exists in our world. But when we are full of the presence of God, full of Holy Spirit, we are no longer afraid to confront the hellish darkness.

Once I visited one of my favorite churches in America and gave an altar call for the young people. Many came forward, but I noticed one young man who was reacting strongly to God's presence. I love it when the joy of the Lord comes or when His peace comes and people are resting in His presence. But I love it more when the ballistic power of Holy Spirit comes, and I can see something powerful is happening. This young man was literally vibrating under the power of God and yelling out. It looked frightening if you'd never seen it before—and even if you had.

I went over to pray for him and asked him what was going on. He said God had told him to help me bring in all the children He wanted to rescue. He was saying yes to God. He was prepared to give his life away to do what God wanted him to do.

I have heard a lot of people say a lot of things while they are being touched by God. I've also witnessed a lot of people abort the promises of God in their lives before they reach full term. But I was thrilled to see this young man's authentic commitment. He came out to Mozambique. He watched, listened and learned. He spent time with us. He spent time with the poor, and he began rescuing kids off the street.

He was around 22 when I met him. Now, at the age of 28, he is living in India. He has over three thousand children in his care, many of whom he has "bought" out of the sex trade. He is winning little children back for Father by the power of the Gospel. God has taken his radical commitment and used him to save many lives.

This teaches me that, regardless of the context of our lives, we should never stop believing God can both fill us and use us for His glory. God is able to display His glory through you, if you will cooperate with Him. He may take you to the other side of the world to do something for Him. He may use you to do something you never expected in your own neighborhood. The what, where and how don't really matter. What matters is that you come to Him and surrender yourself to His purposes. Then He can make something amazing out of your life.

Fresh Oil

God wants to pour fresh oil into you today. We read in Acts 2 about the Holy Spirit coming at Pentecost and filling Jesus' disciples, empowering them to go out and plant the Church. But it is still Pentecost. God is still anointing, filling and empowering those who belong to Him. You can experience Pentecost today. In fact, you must! It's time for fresh oil to be poured into your life until you overflow and the oil runs over, touching the lives of those around you. Holy Spirit wants to fill you with a new passion and change your identity, transforming you and making you new.

I met a young girl from a missionary family who came to Mozambique to spend some time with us. She was from a very conservative background. She certainly wasn't used to hearing people speak or sing in tongues, so she was far out of her comfort zone. But she was deeply touched by Holy Spirit, and we noticed a profound change in her.

She began spending time in our different centers, and gradually God's calling on her life became clear to her. Now she is giving up her American passport to be a North Korean citizen, because Jesus wants to use her to reach out to them.

This is beautiful. Somebody has to stand in the gap. Someone has to say, "I don't care what it costs, Jesus; I will do it."

We need to be so in love with Jesus that we understand His heart. And we refuse to close our eyes to the darkness but instead choose to overflow with His love and let the oil spill out.

God causes people to give up their time and pray and act in such ways for a reason. So many lost, sick and suffering people in the world need Him. When God fills us with Holy Spirit's oil, His compassion comes in. And with that compassion, we start to care about the darkness in the lives of others. And we start to be willing to do something about it.

Let's pray for fresh oil today.

Container

We need to change the way we think.

The widow who cried out for help was consumed by her own self-pity. And why not? Her life was a wreck, and worse was coming. Everything was falling apart around her. Her husband had died prematurely, and with the main wage-earner gone, she had gotten into terrible debt. Now the debts were being called in, and she was about to lose her two sons—sold into slavery to pay off her debts. She would be left with nothing.

But in her self-pity, she missed the fact that she still had a little bit of oil left. She still had something God could use.

God is seeking willing hearts—those who, recognizing they have very little of worth in the worldly sense, are still willing to come to Him to see what He can do with their meager resources.

And God comes.

He comes powerfully precisely because He is looking for empty vessels to fill. He is looking for suitable containers whom He can fill with His oil. He is looking for those people who want to be fully filled with His precious Holy Spirit, those who don't have a whole load of other stuff in the way.

Something powerful happens when we put a stop to self pity in our lives and start believing God can take our tiny supply of oil and multiply it, filling us fully, to His glory.

Ask Father God to empty you of all that hinders His work in your life. Choose to make yourself an empty container. Then Father can come and fill you with His presence, and in a moment, everything can change.

Empty Jars

Having helped her realize she had a little oil in her possession, the prophet Elisha told the widow to go around asking all her neighbors to give her their empty jars.

What an interesting approach to solving her problem! God could have just said to Elisha, "Pay off her debts for her." Or He could have simply said, "Give her some money." He did neither.

Why? Because Father God didn't want to just solve her problem; He wanted to change her life, giving her a completely different outlook and perspective. He wanted to transform her faith and grow her trust in God, removing her anger and bitterness.

The process of gathering up all the empty jars was a prophetic act. She cooperated with God, making the statement that something was about to happen, even if she didn't know precisely what. "Go and ask your neighbors for all their empty jars," Elisha had said, so she did. And, "Don't just ask for a few," he added. He then gave her instructions for what to do next—start pouring the oil into the jars.

It must have been an amazing sight to behold. There she was with one jar containing a tiny bit of oil and numerous other empty jars. She took a step of obedience and began pouring. And the oil didn't run out until every jar she had was full. God had done a miracle.

She now had the resources she needed to pay off her debts and get out of her bad situation. But she had much more than that: She has a firsthand knowledge of the supernatural provision of our incredible Father. She had the faith to believe for His supernatural intervention in her life and the lives of others.

Her empty jar had been filled, her life transformed.

God wants to do the same for you. He wants to fill your emptiness with His plenty, and He's inviting you take a step of faith, to trust Him with reckless devotion.

Burning

God wants to do something extraordinary with you. When He calls you, go. Do whatever He asks you to do. All you need to say is, "Here I am. I'll do whatever makes You happy."

Whether you are an engineer, scientist, musician, dancer, preacher, teacher, K-Mart employee, waitress or restaurant owner—whatever you do in life, do it with all your might for Jesus' glory.

It shouldn't be anyone's goal in life to just be average or mediocre. Why? Because we are children of the King. We are children of our Father, and He wants to fill us so we can burn brightly for Him.

Too many people burn out in life, because they are busy doing the wrong thing or busy trying to do the right thing in their own strength, through self-effort and striving.

Sometimes "doing the right thing" doesn't get us anywhere because we birthed the idea, and God had nothing to do with it. Stop! We must allow Him to fill us, to overflow our hearts with His love and power, to call us forth into what He has specifically for us. As He calls us, He fills us some more and empowers us to do what we are meant to do for Him. And He fills us with joy!

Unstoppable joy characterizes those who have surrendered their all to Jesus and been filled by Him to overflowing.

When we seek to be filled by Him, first and foremost, then we will be happy doing what we do, and we will be effective. We will burn brightly wherever God has placed us, and people will stop and notice.

If you feel like you have lost your way, stop. Go to Jesus and ask Him to fill you afresh. Allow Him to reignite you and set your heart aflame again.

Come Closer

• The Bible depicts the Holy Spirit as being like oil, because He anoints us. Holy Spirit wants to anoint you and me to renew and restore us, to empower and equip us to serve Him more effectively. We need a constant supply of fresh oil, so we overflow and begin to touch those around us.

• God is earnestly seeking those who are willing to be empty containers. He wants somewhere empty that He can fill up by pouring in His oil.

• In the Bible oil was used to light the lamps in the temple of God, as an ointment for healing, as a symbol of cleansing and to signify the calling of priests, kings and prophets. In other words, allowing the oil of the Holy Spirit to flow through you will cause you to be a light to others, will bring healing to your soul, will cleanse you and take you deeper into holiness and will highlight and confirm your calling in Christ.

Buying Oil

Do you want the oil of the Holy Spirit to flow into and through your life? There is only one way to accomplish this: spending time in the presence of God. Remember the parable of the wise and foolish virgins that Jesus tells in Matthew 25:

"At that time the kingdom of heaven will be like ten virgins who took their lamps and went out to meet the bridegroom. Five of them were foolish and five were wise. The foolish ones took their lamps but did not take any oil with them. The wise ones, however, took oil in jars along with their lamps." (Matthew 25:1–4)

Five of the girls in Jesus' story had already made an investment in purchasing oil, so they were ready when the bridegroom came. They were prepared. The other five girls were unwise. They had not invested. When they ran out of oil they tried to borrow some from the wise girls, but they couldn't. Then, while they were out trying to buy some more oil, the bridegroom came and they missed him.

We "buy oil" whenever we spend time in the presence of God and He fills us. He fills and prepares us, so when the emergencies in life come along, we have oil. We are anointed, prepared. This process takes time. It takes an investment on our part.

We can't go to those who've already made that investment and say, "Lend us some of your oil." It can't be done. We have to go and spend time in His presence. That's the only way.

I believe God is saying to you and me: It's time to buy oil. It's time to make time for His presence. To invest in our future. When Jesus comes knocking, I want Him to find me fully prepared. When the sudden circumstances of life happen, I want to have sufficient oil to cope with any emergency.

Make sure you invest enough time in buying oil.

Salt Shaker

In our meetings we like to give Holy Spirit the space to do whatever He wants to do—because He is the boss. Who are we to place restrictions on the Almighty? He can do whatever He likes.

I'm sure some people leave our meetings moaning: Can you believe that? The meeting went on for five hours! Don't they understand we're hungry? That we have babysitters?"

We could stick to time. We could play by normal church rules. But I can't be motivated by that. I don't go to church or any church meeting to give a nice little homily and then go and eat lunch. I go to fully engage with Jesus and to let Him have His way—to see Him touch people in whatever way He wants, for however long it takes.

I live to see people touched by Jesus' presence. I understand that people have homes to go to and things to do, but when I am lost in His presence, time doesn't matter to me anymore. All that matters is Him. I live to be filled with Him and to pour out myself so others can experience more of Him, too.

Some people live their lives like faulty salt shakers—in which the salt has gotten damp and is sticking together. You can shake them and shake them, but hardly anything comes out!

I don't want to live my life like that. I want to be one whose life is easily emptied out for the benefit of others. We serve an extravagant God, so we should give Him an extravagant gift of our lives. Often we think of our lives as being too small, too insignificant for God to use. The way I see it, if my life is so small, why not give all of it to Him?

Ask God to fill you afresh today and to make you easy to empty. Become a person who can overflow and give lavishly of yourself to Father God and to others.

Extravagant

> But for right now, until that completeness, we have three things to
> do to lead us toward that consummation: Trust steadily in God, hope
> unswervingly, love extravagantly. And the best of the three is love.
> 1 Corinthians 13:13, MESSAGE

If God is pouring out oil, I want to be a jar. I want to be an empty vessel. I want to make sure I am fully filled—full of Holy Spirit, fully impassioned with the love of Jesus.

I want to be fully filled with Him, so I am an answer in this world rather than a question. A solution, rather than a problem. I want to be part of Father God's solution to the grief, suffering and sickness that exists in this world—not part of the problem.

I don't want to be a miserable little salt shaker that nothing comes out of! I want to give my life extravagantly.

In Ephesians 1, Paul's passion for Jesus spills over as he writes about the extravagance of our Savior. Verses 3–14 tell us we are:

- Blessed with every possible spiritual blessing
- Chosen before the creation of the world
- Adopted as Father's sons and daughters
- Redeemed and forgiven
- Given the plan of salvation, which is revealed to us through Christ
- Selected to receive the promised Holy Spirit

Here is blessing on top of extravagant blessing, poured out on us by our all-loving Father. How can we not respond to that with an extravagant offering? We love Him because He first loved us.

And our whole lives must become a fitting response to His love. Won't you join me in emptying out your life—in reckless devotion to Him—so He can fill you with all His fullness?

Secret

In the story we've been reading, in 2 Kings 4, the widow gathered all the empty jars she could find from her friends and neighbors. Then Elisha gave her specific instructions: "Shut the door..." (verse 4).

Why was it important for her to shut the door in order to witness the miracle about to take place? I think it was because it was a "secret place" kind of thing. It was personal. God wanted to win back her heart and show her that, though she no longer had a husband, He was still her provider. He wanted her to seek Him out, in secret, and come into a new understanding of her dependency on Him.

The pursuit of God's presence requires us to press in, press in and press in. But if we persist, suddenly we know—we've entered that secret place of His presence.

Once we're there, everything else pales into insignificance. Everything becomes less important. Eating, sleeping, drinking, ticking off tasks on the to-do list—they are all lost as we encounter the revelation of our dependency on Him.

The secret place puts everything into perspective. I live for that. To be fully engaged with the presence of God. Enraptured with the presence of Jesus. For me, it always comes during times of worship. That's why we need to invest time simply adoring Jesus.

We are becoming a company of worshippers, wholly given to God, because He is worthy.

And in the secret place of His presence, we are made complete.

Miracle

Once, while I was speaking at a conference in the U.S., I was introduced to an incredible lady. I was thrilled to meet her, because she had the heart of a mother and had invested her life into rescuing some desperate children. She was mother to nineteen kids. She had witnessed the great need in Mexico, so she began rescuing orphaned kids from the garbage dumps, adopting them and taking them home to live with her.

I was humbled to learn she had heard my story and been inspired to act. We had a wonderful heart-to-heart connection, one momma to another.

What was really amazing, however, was that this lady was committed to pouring herself out despite overwhelming odds. She was in a wheelchair, paralyzed from the waist down. She couldn't do much at all, physically speaking.

Her kids loved her though, and they urged me to pray for her. I began to pray and got all her kids involved, too. We prayed and called on the Lord. As we did, suddenly she started to move her toes—the toes that hadn't moved in years. We got excited. We rejoiced. We should rejoice over the small things, not just wait for the big things.

We continued to pray, praise, rejoice and express our gratitude to Jesus. Then a miracle happened. This woman was not a small lady; she was a big momma! But suddenly God propelled her out of that wheelchair and got her on her feet. Then the most extraordinary thing happened. She began to dance.

She wasn't a trained dancer; she had never danced professionally in her life. But she began tap dancing like an old time Pentecostal. I did train as a dancer, and I can say it was the most incredible tap dancing I'd ever seen in my life, with skill and anointing.

She went on dancing for over an hour. Holy Spirit fell on everyone around her. The presence of God came crashing in. He delights in pouring His abundant life out on those who are pouring out their lives for others.

God can show up anywhere.

So why not here? Why not now?

Kenosis

Imitate God, therefore, in everything you do, because you are his dear children. Live a life filled with love, following the example of Christ. He loved us and offered himself as a sacrifice for us, a pleasing aroma to God.
Ephesians 5:1–2, NLT

Jesus provided us with the perfect example of how we are to live our lives. He is our model, the one we are to follow.

The biblical word kenosis describes what Jesus did. It is derived from the Greek word for "emptiness" and describes the self-emptying of one's own will to become entirely receptive to God's divine will.

Paul writes of Jesus that, "He gave up His divine privileges; he took the humble position of a slave and was born as a human being. When he appeared in human form, he humbled himself in obedience to God and died a criminal's death on a cross" (Philippians 2:7–8, NLT).

Then Paul echoed this in his own life, as he states a few verses later: "But I will rejoice even if I lose my life, pouring it out like a liquid offering to God, just like your faithful service is an offering to God. And I want all of you to share that joy" (verse 17, NLT).

Jesus emptied Himself and became nothing so He would be totally dependent on Holy Spirit, totally reliant on listening to His Father's instructions. Why did He do that? So you could follow Him.

He didn't have to do it. He could have accomplished His mission another way. He could have shown up in gold robes and said, "Listen to Me! Do what I say!" But instead He chose to come as a baby, live among the poor, learn languages.

He did it for the sake of love, so we could imitate Him. So we too could walk in faith, pray for the sick in His glorious name and see them get up and run. So we could pray over a lunch and see it feed a multitude.

What kind of people does God fill? Empty ones.

Come Closer

• When we regularly "buy oil" by spending time in the secret place of His presence, we will be prepared for whatever life brings. We will be ready to respond with the heart of Christ and to trust our Father in the midst of unexpected difficulty.

• Jesus demonstrated it for us. The biblical word kenosis describes how He emptied Himself of His will and desires to become entirely focused on and receptive to Father's will. As He emptied Himself, He was filled. Whoever got in the way of the overflow of His life was marvelously touched by heaven.

• This week, read Ephesians 1 and meditate on the truths it reveals about the extravagant love of Jesus that Father God has poured out on you.

You are blessed with every possible spiritual blessing.

You have been chosen before the creation of the world.

You are adopted as one of Father's children.

You are redeemed and forgiven.

You have had the plan of salvation revealed to you through Christ.

You have received the promised Holy Spirit.

• Consider what steps you can take to go lower, to empty yourself more fully so you can be filled with all His glorious fullness.

More Chicken

Sometimes our attitudes are far from perfect, yet God still moves. It is both humbling and a relief!

Once, I was due to be at a meeting, but I was late. A group of foreign visitors had come for our Bible School graduation ceremony. We were planning a celebration, with an accompanying meal.

At the time, we were able to eat chicken about twice a year. That night was one such occasion. Our kids were really excited about the chicken. Most of the year they eat a vegetarian diet, but not by choice. They love chicken!

Because we are subject to constant power cuts and have basic kitchen equipment, it took eighteen cooks all day to cook it. Consequently, the kids were camped out around the kitchen. They smelled the chicken; they talked about the chicken; the chicken was their delight!

Then the foreign visitors, not understanding protocol, went into the kitchen with the graduating pastors and ate all the chicken. My kids were distraught. I arrived at the meeting and was quickly surrounded by upset kids. "Mama Ida," they yelled, "Those foreigners ate all the chicken—and they're fat!" They were upset and angry, so I became upset and angry. I couldn't believe they had done that.

Generally the cooks will "hide" some small pieces of chicken in their robes and save them for later. So I marched into the kitchen and demanded, "Where's the chicken? Hand it over!" I ended up with a small box of cold chicken.

I was in a rush and not in a good mood. I sat down those dozens and dozens of kids and prayed an irritated prayer: "Thank You, Jesus. Make more chicken!" Then I began handing it out—"Here you go, bless you. . . here you go, bless you." I got to the last person after a lot of kids had been fed—a widowed lady who had been watching. I hadn't even been looking at the chicken, but I realized I was picking up the last piece and giving it to her.

Even though my attitude wasn't right, Jesus had answered my prayer: "Make more chicken!" What a gracious, loving Lord. He will do it for you, too.

Keep Pouring

We need to position ourselves so we keep on being filled, so we are in the right place to continue receiving the blessings of God. How do we do this? By depleting the supply of oil God has given us—by pouring ourselves out. We pour out our lives in His service in order to empty ourselves, so there is room for Him to fill us again, so we can pour ourselves out, and so on—over and over.

The more we pour out, the more we receive.

Elisha instructed the widow in 2 Kings to go home and shut the door—representing the entering of the secret place of God's presence—and "pour oil into all the jars, and as each is filled, put it to one side" (2 Kings 4:4).

Since she had just a tiny amount of oil left, one might think this lady would be delighted to have even one extra jar of oil, but this wasn't what she'd been instructed to do. She had been told to gather together as many jars as possible and to keep pouring until they were all filled.

So she kept pouring.

Holy Spirit will keep pouring Himself out as long as people are willing to be filled and willing to be poured out themselves. As long as He can find those who are wholly given over to God to be used for His purposes.

God will keep pouring out His presence as long as there are vessels to be filled. But He can't pour Himself out where there is nothing to contain His presence.

"When all the jars were full she said to her son, 'Bring me another one,' But he replied, 'There is not a jar left.' Then the oil stopped flowing" (2 Kings 4:6).

Holy Spirit's oil stops flowing when there are no more vessels left to fill. Let us be those who constantly empty ourselves to make room for more of His presence. Let's make it our aim to be empty so we can be full!

Snakes

One Sunday morning our church was filled with hundreds of excited people. We were celebrating a double wedding. The two brides and grooms were standing at the front of the congregation, ready to be married, and the service was well underway, when there was a sudden interruption.

My eldest adopted son was leading worship on his guitar. I had found him on the street at the age of fifteen, an unwanted orphan street bandit, and I took him in. Now he is a fiery evangelist who preaches the Gospel all over Asia. He really loves his guitar, so I was surprised to see him suddenly drop it on the ground. Simultaneously, a huge section of the church jumped up and ran out screaming.

A snake—a deadly Black Mamba—had crept into our tent and was moving among the congregation. If it bites you, you'll be dead in half an hour.

My son had been worshipping with his eyes open. He spotted the snake and knew what to do. He ran forward to avert a tragedy, beating the snake repeatedly until it was dead. Then I looked down and saw another snake right below my pulpit. Immediately I jumped down and whacked the snake so its head came off.

This was a real event. Most likely an angry witchdoctor had them in a bag and set them loose near our tent. It painted a vivid spiritual picture: The snake comes to destroy the intimate wedding.

God wants us to be engrossed in His presence, completely enraptured by Him and in tune with His heartbeat. We are working toward a glorious union with Christ. The enemy's whole desire is to prevent it from happening.

The enemy sends "snakes" into our churches all the time—demonic attacks designed to derail us. We won't see them unless we have our eyes open and are vigilant. It is the worshipper whose eyes are open who knows what to do. We must not be naïve to the enemy's schemes but stay alert and be constantly in prayer.

Defeated

After we killed the snakes in the congregation, a disaster was averted, but still all was not well. One of the brides was very upset and began to hyperventilate. Her family members were not believers yet, and they had perceived this as a bad omen—a snake at their daughter's wedding. Someone was trying to curse and kill her. The other bride was crying, and both grooms looked so sad that their special day was being ruined.

"What am I supposed to do, Lord?" I wondered. The snakes were dead, but the joy had gone out of the meeting, and I sensed a great feeling of defeat and fear. Then God told me what to do. He wanted me to stab the Mamba and hold up the headless body of the snake.

The body was still wiggling, but the snake no longer had a head or fangs. It didn't have the ability to bite anyone again, ever. It was a sign.

The enemy has lost the war. He has been defeated and is now under our feet. But we need to declare who we are in Jesus' name. God told me to shout out a declaration, so I began yelling, "We are more than conquerors in Christ Jesus!"

As I did, the hundreds of people who had fled the tent began to flock back in, the celebration resumed and the atmosphere of joy was restored.

When the unexpected is thrown at us and we feel threatened, intimidated, afraid, we need to remember that our enemy has been disarmed and defeated. He can try to attack and intimidate us, but our God is in control. The intimate wedding He is planning will go ahead, and we will rejoice.

No More Fear

Lots of people are afraid in life. Afraid of many things. Usually we are afraid of things that haven't even happened yet. What if I get sick? What if I lose my job? What if this happens? We fear not getting what we need in life, not being in control and a whole host of other things, rational or irrational.

Over seventy times in the King James Bible we read the command, "Fear not." And more than twenty times it says, "Be not afraid."

God doesn't want us to be afraid, because fear cancels out trust. Fear urges us to try to take control of our circumstances, so we won't be afraid any more. But this robs us of the joy and freedom of giving God control of our lives. It undermines our trust and total dependency on Him.

The solution to fear is not courage but love.

Perfect love casts out all fear. "There is no fear in love. But perfect love drives out fear..." (1 John 4:18).

The more we allow ourselves to be filled with the love of God, the less room we will have for fear. When we are confident in our Father's immense, complete, constant love for us, we won't be afraid anymore.

The Message puts it this way:

"God is love. When we take up permanent residence in a life of love, we live in God and God lives in us. This way, love has the run of the house, becomes at home and mature in us, so that we're free of worry. . . . There is no room in love for fear. Well-formed love banishes fear...." (1 John 4:17–18, MESSAGE)

Let's persist in pursuing God's presence and being filled with His love, so we will be "well-formed" in love, with all fear banished. Free to live and love as Father intended.

Full of Love

When love reigns in our lives and fear is dispelled, we can go into the darkest places on the planet, confident in the knowledge that we carry the glory of God into those dark recesses. In our movement, we actively look for the darkest disasters around the world so we can go there, carrying Jesus' light.

But we have to be full of the love of God. Going into the darkness without being fully filled is inviting trouble, and we won't be effective.

My life message is to stop for the one. To not pass by anyone who needs a touch from the love of Christ. We must stop for each one, genuinely caring and demonstrating the love of Jesus with actions, not just words.

But first we have to stop for the One. We stop for Him and let Him love us.

Don't stop for anyone until you have first stopped for Him. Let the lavish love of your Father, Daddy God, fill you, overflow you, overwhelm you.

The most important thing you can know today is that you are adored and loved by your Father. Until you know this, your love and care for others will be far less effective than it could be.

Get full of God's love. Then you can let that love spill out and touch others. As you do that, the flow of the Father's love through you will increase. As you give that love away, you will receive even more love to give.

Be full. Give. Receive. Give more. Receive more.

His love can never be extinguished.

"See how very much our Father loves us, for he calls us his children, and that is what we are..." (1 John 3:1, NLT)

Come Closer

• We abide in Jesus and spend time, specially set aside, in the secret place of Father's presence so we will be correctly positioned.

• By abiding, we position ourselves "in the way" of God's blessing. We are in the right place to be filled with His Spirit and showered with His blessing.

• But this is not just for us. We are meant to pour ourselves out, so God can fill us once more. We give away God's blessing and favor freely to others, and as we do, He calls us close to Him so we may be filled up again. Thus, He establishes a beautiful cycle of abundant grace.

• When we are filled up with God's love, we have no room for fear in our lives. We can live confident in our Father's care for us. And we will be free to live and love with reckless devotion, as the Father intended.

• Let us embrace this cycle of fullness and emptiness: Full—empty—full.

Water

Have you ever tried to survive a week without water?

We had to teach our pastors to drink water when they fasted. They would attempt thirty-day fasts and not drink because they didn't understand they could have water. I told them, "Jesus had some water; it's okay!"

Some hadn't had any water for over two weeks, in the punishing African heat, before we realized what was happening—but God supernaturally sustained them, and no one died.

How do we learn to live? Just as these pastors had to learn to discipline themselves to drink, we need to discipline ourselves to drink daily of the water of life.

In Numbers 20, we read about the time when God instructed Moses to strike a rock in the wilderness. Water gushed out from the rock so all the people and all their livestock could drink. This event is recalled by the psalmist in Psalm 78:15: "He split the rocks in the wilderness and gave them water as abundant as the seas."

The spiritual water we need comes from immersing ourselves in the Word of God and His presence. This water is as essential—as vital to our survival—as natural water is to physical life. We must drink of it daily.

I don't want to be a dehydrated Christian—one who is miserable, parched of life, a spiritual desert. I want to be a container of living water. I want to receive my daily sustenance from the Rock and then be a source of refreshment to others.

Discipline yourself to keep drinking. Stay refreshed. May everyone who encounters you find nothing of dry and dusty religion, but the life-giving, nourishing, sustaining, refreshing waters of life.

Spirit and Truth

When we are confident in our identity as precious, loved, adored children of God, it frees us. It frees us so we don't need to knock other people down. It frees us from the need to scramble for a position in this world in an attempt to feel like a "somebody." It doesn't matter whether we are a somebody or a nobody, because we are somebody in Daddy's eyes—and His is the only opinion that counts!

When we are aware of our identity, we possess incredible dignity. And we confer that dignity onto every other human being we meet, because we realize we are all created in Father's image and loved fully by Him.

When we know who we are, we freely give our lives away for the sake of love. Just like Jesus.

During our ministry, we have been slammed against walls, had stones thrown at us, been flung into jail. But love compels us to continue. Truly we don't count our lives as our own. Our lives don't belong to us. We give ourselves for the sake of love and for the cause of Christ. We bless those who persecute us.

Jesus is looking for passionate lovers to populate His Kingdom—those who will lay down everything for the sake of His cause, those who don't love their own lives so much that they're not prepared to count the cost and give it all away for Him.

"The time is coming—indeed it's here now—when true worshipers will worship the Father in spirit and in truth. The Father is looking for those who will worship him that way. For God is Spirit, so those who worship him must worship in spirit and in truth." (John 4:23–24, NLT)

Spirit-and-truth worshipers revere Father God with all their hearts, minds and beings. They are fully committed, holding nothing back. They worship Him with reckless devotion.

Let's continue to give what we cannot keep in order to gain what we cannot earn.

The Secret of Staying in Love

People often ask me, "How do you continue to stay in love with the Lord like you do?" Really, it's very simple. I do it the same way people have always stayed in love.

- I spend time with Him.
- I listen to Him.
- I let Him love me.
- I thank Him for the things He does for me.

I love just spending time in Jesus' presence, with no agenda other than being with Him, worshipping Him, being in tune with His heartbeat. I talk to Him; I listen; I worship. I let Him fill me with His love.

I don't look at my watch when I pray. I have no idea how to compartmentalize God. I don't separate out my time with God and say, "Here You go, Lord. This is Your special time." All my time is His time. He is my everything. He is like breathing to me.

How could I say to the one I most love: "You can have this half hour, but I'm busy; I have a lot of stuff I need to do today." I wouldn't dream of it. If we treated our spouses like that, our marriages wouldn't survive long!

Jesus is the one who loves us more than anyone, the one who gave His life to save ours and has invested His entire being in loving us completely. Surely this demands our full commitment in return?

But more than all of that, I stay in love with Jesus because the more I get to know Him, the more incredible I realize He is. Just when I think I know Him pretty well, another layer of incredible, unsurpassed beauty and majesty is revealed. His love and grace know no bounds. We've barely scratched the surface. One reason couples stay in love and married for so long is they keep discovering new things about each other, so it never gets boring. This is our Savior. There is always something new to discover and be thrilled by.

This is how we stay in love.

Genuine

Our witness for Christ is only effective if we have genuine love for others. We cannot manufacture authentic love. We can't force ourselves to love others because the Bible says we must and it's the right things to do.

The one thing the world is looking for is authenticity. People recognize something genuine when they see it. People don't want to be "projects"—statistics for the enthusiastic evangelist. They want to be genuinely loved, understood and accepted for who they are. They want to be cherished.

Not one of the kids we take in off the streets is an orphan. The term orphan implies they have been abandoned and have no one to care for them. That's no longer true. The term orphan implies they have no one who loves them. That's no longer the case. The term orphan implies they have no place to call home. They do now.

The only day on which any of our kids is an orphan is the day we find them. After that, they are family. They belong somewhere. They have people around them who love, understand, accept and cherish them. They have a home.

And they have a new identity as a beloved son or daughter of Father God. They also know, without a shadow of a doubt, that they have been adopted by Daddy God. They belong to Papa.

It can take some time for kids to shake off the remnants of their orphan identity and come to understand their new identity and status. But eventually they change and are transformed.

How it happens is love, love, love. Pure, unadulterated, genuine love. The love of Jesus poured out, day by day, hour by hour, minute by minute. The love of God transforms people. We can't manufacture it. We can only get it from the source.

Patience and Love

Patience is a fruit of the Spirit, and I constantly have to ask God to give me more of it! When we were busy building a university where we could continue to train and educate people, every aspect of the building work seemed to take so long. I found it very frustrating.

Then it seemed like not one wall that was built was straight! That ticked me off. Why can't they build the walls straight? I thought.

But all the workers were from another faith, and one day God spoke to me. He made it clear to me that my role in this project was to show His love to those workers. "It matters more how you love and treat them than if the walls are straight," He told me.

It was true.

If, by the way I lived and loved, I didn't demonstrate the passionate love of God to these builders—while they were busy building their crooked wall—then I'd lost them. My witness would be totally ineffective.

Jesus summed up the essence of life: Love God, love others. That's it. It's not about complaining because our walls aren't straight; it's not about whether our schedule is running according to plan; it's not about any superficial matter. It's about our hearts.

It doesn't matter how many people we touch in life; it's about how we touch them. Those who are touched by genuine love and compassion will remember it.

But without love, all our efforts profit us nothing. We won't win passionate lovers to the cause of Christ with empty words. We will win them with a demonstration of the tangible love of God.

The kind of love that opens hearts and transforms lives.

Love Your Neighbor

He answered, "Love the Lord your God with all your heart and with all your soul and with all your strength and with all your mind"; and, "Love your neighbor as yourself." "You have answered correctly," Jesus replied. "Do this and you will live."
Luke 10:27–28

Love God and love your neighbor. It sounds simple. It is simple. We constantly overcomplicate the Gospel.

Love looks like something all the time. Others notice the way we love God. The way we love those around us has an impact. The way our lives are poured out in love attracts others to Jesus. In our day-to-day lives, we must be love carriers. We can touch the lives of others profoundly just by carrying the presence of God around with us and being ourselves.

The law expert who spoke to Jesus wanted to "justify himself," so he asked Jesus, "Who is my neighbor?"

I think he was missing the point. It's like he was saying, "Hey, I do my bit. I love those around me." But it's not about doing our bit. It's about living a life. The man was looking for an equation, a method that would win him eternal life. Jesus says there is no method other than a life wholly surrendered to God and poured out for the good of others. If you grasp the bigger picture, you no longer need to ask, "Who is my neighbor?"

Instead, you realize all human beings are created in God's image and, therefore, deserve dignity and respect. They may be living far, far from God; their lives may be twisted, ugly and broken. But they are still Father's creation, still candidates for His powerful redemption.

Therefore, we love God and we love everyone with His indescribable love. The more we love Father God, the more He empowers us to love others.

Come Closer

• Father God desires Spirit and truth worshipers, those who are fully committed, holding back nothing. He desires those who love Him with all their hearts, who follow Him with reckless devotion.

• Being wholehearted, laid-down lovers of Jesus means forsaking ourselves and our small desires in order to exalt and promote Him. Many fear doing this because they think they will lose their identity and become a mindless robot. On the contrary, in Him we truly find ourselves.

• In laying down your life, you truly find it.

• In surrendering yourself to God, you find your true identity and thrive in it.

• Through the act of giving up your small desires, you receive God-given dreams that far surpass anything you had dreamed of previously, in both scope and meaning.

• Rather than losing your character, the person God always intended you to be emerges.

Remember, we give away that which we cannot keep in order to gain that which we cannot earn.

Love Out There

Most people who come to Christ don't get saved in church. As Christians, we place a lot of emphasis on getting people through the doors of our church buildings, and people who do come will often respond to an altar call at the end of a meeting. But many won't even come through the doors.

Generally, non-believers are not flocking to the Church. They have to meet Jesus "out there" in the world. The way they will meet Him is by encountering His love through someone in their daily lives.

As a movement, we conduct a lot of outreach meetings, but we also spend a lot of time just loving and talking to people, one-on-one. Sometimes I take a poll and ask our pastors and leaders how many of them met Jesus because someone visited their home, because a friend told them about Jesus or because they were sick and someone came and prayed for them. Ninety percent of them raise their hands. Someone reached out to them, individually, to introduce them to the King.

Most people are reached when somebody stops for them, steps forward and loves them.

It's great to have the big outreaches, the huge meetings in stadiums. But my favorite thing is to sit with one person, one-on-one, and see that person's life transformed as I share the love of God.

Recently I was staying in a hotel, and when I left my room, I bumped into the maid who was coming to clean it. I heard her Latin accent and so spoke to her in Portuguese. She was surprised, and immediately we struck up a conversation. We talked for so long I was late for my meeting! By the end, she had asked me to pray for her and her family. I had made a friend, and Jesus' love had touched another individual. She didn't know about the meeting I was going to, so she wouldn't have been there. But instead, Jesus set out to meet her that day—right there in a hotel corridor as she went about her work.

What a privilege we have to share the love of God with those around us in a natural, unforced way and to see Him touch and change lives.

Jesus on the Street

Rolland and I lived in London for twelve years and started a church among the poor and homeless. We would regularly go out onto the streets and encounter those living in rough situations.

One day we met a man who had AIDS. He was an educated man who formerly had a good job, but he had lived a crazy, promiscuous lifestyle and had eventually gotten sick. While he was in the hospital receiving treatment, squatters had come and occupied his apartment. In the U.K. it's illegal to simply throw them out, and they refused to leave. Eventually, he was forced out of his home. Then he also lost his job because of his long absences, due to his sickness.

So he was homeless, sleeping on the street. The people who passed by treated him worse than an animal. It was not uncommon for people walking by at night to stop and urinate on him. He would get beaten up for no reason.

This was the condition in which we found him. We stopped for him. We talked to him, held him and just loved on him. He told us he had been contemplating suicide because he couldn't face living that way any longer.

We saw him often and always stopped to speak to him and share God's love. We told him he could stop by our home any time he needed to get food. He wasn't particularly receptive to us. Then one day he appeared on our doorstep.

He had set out to end his life one day, but as he was about to do so, he kept hearing a voice in his head, saying, "Your Redeemer lives. Your Redeemer lives." He had come by to ask us what this meant, as he thought we might know.

He had just met Jesus on the street. Right there and then we prayed with him, and he received the love of God into his life. Through the simple act of stopping for this man, Jesus was able to reach in and touch his heart. Never underestimate what God can do with our simple acts of obedience.

Power of the Gospel

A teenager came into one of our meetings in Australia. The Holy Spirit was moving, and the presence of God was tangible, and I could see this kid was encountering God in a big way—shouting out, tears streaming down his face, totally lost in Father's presence. It was a dramatic sight.

In situations like these, I can't help but go over and ask the person what's going on with them, so I spoke to him, and he told me his story.

When he was just twelve, his own father had tried to kill him and had stabbed him. He survived, and his father was sent to prison. His mom couldn't cope with him and threw him out of the house. He had nowhere to go, so he ended up on the streets, homeless, broken, hurt and confused.

One day a Christian family passed him on the street and stopped for him. They heard his story and decided to take him into their home and care for him. He was fifteen when I met him, and he was now in love with Jesus.

He introduced me to his new family. "This is my dad," he said, pointing to the father of the family who had taken him in. Then he said something amazing that broke my heart.

"I forgive my real dad," he told me. "I'm going to go to the prison and have a meal with him and tell him I forgive him."

This is the power of the Gospel that meets people where they are, lifts them up and empowers them to do extraordinary things. This was a life beautifully redeemed. Who can measure what impact that boy's transformed life will have in this world? Our Lord is amazing.

Love Wins

Jesus told the following parable:

"A man was going down from Jerusalem to Jericho, when he was attacked by robbers. They stripped him of his clothes, beat him and went away, leaving him half dead. A priest happened to be going down the same road, and when he saw the man, he passed by on the other side. So too, a Levite. . . passed by on the other side. But a Samaritan... when he saw him, he took pity on him." (Luke 10:30–33)

Two things strike me in this story. First, a Levite passed by the desperate man on the road. Levites are worshipers. Here was a man who was worshiping God but could not see one broken, bloody, hurting person lying on the road in need of practical help. What good is our worship if it is blind? What good is our worship if it ignores the needy?

Second, the man who stepped in was a Samaritan. Samaritans were hated by Jews because they had inter-married with non-Jews and didn't observe the Mosaic Law. He was an unlikely helper, since he would have known he was despised.

In the same way, neighbors of yours might not like you, work colleagues might not appreciate the values you stand for, family members might hate that you're a Christian. That doesn't matter. What matters is that you continue to demonstrate radical love to them each day, that they experience the kindness of God through you.

Revival comes when believers carry so much of the love of Jesus and are so confident in their identity as sons and daughters of God that every person they touch with their lives encounters something of Jesus. Revival comes when believers stop to touch the broken and bleeding with the kindness of God—even though they know full well that person despises what they stand for.

In the end, love breaks through. Love wins.

Radical Love

One day I was on the street in Mozambique, chatting with homeless friends and hugging a cheeky little teenager. He was an orphan with nowhere to go, so I invited him to come live with us. If love looks like something, then we can't just say, "Bless you, go and be well fed." Love has to be expressed practically.

We took him home, and he was a real rascal. He would constantly steal things from our house. He would torment and harass our visitors. He would run away. But I continued to love him.

One day I was in a very dangerous bush area among an unreached tribe, ministering with a small group of people. It wasn't going well! The people were really angry, and they began shaking my Land Rover and smashing our sound system speakers. They started picking up rocks to stone us, and a group of men came over to me to beat me up.

While this was happening, this kid heard God speak to him, "Go to Mama Ida right now." He didn't have a truck, but he managed to get a lift from a truck driver and somehow got himself to where I was just as I was being surrounded by the angry men who were ready to beat me or maybe kill me.

This young man, who could never understand he was my son, who showed no sign of responding to love, ran to my rescue. He was hopelessly outnumbered, and this group of men beat him and beat him. All the while he yelled at me, "Mama, get in the truck! Go, go!"

Eventually, the police came, and we were all able to get away. My son was badly beaten. Then he said something that left me completely undone: "I'm so happy I was able to be beaten in your place. I'm so happy I could suffer for Jesus."

Words can't express, even now, how I felt at that moment. This is what happens when God's radical love is poured out, day after day. A miracle of transformation takes place, even if we don't see it at first.

Close

Come close to God, and God will come close to you....
James 4:8, NLT

In Mark 14, as Jesus was going to the cross, Peter followed but kept his distance. He hung around, but he didn't want to be identified with Jesus. Later, Peter would boldly declare the Gospel, identify himself with Jesus and even sacrifice his life for his Lord. But for now, he was fearful. He kept Jesus at arm's length. He didn't really understand what Jesus was doing or why. So he kept his distance.

Sometimes we can distance ourselves from God. Not fully. We don't turn our backs in complete disobedience. But we walk a little bit away from Him. We hang around at a "safe" distance, and we watch Him, wondering what He might do, not fully engaging with Him.

Like Peter, often we don't understand what God is doing or why. This makes us hesitant to trust Him fully—though trust Him we must.

We'd like God to act in ways we can easily understand. He doesn't.

We'd like Him to be predictable. He's not.

We'd like to put Him in a box that we can neatly label. He won't be contained.

Some people are glad to have made God's acquaintance but want to keep it that way—as a polite but distant relationship. This can never work. Because God is not looking for friends; He is looking for laid-down lovers. He doesn't want to socialize with us. He wants to engage in a passionate, intimate, adventure-filled love affair that will see us utterly transformed by His love.

In truth, laying down our lives and surrendering our all to Jesus is the only "safe" thing to do. There is no safety in keeping our distance from Him. Instead, we need to be fully engaged; we need to press in to know Him more deeply.

Though at times He seems wild and unpredictable, risky and dangerous, He is still all-loving, full of compassion for us and completely unwavering in His commitment to our wholeness and freedom. Don't hold back. Press in. Get closer and lose yourself in His love.

Come Closer

• Jesus' parable about the Good Samaritan could equally have been called "The Parable of the Unlikely Helper," since the person who stepped in to help was someone who knew he was despised by the injured man.

• If you stop to look around at the people in your life, you may well find someone who does not think highly of you. Despise is a strong word. Maybe someone simply doesn't like you or doesn't respect you. You can fill in the blanks.

• What if, this coming week, that person was the unlikely recipient of God's grace, with you acting as His conduit? What if you were to bestow a random act of kindness on that person, not worrying about the outcome?

• Even our harshest critics are people who live with a level of brokenness in their lives. Look beyond the hard exterior and see the need. Visit that need with the kindness of God. In the end, love wins.

No Fear

Some time ago, we felt prompted to go to a particular village in the bush. A team of a dozen kids came along, as they always do, as the prayer team. They pray for the sick—the lame, deaf, blind, lepers—and Jesus shows up. These little kids are full of Holy Spirit.

This day a number of international visitors also accompanied us on the trip. When we reached the village, however, the villagers became really upset and angry. They began throwing rocks at us. We always warn overseas visitors that this kind of thing can happen, but they weren't prepared for it. It freaked them out. They jumped into our Land Rover, locked the doors and began praying fervently. As a result, though, they locked me and the kids out!

I had one girl with me whom I had rescued from a garbage dump. She used to be sold regularly in return for a single shot of booze or a piece of bread. Now she is saved, healed, restored, and she knows her Daddy God's identity. She isn't afraid of anything anymore. She is full of Jesus, full of power.

Rather than being intimidated, she stood up and yelled to the villagers: "Bring me the blind; bring me the deaf!" She had no fear. She ducked the flying rocks and kept on yelling. Gradually, sick people began to push forward for prayer. She prayed, and Jesus healed people instantaneously. As people began exclaiming their healing, it grabbed the villagers' attention, and the rock throwing began to subside. The people who were being prayed for began to give their lives to Jesus. God was visiting this village.

So often fear can grip us. It's easy to run away and say, "That looks dangerous! I don't want any part of it!" But the more we allow Jesus to fill us, the more our confidence in Him grows. His love leaves no room for fear. When He prompts us to step out in faith, like this little girl, we know without a doubt that He will bring His powerful presence and change the circumstances. Today, instead of asking God to take away your fears, ask Him to fill you full of His love.

Holy Spirit

Shortly after we visited the village where they wanted to stone us, I was praying, "Lord, we are willing to do whatever You want us to do, and we'll gladly suffer what we have to, but is there any way we could avoid the rocks?"

The Lord answered me and simply said, "Holy Spirit." That was it.

I didn't know what it meant. "Help me, Lord," I said. "I know you're saying something, but I don't understand what to do."

Then He told me to gather everyone together—to call every pastor, child, overseas visitor and take everyone to our worship-prayer center just down the road. We did this, and Father's presence visited us in a powerful way. We ended up spending several hours in worship, overwhelmed by Holy Spirit's power and presence. At the end of this time, God prompted us to go back to the village we'd just come from.

So we did. We piled every single person into Land Rovers and flatbed trucks and drove, en masse, back to that village.

We arrived, still worshiping, and began praying for every person we met. God crashed in. His presence came upon people powerfully. This unreached people, ignorant of Jesus, entrenched in their own synchronistic faith, began falling under the power of God—laughing and weeping.

Three big, tough looking guys shouted to me to come over to them. I went to them and hugged them, as I hug everyone. They said to me, "We want you to build a church right here. We want it fast! We don't want to wait."

I began to understand what Father had been saying to me. There had been no throwing of rocks, only Holy Spirit. When His power and presence comes into a situation, radical transformation occurs. The more we welcome and honor His presence—and the more utterly dependent we make ourselves— the more He is able to do. When we make room for Holy Spirit, miracles happen.

Overshadowed

The Holy Spirit will come on you, and the power of the Most High will overshadow you....
Luke 1:35

These words were originally spoken to Mary, the mother of Jesus, by the angel Gabriel. In a similar way, Father God "overshadows" each one of us and implants something supernatural in our lives. It is the word of God, the promise of God to us as individuals.

The Father has a unique calling for us all, and He speaks promises over us that He wants to see fulfilled as we are shaped into the people He destined us to be. Though Father loves us perfectly, just as we are, His purpose is also to transform and shape us, to form Christ in us.

God overshadows us and implants His promises, but sometimes we refuse to cooperate. We can abort the promises of God for our lives before they reach full term. Why does this happen? Because when God works in our lives:

- It can inconvenience us.
- It can stretch us farther than we want to go.
- It takes time for the promises to grow in us.
- It takes patience and endurance to reach our destiny.
- It's costly!

And yet, if we truly believe God has deposited something in our lives to change and transform us—and then to change and transform the lives of those around us—we need to pay the price and carry the promise.

Your calling will be different from my calling; God has placed in you promises and a destiny that are uniquely yours. He has planned and purposed your life to be remarkable, to achieve amazing things. Don't abort the promise. Carry it. Be who Father purposed you to be.

City-Reaching Love

People often ask how the Church can reach their city. Many books have been dedicated to discussing strategies for doing this. I only believe in one method.

It begins with a holy hunger among God's people to be filled with Him, to be filled with His Spirit to overflowing. To be filled with His loving-kindness. To be filled with Him and yet want more and more and more of Him.

Where God's people are filled to overflowing with His presence, it will spill out everywhere.

Acts of loving-kindness break out all over a city, and people are touched by the love of God. Acts of unwarranted generosity begin to happen everywhere, and people begin to take notice. Radical love is demonstrated practically, and people are amazed and humbled by it. In this way, we begin to reach a city.

As I have said many times, revival has a face and a name.

It is great to bring together the Body of Christ from right across a particular city and meet together to worship God in a big hall or stadium. That is wonderful, but it's often not the solution to reaching a city.

Countless acts of repeated kindness and love can change the atmosphere of a city, and that takes patience, endurance and commitment.

"Therefore, as God's chosen people, holy and dearly loved, clothe yourselves with compassion, kindness, humility, gentleness and patience... Over all these virtues put on love, which binds them all together in perfect unity" (Colossians 3:12–14).

Cities are reached when every single believer is so fully filled with Holy Spirit that He is manifested all over the city, all the time. Cities are reached when we are so full of Jesus' joy that people everywhere are astounded by Him and attracted to Him. Keep on being filled!

"Follow God's example, therefore, as dearly loved children and walk in the way of love, just as Christ loved us and gave himself up for us as a fragrant offering and sacrifice to God." (Ephesians 5:1–2)

Costly

When God overshadows you, He expects you to nurture what He puts inside you. He expects you to carry it to full term, not to abort it. Many of us have been touched by Holy Spirit, but we have forgotten what He said to us in that place of holy visitation. Or what He said to us was too costly for us to carry. Or we lacked the passion to sustain His word to us.

Father God wants to take His Body to a place where we are able to sustain the promises He places within us. He wants us to take His word to us seriously and nurture it, carrying it with us and patiently seeing it come to birth—no matter what it costs us.

No one in the world will ever again have the privilege of carrying the Son of God as a baby like Mary did. But we are all called to carry Christ Jesus inside us. We are called to be possessed by God's Spirit.

This is costly.

But when God takes possession of our lives and turns them into what He intended, it is the most wonderful price we could ever pay.

"And the disciples were filled with joy and with the Holy Spirit." (Acts 13:52)

Individual

God likes individuals. Each of us has been made unique. In conforming to Father's will, we are never asked to be clones. We are called to be the people God has made us to be and to carry His glory in a way that is unique to us.

Collectors of fine art do not want to buy copies. In fact, the idea is ridiculous. If a piece of art is a mass produced copy, it is basically worthless. It's comparable to the art displayed in hotels. Some of those paintings are really pretty, but they are not valuable. You don't find valuable art in a hotel room. Even the most prestigious hotels don't put originals in their rooms.

You, however, are a priceless original—never seen before, never to be seen again. God made you a complete one-off.

God has overshadowed your life. He not only made a unique you, right down to individual irises for your eyes and fingerprints for your fingers, but He then planted inside you a unique calling and destiny. Your calling is uniquely designed for you to fulfill. No one else can do what you do in the way you do it!

Knowing we are uniquely loved and called need not make us arrogant. Those who are confident in the knowledge of who they are don't feel the need to elevate themselves above others; they can stay low. But they also are not afraid to be so possessed by God that He can breathe His life through theirs.

When you say, "God, let there be less of me and more of You," when you allow Him to fill you so His life explodes out of you to others, then you are most fulfilling your calling and destiny. You are uniquely designed, uniquely called by your Father. You are a one-off original called to be a container and carrier of His love.

Come Closer

• God wants to overshadow you with His presence. He wants to implant you with His promises.

• This is costly. It will inconvenience you. It may stretch you farther than you want to go. It will take time to come to fruition, requiring you to learn patience and endurance as you wait on His promises and reach toward your destiny. There's no way around it. Allowing God to bring the fullness of destiny to fruition in you is costly. And sometimes scary.

• You may wish for control and safety, but God is uncontrollable. He is also love. And He is utterly trustworthy.

• The only way you will ever become the person God intended you to be is by allowing Him to change and transform you. God has called you to be remarkable and amazing. Carry His promise. Don't abort it.

You Are

Recently I was very late for a discipleship meeting, because I felt Holy Spirit urging me to spend more time in the villages that morning—sitting in the dirt, talking to people, simply loving them.

I had the privilege of leading about a dozen villagers to Jesus as we sat there, chatting. Then I glanced at my watch and thought, I'm late. I have to go.

As I was walking down the hill, back to our base, I saw an old lady sitting in the dirt outside her hut. I glanced at my watch again, thinking, I am really late! But the Lord spoke to me. "You have to stop for her."

I stopped. Her clothes were nothing but rags, and she was very skinny. I asked her name. I noticed she couldn't look at me; her eyes were milky white, blind. So I held her hand and asked again.

"I have no name," she replied.

I was shocked. How is it possible for a human being on this planet, created in God's image, to have no name? What kind of parents could birth a child and not give her a name? Once I had nursed a little boy who had his face blown off by a landmine—but he still had a name.

I told this lady, "I want to give you a name." And I did. I gave her a name that, translated from Makua, means "You are" or "You exist." As I spoke this over her, she was visibly transformed. Supernatural joy flooded her heart simply because she had been given a name.

Father God calls each of us by name. He sees all His children. He never says to anyone, "You have no purpose!" Our faces are ever before Him. Sometimes we need to stop and hear Daddy calling our names. He wants us to understand that He knows us, loves us, cherishes us. He wants us to understand our identity in Him. You have a name!

Seen

I held the hand of the woman I had just named and talked to her some more. She had never heard of Jesus, so I told her all about Him. I told her how often, as He traveled from place to place, He would stop for people, make time for them and often touch their lives in powerful ways.

"By the way," I said to her, "He can also heal your eyes. Would you like that?"

Tears rolled down her cheeks and she nodded, "Yes."

So I simply held her, hugged her tight, loved her and prayed quietly. As I did, I witnessed Jesus' miraculous power as her milky white eyes turned to deep, dark brown.

It was beautiful. She stopped crying and began chuckling to herself with joy. I began to cry. Over and over again she said, "I can see!" She was thrilled to meet Jesus.

God met powerfully with this woman because I stopped. I had my own agenda to attend to that day, and I was late. But Father God prompted me to make time for her, to stop for this child of His and minister His great love to her.

It was so simple, so uncomplicated. All I needed to do was to really see her and love her with the Father's love.

Every person is valuable to our Father. That's why we always say we will take every child who comes to us or whom we find abandoned. How could we place a limit on who can be reached when God's limitless love reaches out to every single one of His children?

Even if today you feel far away from Jesus, you are seen. As with this lady, He is willing to meet with you, wherever you are and whatever condition you are in. He doesn't need a special occasion or big meeting to reach you. He is willing to kneel down in the dirt, right where you are, in order to show you He has seen you.

Yes, Lord

Then I heard the voice of the Lord saying, "Whom shall I send? And who will go for us?" And I said, "Here am I. Send me!"
Isaiah 6:8

God calls us by name and has a specific purpose for our lives. Sometimes that knowledge overwhelms us.

Did Mary feel qualified to fulfill her purpose—to carry the Son of God? No! Was she overwhelmed by the call of God on her life? I believe she must have been terrified! We don't take lightly the overshadowing of God. We don't take lightly hearing God calling us by name. It should undo us.

Why is it that God chooses frail human beings to carry out His will?

It is because He longs for relationship. He longs for participation with us. Father God wants sons and daughters who will bear His name and delight in doing His bidding, not nameless, faceless slaves or mindless clones.

God never forces Himself on us. He initiates and then asks us to respond. We have to choose to participate with Him. Like Isaiah, God does not force us to volunteer. He didn't command Isaiah to go! He simply asked whether anyone was willing to go. Undone by His holiness and overawed by His majesty, Isaiah could not help but respond, "I'm here! I'll go!"

Our Father wants to ignite passion within us, and He longs for us to respond with joyful obedience to His will for our lives.

If Holy Spirit comes upon us, our only response can be yes!

Fun

IRIS runs a number of medical clinics. One of these used to be run by a doctor who came to work with us. But she really didn't want to practice medicine. Her parents had pushed her into a medical career that she didn't want. In fact, she hated it. But she had given her life to Jesus, and if she had to be a doctor, she wanted to serve the Lord doing it.

One day, though, she had had enough. She came to me and said, "I hate practicing medicine!"

"Okay," I replied. "What do you want to do?" I'll never forget her response.

"I want to be Director of Fun!"

God had spoken to me a long time before and told me to never try to control our team. I wasn't to tell them what they could or couldn't do, push them around, or tell them we needed them to stay if they wanted to go. So I said to her, "Okay!" Then I laid hands on her, prayed and said, "You are now Director of Fun."

She changed her wardrobe and began wearing colorful clothes. She started arranging all the birthday parties for our children. I was worried about who would run the clinic, but God said to me, "Because you have released her, I will send qualified people to you."

Later we realized God was taking this lady on a bigger journey, and releasing her to be Director of Fun was just one step in that process. He wanted to bring her into the fullness of His will for her life. Now she is Director of IRIS Relief—our "first response" team that responds to disaster situations around the world.

She has visited some of the worst hell holes on the planet and taken the presence of God there. She is so full of the Holy Spirit, so in the center of God's will for her life, that she has seen hundreds of men, women and children in disaster zones give their lives to Jesus.

How incredible it is when we say yes to Jesus' will for our lives.

Feeling

I met a lady called Agatha who had leprosy. She had lost many of her fingers and toes and had no feeling in her hands and feet. As her nerves were literally dying, she experienced constant, excruciating pain in her legs and, as a result, hadn't had a good night's sleep in years.

I sat in the dirt with her and prayed. I hugged and held her, cried with her, asked Jesus to pour out His love on her and saturate her with His kindness.

Then we had to move on. The next day we continued ministering in the "bush bush," and I was doing one of my favorite things—making coffee! A lady approached me, smiling. It was Agatha. Not only did she walk up to me, clearly free from pain, but she grabbed me and began dancing with me! She told me she was completely healed.

Then she took another step toward freedom. She was from another faith, but that day she met Jesus—there and then in the bush.

In my elation I did something stupid—that happened to prove her healing was complete. I jumped around with joy and accidentally spilled some of my hot coffee near her feet. She jumped and screamed! Previously, her feet were absolutely numb. Now she was well aware that hot water would hurt them!

Like Agatha, many today are suffering from a spiritual numbness. They have lost feeling, lost their sensitivity to the heat of Holy Spirit. God wants to heal us of our spiritual leprosy. He wants to restore our sensitivity, to restore the feeling in our feet and our hands, so we can begin to use them for His purposes, so we can go in His name and reach out to others.

It's time for God's people to wake up, to step into His glory and dance again.

Arrow

God wants to take you and shoot you like an arrow into His purposes, into the fullness of His pre-prepared adventure for your life. What is stopping that from happening?

We can't do it in our own strength. An arrow can't launch itself. It must yield to the archer, comply with being fitted to his bowstring and aimed in the direction the archer wants to fire it. The arrow doesn't determine the direction; the archer does.

Yieldedness is critical. If you yield to Him, God can fit you into His Holy Spirit bow. Bam! He fires you and says, "Go for it!" If you are yielded, you immediately start soaring.

God needs His people to fly like arrows into every sphere of life—science, medicine, media, arts, business, retail, mission.

Complacency is overrated; we have a purpose!

Resistance is overrated; we have to yield if we want to get anywhere at all!

Once we wake up and yield to Him, everything can change. God can fire you like an arrow into your destiny so you can begin living the life He always destined for you, from before time.

Don't hold back. Don't resist.

Fly. Be who you were born to be!

Come Closer

• I pray some of the stories I've shared this week help remind you of these beautiful truths about who you are and who you're called to be.

• You have a name—and because God has given you a name, you have a purpose. You are also utterly loved and cherished.

• You are seen by God. No matter what you are going through or how you feel, you are not forgotten by Him. You have value, just by being you.

• You are qualified by God to fulfill your purpose because of faith in Christ and for no other reason.

• God wants to release you into a destiny you can be passionate about. Jesus offers a life of unparalleled adventure!

• God wants to increase your spiritual sensitivity, so you are more aware of His presence and ready to be used to touch others.

• God wants to launch you like an arrow into His purposes. Yield to the Archer!

Back to Basics

When I first became a Christian in Southern California, I spent a lot of time hanging out with fellow believers on an Indian reservation. Though these Christians looked like hippies, with long hair and outrageous clothes, they emphasized the fundamental basics of the faith.

They said, "You need to fast." The Church has often forgotten about fasting. They said, "You need to read the Word. You need to walk in holiness and purity."

Often we forget to do the basics. People go out and do stupid stuff—like getting drunk or committing adultery—because of a persistent lack of the basics in their lives. We need to remember the simple, fundamental essentials of walking with Jesus:

- Time in His presence
- Prayer
- Reading the Word
- Fasting
- Imitating Him

Yes, we need to get back to the basics—but not to a bunch of rules. Rules and regulations will kill us. But when our hearts burn with holy fire, we will want to do what is right. We will want to walk full of the Holy Spirit. We will want to live filled with the life and beauty of Jesus. We will want to imitate Him and do what He does. We won't want to compromise, go our own way or insist on our will.

The Church is like Sleeping Beauty. We need to allow Jesus to kiss us back to life so we wake up and become who we are supposed to be. Once revived by Him, we need to live, day by day, by simply repeating the basics.

"Then we will no longer be infants, tossed back and forth by the waves, and blown here and there by every wind of teaching and by the cunning and craftiness of people in their deceitful scheming. Instead, speaking the truth in love, we will grow to become in every respect the mature body of him who is the head, that is, Christ." (Ephesians 4:14–15)

A Name and a Face

Daddy God knows your name, and He loves your face. At times, all of us have felt invisible—hurt, rejected, abandoned, cast to one side, forgotten.

But you are not nameless or faceless.

Even the most irresponsible earthly parents still manage to name their kids and recognize them. How much more does your heavenly Father know, acknowledge and value you?

He knows your name; He recognizes and loves your face; He knows all about you; He delights in you.

Once I picked up a dirty, abandoned kid off the street and put him in my truck. He had no one, and no one wanted him, so I took him home with me. I showered him and cleaned him up. Then I proceeded to love Him with Jesus' love and show him how valuable he is.

At first, of course, he didn't understand. He responded to kindness the only way he knew—by stealing my soap and my CD player and running off to sell them.

I brought him back. He did it again.

This went on for some time until the message finally sank in. I knew his name, I loved his face; Jesus knew his name and loved his face. Neither of us was going to abandon him, ever.

Today he is a faithful member of our ministry team. He shares the love of Jesus with others. He prays and sees Jesus do miracles for people. All this happened because he eventually realized he has a name and a face, and he is secure in Father's love. Realize today that Father knows your name and loves your face. You are His.

Dignity

Earlier I mentioned a little boy—I'll call him Joshua—whom we found on the street. Joshua had stepped on a landmine and, though he lived, suffered horrendous injuries as a result. Half his face was blown off in the blast: His eyes, nose and half his mouth were all gone.

His story was that he was kicked out and abandoned after his injury. He had basically been written off by the world at large. He no longer had any value, meaning or purpose. After all, what use was he now?

But Jesus had not given up on Joshua. The Lord brought him to us, and we took him in. We didn't give up on him, either. Suddenly Joshua had a family.

More than that, he was and is still beautiful in the sight of Father God. The Father had conferred the ultimate value on his life, by allowing His Son to die for him. Joshua was valuable to Father. Precious in His sight. Dearly loved. His life still had meaning and purpose.

Every human being on this planet is created in the image of God and is, therefore, worthy of such dignity.

Even those who don't know it.

Even those who deny it.

Even those who don't behave in a manner worthy of it.

Our Father calls them precious just the same.

You have been called from birth. The Lord God almighty Himself has mentioned your name in heaven. The Bible says He has covered you, hidden you with the shadow of His hand (see Isaiah 51:16). He knows you, and He loves you.

Not in Vain

God wants to display His splendor through you and me. He wants us to be carriers of His glory. He wants to shine through you and me into the areas of life that we touch.

Too often we allow ourselves to be weighed down with the cares of life. People moan that they are working so hard for very little return. They complain that their lives and work have no purpose—that it's all pretty pointless. People worry that they are living their lives in vain.

Yet look what Isaiah had to say: "But I said, 'I have labored in vain; I have spent my strength for nothing at all. Yet what is due me is in the LORD's hand, and my reward is with my God'" (Isaiah 49:4).

What if everyone truly believed this?

What if we believed it doesn't matter what salary we make? What if we believed it's not important, in the greater scheme of things, whether we seem to be working extremely hard for very little or no return? What if we believed this because we knew for sure our reward is with the Lord?

If we truly believe it, we will begin to live life differently.

We will do everything as though working for the Lord, trusting He will reward us as He sees fit.

"Don't just do the minimum that will get you by. Do your best. Work from the heart for your real Master, for God, confident that you'll get paid in full when you come into your inheritance. Keep in mind always that the ultimate Master you're serving is Christ." (Colossians 3:23, MESSAGE)

When we trust, we are content to leave our lives in God's hands. We are no longer afraid of poverty—or prosperity.

Even if you feel as though you don't have much, entrust it all to Him. Trust in Him, and all your efforts will never be in vain.

The Wrong Dream

We all have dreams. Some people are more open about it than others. Some have secret dreams; others shout about theirs from the rooftops. But we all have dreams.

Some people hold onto their dreams and refuse to let go. But sometimes it's the wrong dream. God has dreams for us that are way bigger than ours.

I dreamed of being a successful dancer, but God had other plans for me. When I became a Christian, He made me put my ballet shoes on the altar and sacrifice that dream. He wanted me to give up my dream, because He had planned a much greater adventure for me than being a professional dancer.

Don't get me wrong; it wasn't easy. It hurt terribly at the time, because dance was everything to me. But it was a good thing. I'm glad I yielded my dream to His.

I have since had the privilege of preaching the Gospel in many nations around the world, and I've seen God do incredible things—heal the blind and deaf, raise the dead, cause paralyzed people to get up and run. I've seen God save countless lives.

I'm not sorry I lay down and sacrificed my little dream. Dying was a good thing!

God wants you, like me, to surrender your dreams to His greater dream for you. He wants you to allow your dreams to die, so His dream can live in you. Yes, God wants to kill you! It's the only way He can cause you to truly live.

I had a dream of being a prima ballerina. God had a different dream for me.

Today I invite you to examine your dream and see whether it's too small, too restricted, too self-indulgent. Come before Father prepared to lay it all down and invite Him to fill you with His dream. When you position yourself at the very center of His will, having surrendered all, that's when the real adventure can begin.

Burning

Once, Rolland and I ministered in Bulgaria in the dead of winter. Without doubt it was the coldest either of us had ever been. The temperature was around thirty degrees below zero. We'd come directly from Mozambique, where it was forty degrees, to a freezing Eastern Europe, and we didn't own any proper winter clothes.

Then we heard the theatre we were due to minister in wasn't going to turn on the heating for us. When we arrived, we were confronted by a gloriously beautiful building—that was as cold inside as out. It had no heat at all.

The building filled up with hundreds of Bulgarian believers and many Bulgarian gypsies. The meeting began, and the presence of God came. Then everyone began dancing.

It was an amazing sight to behold. At first we danced just to stay alive, because we were about to freeze to death! But then, as we danced, something happened. We caught on fire with joy. Something holy happened. People began to laugh and shout, filled with divine, inexpressible joy.

I noticed just a few people, about a dozen, not joining in. They sat in their little theatre seats with their teeth chattering, but they were not about to dance.

God took hold of those who danced before Him with joy. He heated us up from within and set us ablaze.

God is calling you to dance before Him as though your life depended on it, to dance and praise Him in order to be filled with holy joy.

God wants to turn up the heat in your life and cause you to burn for Him, with reckless devotion, because that's what you are designed to do!

Let God's Spirit overwhelm you and cause you to burn brightly for Him!

Come Closer

• Remind yourself this coming week that you can keep abiding in Christ simply by observing the basics of the Christian life: time spent in God's presence, prayer, reading the Word and reflecting on its truth, fasting and imitating Jesus.

• These basics are so simple that they can be overlooked, ignored or forgotten. But they are incredibly effective in helping you walk steadily with God and stay connected. You don't need to tick these off a to-do list or follow them slavishly. You are looking for relationship, not rules and regulations. But when simply observed, the fundamentals will keep you on track and prevent you from being distracted or side tracked.

• Have you laid down your dreams in order to embrace God's dream for your life? Is your dream too small or limited for such an amazing God? Allow Him, this week, to fill you with the incredible dreams He has for you.

• When you leave your life in God's hands, you can trust your life is not in vain—even if it feels like it. Your reward is from Him.

Boast

We, however, will not boast beyond proper limits, but will confine our
boasting to the sphere of service God himself has assigned to us. . . .
But, "Let the one who boasts boast in the Lord." For it is not the one
who commends himself who is approved, but the one whom the Lord
commends.
2 Corinthians 10:13, 17–18

When it comes to computers and technical stuff, I'm easily lost and confused.
Recently I forgot my Facebook password and couldn't get online. I asked
Rolland; he didn't know what it was. I asked some others on our team; they
didn't know what it was, either. Eventually I prayed and asked Jesus for help,
and in due course the answer came.

A lot of people use social media to talk about what they're doing. Today I'm
doing this; I'm doing that; I'm here; I'm there. There's nothing wrong with
that, but I don't want to go on Facebook to boast about what I'm doing or
what my friends are doing. When it comes to broadcasting to the online
world, I have only one aim, summarized in 2 Corinthians 13:17—to boast
about the Lord.

I don't ever want to boast about me. But I will boast all day long about Jesus.
I will boast at the top of my voice about Him!

He is good all the time. He is the most beautiful Savior I could ever have
dreamed of or imagined. He is worth every little breath of my life. I love Him
more today, after 37 years of preaching His Gospel, than I ever have before.
I never want to be intimidated or afraid to keep on sharing who He is with
others, because He is altogether beautiful.

Sometimes when people speak about what God is doing in or through their
lives, it somehow gets turned into a conversation about them. Instead, our
aim should be to direct all the glory toward Him. We remember we are but
dust and are powerless to accomplish anything of real value without Jesus.
Therefore, let us boast in our God. Let's keep boasting about Jesus. The more
we direct people toward Him, the more His glory can shine through our
lives. He is beautiful!

Off Day

I travel a lot. On average, I spend at least four nights a month on a plane, flying to speak somewhere. Because I spend so much time speaking and preaching, I like to sit quietly on the plane. I rest and save my voice.

I am seated, and if a person is next to me, I'll say, "Hello! How are you?" and then, "That's wonderful. God bless you." Then it's lights out. I'm done! The sleeping blindfold goes on, the neck pillow comes out and I settle down for the flight.

That's what I prefer to do. However, I'm always willing to talk if God prompts me to. On the last few flights I've taken, people have wanted to talk. Very recently, the girl sitting next to me on a flight knew who I was and began chatting with me. I was tired and wanted to sleep. I could have said, "Leave me alone. I'm tired right now!" The trouble is, if you're known for your love, it doesn't work to be grouchy with people. You can't ever be grumpy or short tempered.

It made me stop and think.

All of us should be on all of the time. Wherever we are, whatever we are doing, people should know we are in love with Jesus. It should be self-evident. We should so radiate the love of Jesus that people can't miss it. In fact, they should be drawn to it. We are never meant to have a day off or an off day! Not off in our spirits, in our attitudes or in anything we do.

How do we stay on all the time? We live moment by moment in His presence. We live, day by day, under the cover of His amazing grace. We can't do it through self-effort or by telling ourselves to do better. That doesn't work. Instead, we have to lay down our lives daily and allow Jesus to shine through them. We remain on as we remain in His presence, as we abide in Him. In that place of rest and peace, all the pressure of needing to perform is taken away, and we can just be ourselves. In Jesus' presence, every day is an on day.

Worth It

I was tired and ready to sleep, but the girl next to me on the plane wanted to talk. "Are you Heidi Baker?"

"Yes, I am."

She launched into her story. It quickly became clear she loved Jesus and followed Him in challenging circumstances. She began telling me her mother's wife's (yes, that's correct) daughter was getting married, and she was supposed to be the bridesmaid.

She fired question after question at me. "What am I supposed to do in that situation? How do I demonstrate my love for my mother, while not compromising my Christian values?" As she continued to talk, compassion from God rose up in me. I began to pray silently and ask Holy Spirit to give me the answer for this girl, because I didn't want to get it wrong, and I wasn't exactly sure how to navigate her particular dilemma.

"You know," I said, "I think the only answer is to pour out love on your mother. Don't demonize her. Don't condemn her for her poor choice of lifestyle. Instead, love her radically."

We both recognized that the way her mother was living was contrary to biblical standards, but she still needed to pour out love on her. In the end, only the love of Jesus could impact that woman's life. She might expect to be judged. She might expect her Christian daughter to disapprove of her lifestyle. She probably wouldn't expect her daughter to demonstrate non-judgmental, unconditional, radical love.

This encounter reminded me of two things. First, when we pour out love on others, their sin doesn't tarnish us. Our love for them doesn't condone their sin, just as God's love for us doesn't condone our sin. He just loves us.

Second, so often we are tempted to judge. Is this person worthy of my love? Of the love of God? The answer has to be yes! None of us are worthy in the sense that we earn or deserve God's love. But every precious soul who lives was created by the Master. And no soul who lives is beyond redemption. Therefore, every living human is worth the effort of pouring out the love of Jesus.

Love Carrier

But God shows his love for us in that while we were still sinners,
Christ died for us.
Romans 5:8, ESV

Should we just love people with God's love, or should we point out the error of their ways? Shouldn't we preach more about hell? After all, it is a real place, and it's necessary for people to understand it, so they have the opportunity to avoid it.

Or instead, should we just carry them into an experience of the love of God?

We could make it our aim to scare people into the Kingdom. I know how to do that. I've had plenty of practice in the past. But here is the thing: I never found it to be fruitful.

Real fruitfulness flows from intimacy. When we are intimate with Jesus, He fills us with His passion and compassion. Then, when we demonstrate His immense kindness and compassion to others, people are naturally drawn into the Kingdom. We don't have to shout at them or condemn them. We just love them, and they naturally begin to desire God.

If we are armed with love, we have a weapon much more powerful than judgment. Jesus' love is powerful, completely disarming, totally compelling.

It will attract rather than repel. It will break down barriers, not create them. It will soften hearts, not harden them. The girl I met on the plane stepped off the plane a different person—ready to carry the love of God into the chaos of her domestic life.

Remember today that you are a love carrier; you are also the channel through whom God can deliver someone's miracle.

Story

People often want to visit us in Mozambique, because they have heard about the miracles God does. They want to see for themselves. If they come, they will see some miracles. That's certain. But why shouldn't they see miracles where they are, especially in the West?

It is no less possible for God to move where you are than for Him to move where I am. All that is required is one person carrying His presence. We should all carry His love every day.

God can heal anyone through anyone who loves Jesus and is prepared to stop and pray. You don't need to be especially gifted. You don't need to be especially called. All you need to be is someone who loves His presence and is willing to be a conduit of His love. I passionately believe all of us are called to carry the glory of God. We are all glory carriers.

Every single believer has a story to tell. A story of how Christ has transformed his or her life. A story about what God has done. Not every person's story will touch everyone's life. But every person's story will touch someone's life. This is why miracles are waiting to happen for you, right now. You have the unique ability to reach certain people with the love of God—people who will be impacted by your specific story. You need to discover how best to tell your story, how to speak about what He has done in you. Then boast in the Lord. Tell anyone and everyone about the miracle Jesus has accomplished in your life.

Be natural. You don't need a soapbox or a crowd. Just be yourself and tell your story. Then leave the fruit of that in Father's hands. You will be amazed at what He can do through you. It's time to boast in the Lord!

Far Reaching

When Paul wrote that we should boast in the Lord—talk continually about what He has done—I don't know if he anticipated the lifestyle we live today, in a world where messages can be broadcast very quickly and reach many people. Words have never been able to reach so far and have such an impact.

Once, in a meeting, God moved me to prophesy over a couple. I remember saying some crazy things. Such as, they were going to reach many unreached people. I said something outrageous like, "You'll touch millions of people." I said what they'd been doing so far was just the tip of the iceberg. I made some pretty far-reaching claims.

Time went by—maybe a year or more. Then one day my assistant told me she'd had an email from the same couple I'd prophesied over. She suggested we should meet with them, so we moved things around in my schedule to make it happen. In due course, we all met in a hotel room. When I arrived, I could see a number of items laid out on a table. In Mozambique we've had solar powered speaking Bibles for a while, which have been an amazing resource, but these people had gone much farther.

From the day I prophesied over them until that day in the hotel, they had been busy developing specific technology designed to reach the masses with the message of Jesus. They had created solar powered projectors to show the Jesus Film that could fit into a backpack, so a person could walk into the bush without the need for a truck or a generator. They also had a number of other cutting-edge devices that could be used to spread the Gospel via the cell phone network.

Most amazing of all was their statement: "We've developed these things for your movement!"

Stunned, I said, "But not just for us! We need to give it away to everyone who can use it for Jesus."

When we are obedient to God and act on His Word, we never know how far-reaching the consequences will be.

Come Closer

• Stop for a minute and take some time out with the Lord. Search your heart. Quiet your soul. Be still.

• Are you facing something right now that is making you angry, hurt and upset? Is a problem in your family, in your friendships or at work driving you crazy? If so, bring it to God right now. Lay it before Him. Tell Him.

• God is teaching me more and more about the need to run right into those frustrating situations around me. Not with loud resentments or bitterness but armed with the radical, sweet-natured, disarming love of Jesus! Do you know what the answer to your problem is? I can assure you, it is not judgment or trying to convince others of the error of their ways. The call of God on our lives on days like these is to get on our knees and ask Him for His beautiful, powerful and overwhelming love for the people involved.

• I have been challenged to give people, even those who don't like me, real blessing and favor. I have been called to share my best stuff with those who don't bless me back. That is what God is like. That is who He is. We are made in His image, and we need to be those who radically follow His character and His ways.

Pray with me:

Lord, only You know what is getting to me right now—the niggles under my skin, the naysayers, the critics, the difficult, the unlovely. Thank You that Your love reaches out to all of them, as it does to me. Transform my heart today so I might be someone who offers outlandish joy and love in unexpected ways to those whom You have called me to serve and love. Amen.

Compassion

One Monday I woke up, as I always do in Mozambique, at 5 A.M. I slapped my face, drank my coffee and made some eggs for the many children who had stayed over the night before. I had not had much sleep, as some of the kids had needed to talk and pray with us until the early hours of the morning.

We start church early, and we had three services that morning, as usual. It was powerful seeing several thousand kids (and chickens and dogs) worshiping Jesus—or just running around. It was loud. It was holy, and it was chaotic.

After those three services, I always go out. Every Monday it's the same. I want to keep in touch with the simple goal—to love those around me with the deep compassion of Christ. If I stopped understanding my neighbors, I would lose what God is asking me to remember. Every talk I gave would be hollow and empty. Every Monday, unless God tells me otherwise, I am in my village. And I take my time. People are suffering. They need me to not be in a hurry.

This one day, I knew I had to visit my friend Tina. She is an old, old Mama. Our team had built her a house a long walk away on the other side of the village, and I was on my way to dedicate it. After a long, tiring walk, I arrived. I am not exaggerating when I tell you how simple this little place is. It is made of bamboo and mud. But when I got there, my friend burst into tears: "I never dreamed I would live in such a palace," she cried.

I stared again at her house, and my eyes filled with tears. I was not looking at a palace. I was looking at a sturdy, well-built shack. But to her, it was a thing of beauty, symbolizing her independence and freedom. And more than that—it reminded her she is loved by a man called Jesus!

It matters how we look at things. It matters how grateful we are. It matters that we are full of compassion for those around us.

Caring for Others

My friend Tina was thrilled with her new home, but she did not have water. She did not have money to pay someone strong enough to bring water to her. As she told me her dilemma, my heart broke for her.

I asked the Lord what we could do to help. I was on the hill, next to the stinking latrine, picking up garbage and throwing it into the pit. As I was doing this, some of the nearby villagers began to notice me. I knew what they were saying, as I can understand some of their dialect.

They spoke among themselves: "Why is this pale woman helping Mama Tina? Why is she throwing rubbish in the pit? What is she doing here?"

So I greeted them in their language and asked them to sit down with me on that hill. They asked me questions about the new house. I shared with them that Mama Tina was so loved by a man called Jesus that He had blessed her with this place to live. They wanted to know more and asked me many questions. Some of them began to have their eyes opened and asked if they too could trust in Jesus. As I led them to the Lord, I asked them to do something for Him.

"Do you see this woman?" I asked them, motioning to Mama Tina.

"Yes," they said.

"Jesus loves her, and He wants you to help take care of her. Can you do two things for her? Can you tidy up this rubbish outside her house and burn it in the pit, and can you bring her clean water every day?"

"Yes! Of course!" they said.

It was that simple. Every six weeks or so I check up on Tina. "Are they bringing you water?" I ask.

"Oh yes!" she smiles. "I have clean water every day. Do you want a drink?"

Jesus said in Matthew 10:42, "And if anyone gives even a cup of cold water to one of these little ones who is my disciple, truly I tell you, that person will certainly not lose their reward." Love like this is so very powerful. We cannot truly love Jesus if we don't show that love to others.

Turn Around

I am not originally from a Christian family, and when I got saved, my parents were not very happy. My crazy new-found faith rather upset them.

I was a full-on devotee with zealot tendencies! I preached hell fire and all that stuff. They put up with it for a while, but when I told them that I wanted to be a missionary, things unraveled. I remember their faces staring back at me.

"What? You want to work with pitiful, poor, uneducated people in some dirty, dusty un-mapped place somewhere?"

I simply nodded. It was like the reddest rag to the angriest bull.

"Why? What is the matter with you?"

I laugh now to think about it. They tried everything they could to set me straight. They even went as far as getting a psychiatrist to try to "de-program" me. They assumed I was in some kind of cult and hoped I would grow out of my "Jesus phase."

I never did.

My Jesus is not a phase! He is not someone I could ever give up on, because He has never given up on me. Instead, He has only increased my reckless devotion to Him as I have experienced His sheer goodness and overwhelming love.

Some twenty years later, I had the privilege of leading some members of my family to the Lord. God rocked their world and turned it upside down. Now I know they are in heaven, clapping us on, cheering and shouting, "It's all true, Heidi. You go girl!"

The truth is, no one is outside the reach of the Lord. Even the toughest Satanist or atheist can melt at just one touch of His transforming power. If you are praying right now for someone who thinks you are on the nut list, don't give up! That person's testimony may one day be, "She never gave up praying for me, and look what God did!"

Turning No to Yes

As kids, my sister and I were close friends. We are less than a year apart in age. But when I turned to Jesus, she became very angry at me. "I hate your guts! I used to idolize you. But not now!"

I shouted back, "If you don't receive Jesus, you will burn in hell." Perhaps that was not the most gracious thing I could have said.

She stared at me for a second, and her eyes widened. "I don't want to burn in hell," she whimpered, suddenly quiet and thoughtful. Right then, she prayed the sinner's prayer. That was all she did for 37 years. She just had fire insurance.

I was totally surprised when she told us she was coming to visit us in Mozambique. At the time, she had hurt her heel and had a cast on her foot. She hobbled on crutches into one of our crazy Holy Ghost meetings and immediately hated everything she heard and saw. I could tell how uncomfortable she was. Sure enough, it wasn't long before she was whispering to me, "You will never get me speaking that mumbo jumbo!"

At the next meeting, something softened in her. "I really feel the force!" she smiled. I knew she was searching for ways to explain what she was experiencing.

At the next meeting, God had a little fun with her. He pretty much slammed her to the floor! She was laughing and flopping around like some kind of demented landed fish, fighting for air. But she was totally at peace. "This is better than being wasted!" she shouted in a way that showed she had no idea how to control the deafening volume of her voice. "I'm loving it!"

My sister, who had said no to God every day for 37 years was suddenly saying yes.

Threats of hell hadn't change her life. An encounter with God did. Rather than trying to twist people's arms by scaring them with hell, let's introduce them to our Father. His love is enough to turn any no to yes.

Rejoicing with Those Who Rejoice

When my sister came to know Jesus, I could have been like the older brother in the story of the prodigal son. When the younger brother returned home:

"The older brother became angry and refused to go in. So his father went out and pleaded with him. But he answered his father, 'Look! All these years I've been slaving for you and never disobeyed your orders. Yet you never gave me even a young goat so I could celebrate with my friends. But when this son of yours who has squandered your property with prostitutes comes home, you kill the fattened calf for him!'" (Luke 15:28–30)

I could have reacted in this way. I had worked all those years for God, and here was my sister, drunk on the Holy Spirit for the first time, telling me what it felt like. (As if I didn't know!)

I didn't feel anything that night. I was not knocked over by the power of God. But I was truly happy. Feelings of resentment had no place in me. I was so thrilled for her and for myself. It was as though she had been restored to me, as well as to Papa.

When she fell on the floor, I was probably the most shocked person there. This was my sister. The one who had declared how much she hated me. The one who had despised Christians and tried hard to avoid God for all those years.

I could have reminded God of how long I had been on His side and demanded better treatment, but instead, I found myself feeling blessed. "Thank You, Jesus!" I shouted. "Thank You for answering my prayers."

We must be careful to rejoice when the long lost sons and daughters come home. If we feel resentment or anger over the Father's blessing toward a newly saved lost one, it is a sign we have not yet become certain of the depths of His love for us. When we are secure in our identity as Daddy God's children, we will rejoice extravagantly with Him when the lost ones come home.

To Such as These

The night God floored my sister He also touched her foot. Suddenly, as she was giggling and writhing on the floor, all she said was, "Heat! Heat! Heat! Heat!" Off came the cast! She clearly did not need it anymore, as she danced around excitedly with no pain and stiffness. It was a beautiful thing to see. That was day one. When day two arrived, I said to my sister, "Honey, it is time to go on outreach." She agreed happily, not knowing what was ahead. We climbed into my Land Rover and began bumping along through the potholes and muddy dirt tracks. I saw her come off the seat a few times and nearly hit her head on the roof. "Where are we going?" she asked, holding on to the vehicle for dear life. It was a perfectly reasonable question. Most people know where they are going when they set out. But I honestly did not.

"We will drive till we get there," I said.

"Where though?" she enquired again.

"Don't worry. It will all become clear," I explained. Eventually we stopped at a village—probably the darkest and most challenging place I have ever encountered. Everyone seemed to be infested with a plague of worms. They had worms in their feet, hands, elbows, arms, legs. Everywhere.

"Where are we going to sleep?" she asked staring at the broken down huts. "Anywhere you like. You're my sister. Pick a place," I replied.

"Err, Heidi... where's the bathroom?"

I smiled a little mischievously, "Again. Anywhere you like. Pick a place."

"What do we do now?" my sister asked.

"Follow the children," I answered. "They will show you the way. I have read the book, and that's what it says." Jesus said, "Let the little children come to me, and do not hinder them, for the kingdom of heaven belongs to such as these" (Luke 18:16). Sure enough, the children led my sister to people who needed her prayers. She saw her first healing that day and it changed her whole life.

After we encounter the goodness and love of the Father, the first thing we need to learn to do is give it away.

Come Closer

"Restore to me the joy of your salvation and grant me a willing spirit, to sustain me." (Psalm 51:12)

• That kind of joy—Psalm 51 joy—is possible now. Aren't you glad you don't have to wait 37 years to see the goodness of God in your life? I know I am. My sister was as far from God as she could get, yet in one moment she was undone by His holy, wonderful power. No one is too hard for Him to change and reach with His incredible, miraculous, healing love.

• As I reflect on the amazing testimony of my sister's transformation, I am reminded of this wonderful truth: "Therefore, if anyone is in Christ, he is a new creation; old things have passed away; behold, all things have become new" (2 Corinthians 5:17, NKJV).

• This is now true for my sister, as it is true for you and me. But sometimes we can take this beauty for granted. Consider afresh today: How long have you been in Christ? What does that look like for you? In what ways has God made you new? What old things have passed away?

Take some time to be reminded of the joy of your salvation, and praise God for all He has done—and undone—in your life. Now pray:

Papa, thank You today for my salvation and for stopping and stooping to pick me up and carry me. I pray today that You would restore to me anything that the enemy has tried to steal kill and destroy and that I would have a fresh joy and awareness of all You have died to save me from and for. Amen.

Knowing Who Is the Savior

God has called us to shine in the darkest places on this planet with His hope and light. Sometimes in my work, I come across villages that cry out to me.

Soon after arriving at one, I saw an old man sitting in the dirt dressed only in shredded rags. He was clearly dying. His whole body was infested with worms. I sat down next to him and began to speak to him. He had not had a drink for a long time. The lethal amount of worms in his system was preventing him from the slightest movement, and even crawling to water was not an option.

Whenever I find myself in a situation like this, with a dying or needy person, I ask the Lord, "What is it You want me to say? Show me what You are doing."

I could just fall apart and do nothing but cry. I could get stressed out and shout. But I have learned I am not the savior. God is the savior. But there is always something God wants me to do. There is a purpose in me being there at that moment. My reason right then was to find water and give him a drink. So I found a bucket, filled it and brought it to him. He drank as though he had never had a drink before.

I started crying. If I can't cry at such desperate need, I am in big trouble. How can a world with liposuction and diet pills also have people who are dying from lack of care and clean water? I am not angry with God or His people. God is calling all of us to stop for the one, to feel what Jesus feels. We don't have all the answers.

Philippians 2:14 says, "Do all you have to do without grumbling or arguing, so that you may be God's children, blameless, sincere and wholesome, living in a warped and diseased world, and shining there like lights in a dark place" (PHILLIPS).

This is what we can do. We cannot be the savior, but we can find His purpose wherever we are. We can do our best as His hands and feet, even though we don't have all the answers.

The Size of God

The day of my sister's first outreach was more than just an eye-opener for her. It was a rude awakening. She had no idea about the injustice, poverty, pain and suffering of some of the most beautiful people on the earth.

As she ran round that village, with the children guiding her to the broken and the dying, she was filled with the horror and magnitude of their suffering.

She later described it as the best and the worst day of her life. And I see why. Understanding the nature and scope of the problem is always overwhelming, but seeing that you can make a difference and obey the call of God is totally exhilarating.

When godly compassion hits us, it does more than make us cry. It makes something rise up within us, and it moves us forward.

I believe we are all called to reach the unreached, whether that is in a wealthy mall somewhere in Florida or along a dusty road in Africa. We can all make sure our actions match our faith.

My sister was arrested that day by the depth and breadth of God's love for His world in a way she had never experienced, and it opened up totally new thoughts and feelings for her. She suddenly knew why she was alive.

She met a crippled lady and told her what God had done for her. She absolutely believed this lady could also receive her healing. And God did not disappoint her. My sister prayed for the lady, who was healed and started jumping around.

"Heidi, this is real! This is real!" she shouted. "Let's do it again!"

And we did. We sent in team after team who exterminated all the worms and treated the people. The leaders of another village (who were from another faith) came to the Lord and gave us a place to build a church.

Light shone in the darkness.

You can be a light in the darkness, too, wherever you are, if you will simply let your actions match your faith.

Wake Up Sleeping Beauty

We all know the fairy tale story. The prince discovers a kingdom asleep and a castle in slumber. He finds the tallest tower, climbs to the top and discovers a beautiful princess. He bends down and kisses her, awakening not just her but everyone in the kingdom, too.

Sometimes I see the Church in the West in this way. The Church is so beautiful. It was God's idea, His invention and His bride. But it is often not awake to the needs of the world and the call of the Bridegroom.

In Matthew 16:18, Jesus said to His disciple Peter: "This is the rock on which I will put together my church, a church so expansive with energy that not even the gates of hell will be able to keep it out" (MESSAGE).

I love the fact that God's Church is "expansive with energy." Nothing, not even all of Satan's assignments or the powers of darkness, can get in the way. Nothing can overpower it, be stronger than it or hold out against it. The Church is invested with the very nature and character of God Himself.

Why? Because He calls it His own. Anything that belongs to God is subject to Him and, therefore, protected by Him. This means you and me, too! We may be small, but we are meant for big things.

I love it when I see western Christians waking up, coming to and realizing more of God's eternal plans. Everything here is temporary, but God's purposes are forever. And we can only see a small portion of what He is doing: "For now we are looking in a mirror that gives only a dim (blurred) reflection [of reality as in a riddle or enigma], but then [when perfection comes] we shall see in reality and face to face. . ." (1 Corinthians 13:12, AMP).

You are meant for big things!

Lost and Found

The Bible contains so many passages about things being lost and found. Wherever I go, I urge people to understand God's heart for the lost. There really is such a thing as being lost, and there is also such a thing as being found. I ask the Holy Spirit to reveal it to people. And He loves to do it.

Some of us need a reality check on this issue, because we have stepped away from the urgency of it. We have chosen instead to busy ourselves with mere trifles and not use our days in eternal and lasting ways.

I know why I am on earth, and I constantly need to remind myself. Many things could distract me from my ultimate life goal and purpose. I have to keep the lens of my focus clear.

My purpose is adoring the one who is worthy and bringing the lost into a place where they know He has found them. They are the pearl He gave everything for. They are just as important to Him as I am. They are the apple of His eye and the object of His affection.

Maybe we need to pray more regularly, "Lord, break my heart with what breaks yours."

The evangelist Sammy Tippet is said to have written, "Too many in the West desire to know the manifest love of God without the manifest holiness of God. We have lost the message of repentance. Now the Church in the West is the sleeping Giant. The Church in the East sends a strong message: The repenters must repent!"

We need God's help to understand our own personal mission in this world and to be able to make a difference for Him. Not out of duty but out of sheer joy. The good news is we have everything we need. All the resources of heaven are ours in Christ Jesus. Heaven contains enough passion, gifting, anointing, worship, purpose and glory for each of us to have all we need and more.

The Widow's Mite

I sometimes wear a little necklace that carries what I call my "widow's mite." I am not a widow, but I like to share and emulate her story:

"Just then he looked up and saw the rich people dropping offerings in the collection plate. Then he saw a poor widow put in two pennies. He said, 'The plain truth is that this widow has given by far the largest offering today. All these others made offerings that they'll never miss; she gave extravagantly what she couldn't afford—she gave her all!'" (Luke 21:1–4, MESSAGE)

Don't you love that story? It is not about the amount we give but the place we give it from.

Did you know God loves it when we give extravagantly—over and above what would be expected? That is why this book is called Reckless Devotion. It is about being over-the-top silly in the amount we love God and give to Him! We need to be marked by a kind of unthinking boldness when it comes to the Lord.

One day I was weeping on the floor and asking God how He could possibly use my tiny life for His amazing plans. I was feeling small and sad. I knew there was a sea of humanity out there in desperate need. Do you know what He said to me? I heard Him speak these beautiful words:

"Heidi, I like your little life. And I accept your offering. I'm going to take it, and I am going to multiply it for My glory."

Only God can make something out of nothing. Only God can multiply a tiny seed and make it grow. He can provide what was not there before, and He can use something small and seemingly insignificant to grow something vast and full of purpose.

Don't be afraid that all you can offer is yourself. He can do "immeasurably more than all [you] ask or imagine" (Ephesians 3:20) with your laid-down life. Throw yourself into the offering today. Not as a tithe, but as a whole sacrifice to the Lord. Give yourself and watch what God does with you.

Godly Teamwork

I love the Church, and I love my Christian brothers and sisters all over the world. I know not all of them feel the same about me, but I don't let that bother me! I am called to love people, not judge them or find differences between us.

The Bible says we are "all one in Christ Jesus" (Galatians 3:28).

I love it when I see people giving up their lives in the service of God, whatever flavor of church or stable of theology they come from.

Recently, I met up with some Wycliffe Bible translators, and it was such an honor. They work year after year, often in terrible conditions without power, sanitation and friendship among some of the most difficult and hostile tribes in the world. But they see that as their joy and calling. I love to hear about people passing on the baton of faith in this wonderful way.

We could not do what we do without the help of such translators, who have enabled our tribe to run with Jesus. I can't fathom what it takes to reach a people group with 26 languages, like those in our area, but these men and women of God make that their life's work.

When we arrived in our area ten years ago, these people had already translated four books of the New Testament. What a blessing that is to someone like me! It is totally necessary for our evangelistic work.

So I choose today to honor and remember such people of faith who have gone before me, and I praise God for their gifting. I pray they and you would never feel discouraged and would continue to "live a life worthy of the calling you have received. Be completely humble and gentle; be patient, bearing with one another in love. Make every effort to keep the unity of the Spirit through the bond of peace" (Ephesians 4:1–3).

We are all called to preserve unity wherever we are, whether in a small, rural church in England; in a mega-church in Texas; or in the bush somewhere. We must speak well of our brothers and sisters and make every effort to show them godly kindness.

Come Closer

• I recently saw a picture of a small child standing on her father's feet and allowing herself to be taken wherever her daddy went. Perhaps you can remember doing this as a child, too. Your hands were firmly held, and your feet were planted on someone solid and sure.

• Yielding ourselves to God in this way brings great blessing and takes away the strain and stress of trying and striving that so many Christians seem to be wrapped up in. When we yield to God, we are surrendering to Him, submitting our will and our desires and allowing Him to have His way.

• But there is a further meaning of that word. In agricultural terms, a yield is about producing something. When we turn our lives over to God, He is in charge of the fruit that is produced. Spectacular things begin to happen when we tell Him He is in charge.

Join me today in speaking out over yourself:

Lord I am Yours. I submit my whole life to You. I offer You the size and shape of my little life. I offer You my failures and my flaws as well as my talents and potential. All of it belongs to You, Father. As I yield myself to You, I thank You that I can trust You with the fruit in my life. Thank You that I can be like a tree planted beside water "which yields its fruit in season and whose leaf does not wither"—whatever I do will prosper because You are in charge. Amen.

Now take some time to read Psalm 1:1–3 (which I have based the above prayer on) and meditate on its wonderful truths.

Giving Your All

One time a preacher visited our tribe. He was not from Africa and did not know what to expect. He had prepared to preach on the story of the lost coin in Luke 15:8–10. As part of his talk, he asked if anyone had a coin he could use as a visual aid. Not one hand went up. He turned around and asked the senior pastors on our team for a coin, but not one of them had a coin.

He was getting flustered and incredulous. I watched his face as it suddenly dawned on him. The poverty in that place overwhelmed him. His eyes filled with tears and he wept, right there and then, for the lack he saw in front of him—a lack he had never experienced before, a lack he had never personally been challenged by.

Certainly our tribe is financially poor. No one has anything of monetary value. But that does not stop us from being rich in other ways or making our offerings to God. Our people might not have cash to put in a bucket, but they have a different kind of gift to give to the Lord. They worship Him in dance. Their whole bodies are given over to Him. They might not have money, but they have no shame in dancing as an offering of praise.

They will walk for three days to go to a meeting and dance for God. They will travel through hot and dusty villages, without food or water, to give the only thing they can offer—themselves.

My people are some of the richest on earth. They are some of the most joyful. They do not consider themselves poor. They rejoice that they have been found. They see themselves as blessed and rich and whole. They are full of passion for God, full of His glory and full of His presence. When I look at them I do not see lack, but plenty.

May we all, regardless of our monetary wealth, give all we have to the Lord. May we worship Him with our whole selves, extravagantly, like my people in Africa.

God's Way Is the Best Way

We have an amazing boy who lives with us called Aselmo. I love him so deeply. He is so full of joy and passion for Jesus. He was born with club feet, so he doesn't walk very well. For some reason we don't understand, Aselmo has been in many meetings where healings take place, but as of yet, God has not healed him.

One day we were on an outreach trip, and Aselmo was along. I became aware in my spirit that some of my kids were being given words from God. "Which one of you has a word of knowledge?" I asked and a whole bunch of them raised their hands, including Aselmo.

"God's going to heal someone who can't walk well," he said, brimming over with excitement.

I couldn't help but hope it was going to be him. "Please, Lord, let it be today. Let it be my boy!" I pleaded in the quiet of my heart. No one moved or came forward.

Aselmo spoke the word again, "Jesus is going to heal someone who can't walk."

Out of the shadows came a woman. She was bent over from years of carrying a heavy burden. What looked like a sack on her back was actually a three-year-old little girl who couldn't walk. Aselmo looked at me with his cheeky grin. When the mama put her on the dirt, the girl fell over like a rag. She had no working muscles that could hold her up. She appeared to be lifeless, but she was breathing.

Aselmo put his young hands on this child, and the power of God hit that little girl's body like an electric shock. She moved and strengthened in front of us. Her frame started to take shape almost like a puppet, drawn out of lifeless sleep. She sat up! Her mother started weeping, and Aselmo grinned. This little one was healed. Hallelujah!

God does not do things our way. His understanding and His ways are not ours. I trust Him with my little guy, as I do with everything. You can trust Him with your unknowns, too. He knows so much that we don't know.

Perfect Plans

Many times I have asked God why our beautiful child, Aselmo, has to continue to hobble around on club feet when others are miraculously restored. I have prayed for him and laid hands on him. He is still the cheeky, lovable boy he has always been, and he does not let his condition get him down. But nothing has changed. It is one of the mysteries of the Lord.

Whenever a doctor or a medical person comes to visit us, I always ask if anyone can fix my little guy's feet. Now, due to so many people's love and generosity, Aselmo is finally going to Malawi for surgery. I can't tell you what this means to him or to us. We are all so excited!

Rather than heal him outright, God has perfected a hugely complicated plan in which hundreds of people are involved in the blessing of Aselmo's healing and transformation. When I think of the surgeons, the many people who have given money, those who have prayed, those who will fly him to Malawi, those who will care for him in the six month period of his recuperation, it astounds me that God would go to all this trouble just for us. But He loves us with an everlasting love!

His ways are not our ways. His knowledge is not skewed. His motives are not mixed. His insight is not blurred. His discernment is not warped. He can see round corners, down potholes, into the heights of the galaxies and the depths of the seas.

Instead working in the ways we sometimes hope for and expect—as we did for Aselmo—God works according to His own plan. Perhaps God is showing Aselmo how valued and loved he is by weaving an intricate story through so many other people's lives. I look forward to seeing all God does.

Sometimes it is hard to understand why things do or do not happen in this life, but in those moments, in the midst of those mysteries, we can rest in God's goodness and love for us. What we can know for sure is this: His ways are the best.

Living in Community

Let me share with you one of the reasons for our ministry's success. We love community. We love team. It is one of our greatest pleasures and joys that we are not doing everything solo.

Over the years, we have learned how key it is to share our lives with a group of people we can call our own. "Stopping for the one" doesn't just apply in a ministry situation, but also in spending time with those who uplift us and love us.

I cannot tell you how vulnerable you are to the enemy's attacks if you try to do everything all on your own. He will prowl around you like a roaring lion and pick at you bit by bit, unless you are snuggled up with other believers, safe in the fold.

We have to make time in these busy days to be accountable to those who support us. We have to share deeply with those in our community. We have to come into God's presence together and spend time praying and worshiping Him.

It's not enough to be part of a great church or go to a fabulous conference every once in a while. We have to do life with others in order to be more like Jesus. He chose a small number of people to be intimately connected to. He shared with them on a deeper level. He explained His Word to them. He loved them in a transforming way. They were His team.

The reason we can feed all the children God sends us is because He has given us the most incredible team. We could not do what we do without mechanics, cooks, teachers, pilots, engineers, medics and builders. Hundreds of people make our team work. And each of them functions within a small group that they pray with and care for, where they can be intimate and vulnerable. Not one person is less important, and not one calling is less valuable.

We all need this type of community. If we want to effectively do something for God, we need to also know how to do life with other believers who will love us and keep us strong.

When He Doesn't Make Sense

The Christian life is never boring. It is an adventure. You never know what the Lord is going to ask of you.

Some years ago, I was on my face in the dirt, worshiping the Lord, surrounded by some of my kids. They were praying for me. When my kids pray, they are not quiet or respectful. They poke me and pull at me. They shout and dance. It is noisy and chaotic. My face was planted in the dirt, and as the fervor of the prayers increased, my face was getting pressed down deeper into the hard muddy floor. I wanted to tell my kids to stop praying. They were hurting me.

But what God was saying to me at that very moment was even more painful. As the children were shouting, "Lord, speak to Mama Ida," I heard His voice loud and clear. I started seeing nations in my mind, and I heard God say, "I am sending you back to the multitudes."

I did not receive that word with joy and hope but with fear and sadness. I didn't want to leave the children. I did not want to go elsewhere. These were my little ones. This was my flock now.

I was battling in my heart. God must have gotten it wrong. Maybe I heard Him wrong. But the very next time I turned on my computer, I found emails containing over thirty invitations to speak in various countries. This had never happened before.

Unbelieving, I questioned God again: "Why would you take me from the poor? Even for a day of my life? I don't know why or how."

But He was right.

God had big plans that, at that moment, I could not see. He knew I needed to spend time in the developed world for the sake of the developing world, and vice versa. But it took me a while to agree with Him!

God's plans don't always make sense, but they are always best. When He speaks, you can trust Him, even if you don't understand the purpose of His plan for you, either.

The Power of Agreeing with God

Sometimes I have been an unwilling participant in God's plans for me. But over the past ten years or so, God has changed my heart on one of my most significant battles.

After God told me He was "sending me to the nations" and I argued with Him, He made it clear I needed to speak at a number of conferences.

I used to hate these things with a passion. I would arrive, fuming. I would sit, fuming. I would stand on the stage, fuming. I was angry that I was even there. I wished I was at home. It was like I was saying, "Lord, please use me today. Take my life as a living sacrifice. And please note the size of my sacrifice! Amen."

I had no idea some people paid for the conferences they went to! I did not realize people in the West charge for a seat at these things. Here I was moaning my head off about being there, in front of people who had paid for the privilege of hearing me whine!

But that realization made things worse. I was desperately asking, "But how do the poor get in? How do they get teaching?" Then I would complain to the organizers, get them to go out into the street and bring in anyone who could not afford it. I would slap down my credit card at the front desk and tell them I would pay for anyone in need. I still feel that way.

After a few years, the Lord spoke to me about my attitude. "I have asked you to go, Heidi," He said gently, "and I want you to be joyful about that."

I chose to obey Him, and now I am so joyful about going to speak to people about Him, whether they are in Texas or Bratislava or Malawi.

It is important for you to carry joy, too, whether you are a musician, a dancer, an advertiser, an electrician or a nurse. That is your destiny.

God didn't want me to be a miserable missionary. He wanted me to share the good news of His love. I needed to get on board!

Come Closer

• Let's take some to sit with Papa God for a minute. I don't know what your life has held today, whether it has been a rushed or a quiet, thoughtful kind of day. However you are feeling, just reach out to Him now and offer Him your thoughts and the attitude of your heart.

• Ask Him to speak to you right now. Ask Him to tell you something He has planned for you. Speak out loud: Holy Spirit, come and inhabit this space where I am right now.

• What is God drawing your attention to? What is His challenge to you?

• We have talked about being ready and willing to trust God in recent days. We have looked at stories where God showed His infinite power and wisdom. I have shared parts of my life where I was not willing to let Him be in charge. Perhaps there is an area of your life that God does not have full access to. Is there a room within the house of your heart that says DO NOT ENTER?

• Tell God today that He can go into that room, that He can take the sign away. You might like to write a prayer down to remind yourself that God has an "Access All Areas" pass to your soul.

Little People, Big God

Whatever your experience—however many years you have been a Christian or studied the Bible or understood deep things in God—you are still small. Once we understand and accept that, God can really start to do what He needs to do and be what He needs to be.

Did you know when Jesus sees your life, He already has in mind what He is going to do with it? That's what it says in John 6:5–6: "When Jesus looked up and saw a great crowd coming toward him, he said to Philip, 'Where shall we buy bread for these people to eat?' He asked this only to test him, for he already had in mind what he was going to do."

Jesus sees a multitude before Him. He knows what is going to happen, but He wants to involve His disciples. He asks Philip what he is thinking. The "where shall we buy bread?" question is a test. It is to see if Philip can remember who Jesus is and what Jesus can do—if he can remember where all provision actually comes from. It is to remind Philip of how small he is and how big God is.

We are all little people, and we have a great, masterful God. It is incredible that God likes us and wants to use us. But it is true!

Our lives are precious to Him. If we remember how small we truly are, God can use us for His glory in the world, and the miracles can happen not just to us but through us.

Carry On

We all carry something. Did you know that? Some of us carry pain. Some of us carry joy. Some of us carry life. But we all carry something.

Can I ask you today what you are carrying with you? If I were to unpack your spiritual backpack, what would I find? What would I see?

I have already said I used to be a pretty miserable missionary. I would fuss at God and complain to Him about all sorts of things. I carried a lot of grievances, I guess.

But over the years God has taught me so graciously through the love of His Holy Spirit how to be a joy carrier, a presence carrier and a fire carrier. And do you know what is beautiful about those aspects of God's character? They are unending. They flow and are never diminished or hidden.

Romans 15:13 says: "May the God of hope fill you with all joy and peace as you trust in him, so that you may overflow with hope by the power of the Holy Spirit."

I want to be like that, to overflow in that way. Don't you?

I laugh now when God sends me all over the world. I used to cry. I enjoy seeing people in many nations. I love responding to their needs and questions and fears. It is part of my mandate. It is not a bolt-on extra to my life any more. God showed me that.

But I have to do it with joy, not with loathing or apathy or tiredness or a lack of peace. I would be nothing more than a "sounding gong" doing it without love.

Have a good check today about what you are carrying. Ask God if you have the right things in your luggage, and ask Him to reveal to you what you bring to those around you.

God Likes You

Some of us have a very warped understanding of God. It sometimes stems from our earthly fathers or from a past authority figure. If we are honest, we really don't believe God actually likes us.

We know He loves us, because the Bible tells us so, but maybe we think, God has to love me. That's His job. Perhaps deep down we are a little confused about the way God feels about us.

I realized a long time ago that God doesn't just love His children. He likes us, too.

Think about it. He chooses to use us and partner with us. He doesn't need us to accomplish anything on earth. He could just command a few thousand angels to scurry around and get all His jobs done. They would do it perfectly, with no poor understanding of what He had asked, no mixed motives, no struggle, no self-image problems. It would be a breeze! Surely that would be easier for God, right?

But He is not interested in things being easy for Him. He wants us to grow in Him, be loved by Him and understand the fundamental truth that He likes hanging out with us.

Perhaps you are someone who can believe He likes your best friend Clare. Clare is pretty. She is holy. She has nice jeans. She volunteers for the homeless shelter. What's not to like? But maybe, for some skewed and messed up reason, you have a problem really believing God likes you, too.

Let me tell you something true. God desires you. He loves you. He has amazing plans for you. And He likes you! He likes me, too.

His liking of you is not based on how clever you are, how well you can serve Him or what you look like. It's not about who you know and can influence for Him. It's not about your gifting or your preferences. He likes you because He made you. Like an artist finishes His work and signs it proudly with His name, God has written His name of love across your life.

Do It Now!

Everyone who knows me understands very quickly that I live my life in a strange paradigm. I am always in a hurry to reach the lost, but when I find them, I pray with them like I have all the time in the world. It is one of the things that makes me, me!

Do you realize you won't need any faith in heaven? You won't need to trust in God in heaven because He will be right in front of you. You only need faith and trust on earth. You will be able to demonstrate what you think and believe in heaven, but you won't need to use it in the same way.

We will worship God in heaven in much more of an incredible way than we have been witness to on earth. But one thing we cannot do in heaven is share our faith with a non-believer. We won't be able to reach anyone who is lost from heaven because only the found will get there!

When you breathe your last breath, that is it. You will no longer be able to pray with or talk to a lost person. How does that make you feel?

I am so sure my life is all about taking as many people to heaven with me as possible that I ask God to help me keep breathing.

In 2 Timothy 4:2, Paul tells us, "Preach the word! Be ready in season and out of season..." I find this funny. There are only two times to share the Gospel with people—when they want to hear it and when they don't!

Do you know what will matter in a few million years? Not whether you made Board of Directors or whether you bought that lovely new car or whether your kids got into that prestigious university or whether your wife wrote a book. All of that matters to God, of course. But what will matter to you in eternity is how many people you brought with you. Maybe you need to make a change in your attitude or your heart today and reorder some priorities in your life.

Bean Counters

I love what I call bean counters—the financiers, the money checkers, the treasurers. They don't always get good press, but actually we could not do what we do without them.

Our team was recently asked to come up with a budget. I had to chuckle. When I read the Bible, I sometimes question, "What happens to the budget when the Spirit of God shows up?" I am sure Philip asked this same question in John 6:5–9:

When Jesus looked up and saw a great crowd coming toward him, he said to Philip, "Where shall we buy bread for these people to eat?" He asked this only to test him, for he already had in mind what he was going to do. Philip answered him, "It would take more than half a year's wages to buy enough bread for each one to have a bite!" Another of his disciples, Andrew, Simon Peter's brother, spoke up, "Here is a boy with five small barley loaves and two small fish, but how far will they go among so many?"

Jesus saw the many people in front of Him. He knew what God was asking of Him. He knew what to do. He already had it in mind. Philip, however, was looking at the masses from a different perspective. He was a bean counter. He knew how much things cost and what their value was. He was a financier. He was a businessman. His perspective was hampered by what he knew. Jesus' perspective was heightened by who He knew!

Let's not be so caught up with what is possible, but instead with what is God's purpose. We work for someone who is life manifest on earth. There are no limits to what we can achieve through His incredible power.

Different Lenses

One time a sweet evangelical young man around the age of eighteen came to serve on our team for a short time. He did not know what he had come to or what to expect. We had him serving in the kitchen. Now this young man was a bean counter. He knew how much food we had and how much we needed. He had worked it all out.

One night, trouble arrived. Some major alcoholics came to the meeting. They were so drunk and angry that they started to beat up some of the senior pastors.

Sometimes we need to see things from God's higher perspective. It can be hard to do when things happening in the natural look wrong, but that does not mean God is not at work. Far from it!

I knew we first had to serve food to those alcoholics and the girls in "short clothes" who had arrived with them.

Then this young man came marching out of the kitchen to me. "Mama Ida! What are you thinking? There are 864 pieces of chicken, and there are 1459 people. What are you thinking? There is going to be a riot!" (I don't remember the exact numbers, so this is a hazy guess-timate; the point was, we were far short.)

He was not very happy. It looked like we were not in control of the situation. In fact, we weren't! God was. I replied to him, "Sweetie, listen. When we don't have enough, Jesus makes some more."

He looked at me with this look that said, You are a crazy woman! And he stormed back into the kitchen. We fed the ones who were abusing us first. And there was more than enough for the rest of the people.

Afterward, this precious young man came back to me, weeping. It had been documented. He had counted. He knew there had been a miracle. I thought it was good of God to send me a bean counter that day.

Come Closer

• As your draw near to the Lord today, be aware of what He is saying to you. James 4:8 says, "Draw near to God and he will draw near to you. Cleanse your hands, you sinners, and make your hearts pure, you double-minded" (NET).

• In what ways has God felt near to you this week? How have you noticed Him at work in your life? What areas is He challenging you about?

• We have looked this week at how God takes the small and seemingly insignificant offerings in our lives and multiplies them for His glory. Like the little boy who offered his packed lunch to Jesus and the disciples, we all possess things that have great potential to achieve when placed in the hands of our living God.

• Perhaps you have discounted the gifts you have—the things you can do— from God's plan for you, because you have wondered how He could possibly use them for His purposes. Take some time to consider what you need to bring to Him afresh—the small things and the big.

Join me in praying now:

Father God, I thank You that You can turn even the smallest gift made to You into something so precious and eternally significant. Father, please help me to work out how to allow You to have everything I am and everything I can bring. Help me name out loud now the things I have assumed You would not use. Give me the higher view; show me what You can see. I thank You that You can use all I am for Your name's sake. Amen.

It's Going to Cost You

I believe in the destinies of young men and women with fire in their eyes who come to me begging to be "sent out." But I always tell them there will be a cost.

I have had people say to me, "Heidi, send me into the Congo. God has anointed and called me to rescue child soldiers." Whatever their nationality, whether they are Brazilian, Italian, Russian or French, if they come to me asking, I think seriously about sending!

Many times we have sent young missionaries out with passion in their hearts and a bit of money in their pockets, carrying nothing else but the prayers of the saints. They come back alive and well, shining with the glory of God and telling us about the many exploits they achieved in His name. It is a truly beautiful thing.

Do you know who my heroes of the faith are? It is these young, spirited people who know the cost but go anyway! They are my heroes, because they are fearless lovers of God. They are reckless in their devotion, totally abandoned to the cause and utterly sold out for souls. They are my kind of people!

Others may wonder if they are ready enough, wise enough, prepared enough or fit enough for such a journey. But my question is, "Are any of us?" We can always make the excuses of some whom we've read about in the gospels.

"[Jesus] said to another man, 'Follow me.' But he replied, 'Lord, first let me go and bury my father.' Jesus said to him, 'Let the dead bury their own dead, but you go and proclaim the kingdom of God.' Still another said, 'I will follow you, Lord; but first let me go back and say goodbye to my family.' Jesus replied, 'No one who puts a hand to the plow and looks back is fit for service in the kingdom of God.'" (Luke 9:59–62)

We live by these verses. I don't want to be someone who—when Jesus says, "Follow Me"—answers back, "Let me first..." I want to follow, and I want to be ready and willing to count the cost.

What about you?

I Don't Have Your Calling

Some people are foolish enough to come to me and say, "You know, Heidi, God hasn't called me to do what you do. I don't have your calling."

I smile. Then I explain why Scripture tells me they are wrong. I agree that not everyone is called to an overseas mission. Some of us are called to an over-the-road mission or an across-the-playground mission or another kind. But we are all called to a mission.

The great co-mission in Matthew 28:19–20 records Jesus saying, "Therefore go and make disciples of all nations, baptizing them in the name of the Father and of the Son and of the Holy Spirit, and teaching them to obey everything I have commanded you..."

The fact is, we are all called to share our bread with the hungry. If we know Jesus, we are well-fed spiritually. How can we look into the faces of the spiritually hungry and do nothing? Jesus is true food and drink.

John 6:35 says, "Then Jesus declared, 'I am the bread of life. Whoever comes to me will never go hungry, and whoever believes in me will never be thirsty.'"

Isn't that an amazing truth?

Everyone who is a Christian has fresh bread for the hungry. It may look to you as though what you have to offer is only a small loaf, but it is enough to give away. It is enough for God to multiply.

This means we can go to Mecca or to the Mount of Olives, to Somalia or the Sudan, in the confident knowledge that we have something people need!

Position Yourself

Over many years, I have learned I need to position myself well in order for God to use me. This means I cannot waste my time worrying about how important I am, what people think of me or what my ambitions are.

Fortunately for us, we don't have to guess what Jesus requires of us in this area. The disciples were, at times, learning what He expected of them, too. We see this in Matthew 18:1–5:

"At that time the disciples came to Jesus and asked, 'Who, then, is the greatest in the kingdom of heaven?' He called a little child to him, and placed the child among them. And he said: 'Truly I tell you, unless you change and become like little children, you will never enter the kingdom of heaven. Therefore, whoever takes the lowly position of this child is the greatest in the kingdom of heaven. And whoever welcomes one such child in my name welcomes me.'"

Jesus is very clear here about how He expects us to behave and what He wants us to be like. He is not asking us to try more, to work harder or to court or catch more attention from others. He is asking us to become smaller.

I want to give up my life for the sake of the gospel. I want to position myself so God can use me. Mark 8:34–35 gives us more of a clue about how Jesus feels:

Then he called the crowd to him along with his disciples and said: "Whoever wants to be my disciple must deny themselves and take up their cross and follow me. For whoever wants to save their life will lose it, but whoever loses their life for me and for the gospel will save it."

If we wish to be great in the Kingdom, we need to become small, deny ourselves and sacrifice ourselves. The equation is: He will increase when we decrease.

The Last Day

We all need to get things into perspective. We can sometimes forget our passion for the Lord and why we are alive at all. Those of us in the rich West can easily get bogged down by "...the worries of this life and the deceitfulness of wealth..." (Matthew 13:22).

We forget which day matters. We think yesterday matters—or even today. We can even waste time planning for our tomorrows. But we forget about the last day. Listen to what Jesus said on the subject John 6:37–40:

"All those the Father gives me will come to me, and whoever comes to me I will never drive away. For I have come down from heaven not to do my will but to do the will of him who sent me. And this is the will of him who sent me, that I shall lose none of all those he has given me, but raise them up at the last day. For my Father's will is that everyone who looks to the Son and believes in him shall have eternal life, and I will raise them up at the last day."

If we get our perspective right and remember how important that last day is, we will get what we need to do today right, too.

So many of us would be happier if we simplified our lives and cut out things that have nothing to do with our mission for God, if we stopped worrying about tomorrow or living in the past, if we focused on the future and had our minds on eternity.

Jesus is very clear that we have a destiny. We will be "raised up" with Him on the last day. Won't that be an incredible thing? But look at what it says earlier in the passage: "This is the will of him who sent me [God the Father], that I shall lose none."

God's heart and passion is that none will perish but all will come and bend their knee. What are you doing about that desire? What are you living for? What passions are you displaying right now? The Bible is clear: "Where your treasure is, there your heart will be also" (Matthew 6:21).

Becoming Less

This has been a season for me of learning about emptying myself, making myself smaller and reducing who I am for the sake of Christ. It is a hard lesson to learn, but there is actually so much joy in it!

Paul said, in Philippians 2:3–4, "Do nothing out of selfish ambition or vain conceit. Rather, in humility value others above yourselves, not looking to your own interests..."

That is such a challenge for us, isn't it? Can you honestly say you do nothing out of selfish ambition, that you never try to raise yourself up or make others think well of you? Can you say you do nothing from a motive of self-promotion?

God wants us to live so deeply inside the heart of Jesus that we can hear His heartbeat. He wants to help us make sure no man, woman, child, charity, movement, ministry or church can turn us away from the simple rhythm of that call.

God does not want us to be a people of complaint or comparison. He does not want us to be busy looking at one another and fussing because we don't appear to have the same anointing or favor or gifting as someone else. Do you know why we won't have what someone else has? It is because God has something different for each of us. But our destiny starts with becoming less, not becoming more.

It is a paradox that when we give everything and empty ourselves we will be fuller than we have ever been. But it is also radically true.

Laid Down

The Christian life is not about standing up and being important and well known for God. It is about laying yourself down and being unknown for Him! It is the exact opposite. This is the deal. I have to decide to think this way.

You may ask, "How do we consider others better than ourselves? What is the secret to that?" My reply is: He showed us how. He was the servant of all.

I often find myself praying kenosis prayers. This kind of self-emptying of one's own will and becoming entirely receptive to God's divine will is something I am just beginning. It is so radical, so exciting and such an adventure to do this with God.

As imitators of Christ we are meant to copy His every move. So I have tried a little self-emptying. I have attempted to lower myself for His name. I am already seeing that when I am empty, He can truly fill me. The emptier we are, the more room there is for Jesus and the less complicated life becomes.

There is an old adage about the word joy. It is said that true joy is spelled:

Jesus first.
Others next.
Yourself last.

Never have I found that to be truer than in this season of kenosis.

Come Closer

• God doesn't want a people of false humility. He wants us to be those who know who we are in Him. We are sons and daughters, heirs to His throne. We are also His servants.

• If Jesus knew He needed to make Himself nothing and serve us, how much more do we need to do that? There is no room for ego in ministry!

• In what ways have you been impacted by the past week's teaching on being lower and emptying yourself? Can you think of some areas in your life where you need to make yourself even lower than you have already?

Pray with me:

Father God, forgive me. Far too often I am influenced by what other people may or may not think of me. Forgive me that deep down I pretend to be so many things I am not. Please prevent me from constantly trying to attract attention to myself and not to You. Help me to not fall into a pit of gloating over human praise or being downtrodden by criticism. Please help me not to waste time dreaming about imaginary situations in which the most godly, clever, able or charming person is myself. Lord, in some ways I am scared to ask you to humble me! But I know I want and need to be humbled. So here goes! Please humble me, Jesus. Empty me out so You can truly take all of me and have Your place in my heart. Amen.

Emotional Wreck

I used to apologize for crying when I was preaching or speaking, and I would try to pull myself together. I used to worry people would feel embarrassed at my show of emotion. But now I just cry and let the tears flow down my face. I have preached whole sermons in floods of tears, and I have learned it is okay! In fact, sometimes it is necessary, right and good.

If the almighty, powerful God chooses to pour Himself out and impact my spirit so much that I can't stop crying, how am I supposed to respond? Am I supposed to pretend He is not at work in me in that moment? Or am I meant to go with it and trust Him to speak through that emotion?

I will answer that question for you. I want to know God, and I want to please God. That is my motivation for my life. That is my heart's desire. Psalm 126:5–6 says, "Those who sow with tears will reap with songs of joy. Those who go out weeping, carrying seed to sow, will return with songs of joy, carrying sheaves with them."

I am learning we are allowed to get upset about what upsets God. We don't have to be people pleasers. We don't have to worry about what people think of us. Only what God says matters. It is powerful to "sow in tears" and reap with joy. A beautiful harvest is gathered when we cry the tears of the Lord. If His heart is broken about something and He lives in me, then of course I am connected to that sadness, too.

But we do not cry forever. We will return with songs of joy. "...Weeping may stay for the night, but rejoicing comes in the morning" (Psalm 30:5).

Do not feel ashamed when you feel what God feels, when you weep with His tears. Let it out, even when others are watching, knowing you are sowing with your Father into a beautiful harvest.

"Souled" Out

Sometimes when I am invited to speak at a conference, I catch a glimpse of the brochure. The things people say about me frighten me, because I am just a normal person. They "big me up" to bless me and also—it has to be said—to get the crowds in.

I know I am a carrier of His presence, and signs and wonders happen when I pray. But that is not because of me or any gifting or title I possess. It is because our loving heavenly Father chooses to use those who are sold out for Him. I am not special or any different from you. You too can see blind people healed and dead people raised. Jesus told you that could happen. "Whoever believes in me will do the works I have been doing, and they will do even greater things than these, because I am going to the Father" (John 14:12).

William Bordam, a young Christian missionary in the early 1900s, refused to join his family's wealthy dairy company, instead risking disapproval and loss by travelling to Egypt to continue his ministry and training. Not long after his arrival, he contracted cerebral meningitis and died at the age of 25. After his death, his Bible was given to his parents.

In it were the words, No Reserve. At a later point, he had written, No Retreat, and shortly before he died, he had added, No Regrets. I honor people who have no reserves, no retreats and no regrets in their service of Christ.

Bordam's ambition was not to lean on his family for influence and support but to make himself nothing and lean on Christ. His short life was full, not empty. His legacy was of a life lived well.

I have no ambition but to see the Bride of Christ come home and fill my Father's house. I have no reserves, nowhere to go but to Him. I have no retreats, nowhere to hide except in God. And I can honestly say I have no regrets about what I have chosen to do with my life.

Are you ready to be sent out by God in this way, with reckless devotion, to do all you can to fulfill your calling?

Christlike

Who are you when no one is looking? If you say you are a Christian, are you truly Christlike? Do those you meet and talk with say they recognize something of the divine in you?

It is challenging to think about, isn't it? Many of us wear masks in front of others, whom we are trying to impress, but when those masks come off, we are totally different people.

Paul says in Philippians 2:1–2:

"Therefore if you have any encouragement from being united with Christ, if any comfort from his love, if any common sharing in the Spirit, if any tenderness and compassion, then make my joy complete by being like-minded, having the same love, being one in spirit and of one mind."

So let me ask you. Are you tender? Are you compassionate? Are you like-minded with others Christians, or do you constantly fight with fellow believers about little things?

What are you like when you check out of a hotel or when you buy gas? What are you like with those you think of as "lesser" in your life? Many of us would be shocked to think of ourselves as duplicitous people, living two distinct lives, but it can happen all too easily. Think for a minute:

- Would people be shocked and upset if they saw how you spoke to your kids and treated your family when no one else is around?
- Are there any secret sinful habits in your life that plague you?
- How do you talk about other people when they're not there?
- Are you a bully to yourself? Do you say horrible things over yourself when you fail—things you would never dream of saying to others?

Are you the same person in church as you are at work or at home? We all need to be real and genuine. We need to be those who are like Christ. Thank God today that His desire is to make you more like Jesus (see Romans 12:1–2).

Fasting

I don't get much time to eat. I am such a busy person that sometimes I forget to eat. In fact, I often rely on those around me to remember I need a drink of water or a quick bite. Most days I speak three or four times, and in between, I find so many people needing prayer that I can just go without and not realize it. Until I feel faint and exhausted, that is!

Sometimes, however, God asks me to refrain from food for a reason. Fasting is something I regularly do to help me focus in on what He is saying to me. It makes me dwell on Him in a different way. It sharpens my vision and helps me to see more of what God sees.

Fasting also reminds me just how many people are hungry in our world—not just physically hungry but also spiritually. Multitudes are craving pure spiritual food. It is an appropriate aide memoire for those in any kind of need.

Many of the people I live and work alongside know what it means to suffer true hunger. Some are malnourished; others are desperately ill because their thirst for water led them to drink from a contaminated source.

Telling people like this they can know a spiritual food that will satisfy them has a different resonance. In the West, when we say we are hungry, we mean we haven't had a snack for a few minutes. In my part of Africa, it is common to go for days without food. People truly know what hunger means.

There is a cost to serving Jesus. God might ask us to go without something we love for a while. He might ask us to fast from something we feel we love. Are you willing to give something up in this way for Him?

Writing in his book, Mere Christianity, C. S. Lewis said, "If our charities do not at all pinch or hamper us, I should say they are too small."

True Forgiveness

Some time ago, a terrible thing happened at our camp. A boy we hadn't known for long, who had severe special needs, raped one of our little girls. Then he ran away. It was devastating.

My reaction was different from the reactions of many around me. I went out to look for the boy. Not because I was angry with him, although I was saddened and sickened by what he had done, but because I cared for him. His life mattered to me. I was filled with an inexplicable compassion for him. I couldn't cope with the thought of him out there on his own, wondering about what he had done and not understanding it.

My staff was so upset about the situation and what had happened. They couldn't understand why I was begging God to let me find him.

But I could only hear the voice of God in my heart, whispering to me: "I came for the sick, not the well. I love that little boy in his confusion and struggle. Keep looking."

I continued to search for him everywhere I went. God had etched that little boy's face deeply into my heart. One day, not long ago, I found him. I flew to a town, and there he was. I had prayed for so long to find him, and there he was. I don't know why, but I couldn't help loving him. Not long after I found him, I decided to fly him, at great expense, to one of our camps in the north where he could be cared for more closely. Now he is worshiping God and being transformed.

God's love is big enough to touch any life! His mercy is bigger than disability, pain and anger. Not one sinner can't come back home. Not one!

I am so pleased God went out on a search party for me. He was not content to leave me where I was, but He came looking for me. This is my job, too. Will you join me?

Who Can God Use?

You may believe God will be able to use you when you are older, when you are trained, when you have more time or more money or more of something else.

However, God can use anyone of any age, any background, any IQ level, any status, any socio-economic band, any tribe, any tongue and any skill set. He doesn't have to start with someone who has influence, power, a Ph.D. or a bank account. He can use someone who is totally illiterate, poor and invisible to the world.

He wants people to respond to Him like Isaiah did: "Then I heard the voice of the Lord saying, 'Whom shall I send? And who will go for us?' And I said, 'Here am I. Send me'" (Isaiah 6:8).

When was the last time you waved at God, got His attention and then said, "Here am I. Send me!"

God changes the calls on our hearts over the years. We do not know what God previously said to Isaiah. Maybe he was someone who had been brought up in the schools of the prophets. Perhaps, when the word of the Lord came to him, he had accepted it as a clear and sufficient calling. Now, however, he had a detailed vision and a clear and distinct mission. He was told to go and instructed as to what he was to say.

Here I am, send me!

When we are bold enough to say those words, God will use who we are for His glory. Do you think God can use a dancer filled with His glory? Could He use an artist? What about a teacher?

Of course He can. He can use anyone. He not is not looking for you to make a name for yourself, grow the amount of followers you have on Facebook or get yourself a good website.

Jesus made Himself nothing. He didn't make Himself something or someone. He took on the nature of a servant (see Philippians 2:7).

This is what He asks of us, too. Who can God use? Anyone. Including you!

Come Closer

• Look afresh at Philippians 2:3–4 today, and sit down with the Lord as you pray through it. "Do nothing out of selfish ambition or vain conceit. Rather, in humility value others above yourselves, not looking to your own interests but each of you to the interests of the others."

• God loves to honor those who honor Him and imitate Him as "dearly loved children." He is pleased with the prayers of laid-down lovers who want to go even lower, so He can increase more in their lives.

• Colossians 3:12 says, "Therefore, as God's chosen people, holy and dearly loved, clothe yourselves with compassion, kindness, humility, gentleness and patience." Let's be people who remember today how chosen we are and how to clothe ourselves in the beautiful characteristics of our Father.

Pray this prayer:

Father, show me any areas of my life where I am selfish. Show me circumstances when I put myself above others or value my own advancement more than the advancement of those around me. Help me not to be conceited about what I can do, what I can offer or the skills I possess, but to remember that "every good and perfect gift" comes from You (see James 1:17). Help me to look at others, be aware of their needs and elevate their adventures above my own. Help me to serve those around me whom You have given me to love. Teach me that sense of humility that allows and celebrates others' successes, and help me to stand up for those around me who do not have a champion. Amen.

Fragrance of Christ

If I asked you what you smelled like, you might point to the fact that you had clean clothes on, that you had washed, that you wore perfume or deodorant. But what if I asked you what you smelled like to God?

Ephesians 5:2 describes Jesus as being someone who "...loved us and gave himself up for us, a fragrant offering and sacrifice to God."

God loves a good smell! He loves the smell of a holy offering and a loving sacrifice. But what does this look and smell like? What is it God is looking for here? Another clue is set before us in 2 Corinthians 2:15: "For we are to God the pleasing aroma of Christ among those who are being saved and those who are perishing."

We are meant to smell like Christ, to have His aroma in the world.

Fragrance is hard to describe. You will rarely be able to explain a smell in one word. You need to use a number of words. Perfume is hard to explain, but it is utterly recognizable. Just a tiny scent can bring back vivid memories, sounds and tastes. It can transport us somewhere else in a way our other senses do not.

What is the fragrance of Christ like, then? It is like the Father. It conveys some of the sweetness of His beauty and His love. It is the smell of grace and mercy, the aroma of goodness and holiness.

It reminds us of God.

So let me ask you again. What do you smell like?

Or rather, whom do you smell like?

God's Aroma

Our world is obsessed with valuing things according to their magnitude. Even (and sometimes especially) in church settings, we can be so worldly at times about prizing that which looks and sounds impressive. We can find that we care more about the number of people at a conference than about what God actually did there.

The stadium was full! There were no empty seats! The parking lot was gridlocked!

We ask after a meeting, "How many were saved?" What we mean is, how many hands went up; how many were prayed with or ministered to? The real answer is, we don't know. So much of what God does is unseen by us and seen only by Him. He can do plenty in someone who never comes forward for prayer, and we will be none the wiser.

The fragrance He exudes cannot be measured. You only need a tiny amount of a powerful scent to fill a large room. A very small quantity of good quality perfume can have widespread influence. Just a touch of God is enough.

I am learning more and more that God is not interested in the things we often hold in such high esteem. He does not care about the rubbish that fills our newspapers and the works of humanity that seem so impressive to us.

Aren't you glad He is not asking you to be what the world wants? He is not calling you to be "successful" in the world's opinion. Instead, He wants you to carry His aroma as you go about the world and to realize the power in His smell.

Losing to Win

When we own something of value, like a house or car, we typically want to insure it against loss from any kind of accident, theft or destruction. We insure our possessions because we want some kind of protection against our loss. Paul speaks about loss in Philippians 3:8 in an interesting way. He says, "I consider everything a loss..."

Paul is not saying nothing we have is valuable. He is also not saying everything is worthless. The Amplified Version of Philippians 3:8 explains a little more about what we win and gain: "Yes, furthermore, I count everything as loss compared to the possession of the priceless privilege (the overwhelming preciousness, the surpassing worth, and supreme advantage) of knowing Christ..."

Many things in the gospels do not fit the pattern of the world. The Bible teaches us to love our enemies, to give to those who hate us, to lay things down in order to gain and to become last in order to be raised. This kind of theology only makes sense to those who have the Spirit living within them. To others it appears foolish, unwise, even a little mad.

Paul made the decision not to hang onto these valuable things but to exchange them for Christ. Why? Because there is no comparison. There is "overwhelming preciousness, surpassing worth, and supreme advantage" to being known by Christ and knowing Him in intimacy.

What about you? What are you ready to lose in order to win?

Consider It Rubbish

We have all met people who are hoarders. Their houses and work spaces are a mess of collected items that have little or no value. But for some reason, these items are precious to the hoarders and are kept for a "rainy day."

I cannot afford to be like this. I am not materialistic in that sense. Many of my kids wear odd flip-flops. We do what we can to dress them, but we are not aiming for high fashion. Things like that do not matter where we are. What matters is who we are and what we do for others.

Philippians 3:7–9 says:

"But whatever were gains to me I now consider loss for the sake of Christ. What is more, I consider everything a loss because of the surpassing worth of knowing Christ Jesus my Lord, for whose sake I have lost all things. I consider them garbage, that I may gain Christ and be found in him..."

This kind of attitude is a challenge for so many of us. The Bride of Christ, especially in the West, prizes so many things. Wealth, clothes, shoes, handbags, jewelry, books, people, church buildings, status and friendships can all jostle for position in our hearts. If we are honest with ourselves, sometimes we hold them in higher esteem than we do our Lord.

The Bible says we should consider them rubbish, garbage and worthless compared to knowing Christ. In Wesley's Commentary on Philippians, he points out that the "Greek word here signifies the vilest refuse of things, the dross of metals, the dregs of liquors, the excrements of animals, the most worthless scraps of meat, the basest offal, fit only for dogs."

That doesn't sound like anything of value. I don't need to hold on to those things!

Let us be those today who seek to gain Christ and be found in Him.

Rubbish Heap

Many rubbish heaps exist where I live. People use them to find food, scraps of metal to sell and personal items they can mend or use. It is heartbreaking that many children across the third world live in such dangerous and unsanitary places, where they can easily contract and spread disease to one another.

Spiritually speaking, of course, so many people in the world live on rubbish heaps. They spend their lives searching in the wrong place for the wrong things, because they don't know where else to look. They prize what God has thrown away as worthless garbage. They search for it and make it their goal and their delight. This breaks my heart. It saddens me that so many of my brothers and sisters on earth are buried up to their eyes in the muck and mire of debris.

When the apostle Paul says he considers the things of this world to be rubbish or excrement, he speaks with a tone of revulsion. It is not just that we don't need those things. It is that they are damaging for us, and they leave us and others with a bad smell.

The fragrance of Christ is something hard to describe and explain. So many people are looking for the smell, but they don't know where to find it. They think that elusive aroma will be in an expensive car or a beautiful house or a rich husband. They think this is where their happiness is. But when they possess those things, they find they have the stench of death.

The spiritual rubbish heaps of the world are full of lost and lonely people. Our job is to populate the world and go in search of those who fill their lives with worthless things.

The One God Places in Front of Us

I don't have a romantic view of being a missionary. My life is not filled with easy, sunny days. I laugh a lot, but I cry a lot, too. I see great need all around me, and at times, it is overwhelming.

But I do not stay in that place for long. I remember God has sent me for a reason, and when I lay down my life for Him, He will provide all my needs and the needs of those to whom He has sent me.

When you love God deeply in this way, with reckless devotion, He will always place in front of you someone else to love. It may not be someone you like very much. It may not be someone who smells good. It may not be someone you think of as deserving or worthy or your attention. But then you need to look at God's criteria for salvation.

The most famous verse in all of Scripture is John 3:16. Sometimes it is helpful to remind ourselves of the basics of the Gospel. Here it is in the Amplified, which is so rich in meaning: "For God so greatly loved and dearly prized the world that He [even] gave up His only begotten (unique) Son, so that whoever believes in (trusts in, clings to, relies on) Him shall not perish (come to destruction, be lost) but have eternal (everlasting) life."

God greatly loves and dearly prizes everyone in His world so that anyone who believes in Him—rich or poor, kind or evil, clever or simple, old or young, ugly or beautiful, dirty or clean, well or ill—can come to Him.

My friend, will you be one who stops for whomever God puts in front of you? Will you be a person who determines today not to judge and think, I cannot reach this one for the Lord. She is too far down that road to self-destruction.

We can make excuses for why we don't want to serve the Lord. He reminds us today of the word whoever.

Come Closer

• We have been challenged this week to consider the kind of aroma we give off and what we deem important in our lives. What have you had to consider rubbish for the sake of Christ? What have you had to change your attitude on?

• In our culture, we don't like to lose anything—an argument, a friendship or money. We are not prepared for it. That is why so many get married now with legal agreements about what will happen to their possessions when they split up! What a sad way to start out together.

• I have learned and I am still learning that what I have chosen to give up for God is nothing like what He has given me in exchange. He gives us beauty for ashes every time!

• Read with me the beautiful passage of Isaiah 61:1–3. Read it out loud with conviction and trust. Declare it as God's heart to work in and through you.

"The Spirit of the Sovereign LORD is on me, because the LORD has anointed me to proclaim good news to the poor. He has sent me to bind up the broken-hearted, to proclaim freedom for the captives and release from darkness for the prisoners, to proclaim the year of the LORD's favor and the day of vengeance of our God, to comfort all who mourn, and provide for those who grieve in Zion—to bestow on them a crown of beauty instead of ashes, the oil of joy instead of mourning, and a garment of praise instead of a spirit of despair. They will be called oaks of righteousness, a planting of the LORD for the display of his splendor." (Isaiah 61:1–3)

The Dying Seed

The Gospel contains so many deep and unfathomable mysteries. One such wonderful truth is that we have to die in order to truly live.

Think about a seed. In order to grow it has to be fully dried out and planted in spacious and fertile ground. I expect if seeds could talk they would think they were being buried and left to die!

A seed by itself has no power. But it contains great promise and potential. That enormous amount of locked-in latent power can only come forth in the right environment. Just as a seed has no power to produce life inside itself, until it is buried in the soil, so we cannot be used by God until we are willing to die first and be made new by His Spirit.

Mark 4:30–32 says, "How can we picture God's kingdom? What kind of story can we use? It's like a pine nut. When it lands on the ground it is quite small as seeds go, yet once it is planted it grows into a huge pine tree with thick branches. Eagles nest in it" (MESSAGE).

It is incredible that God can grow something so magnificent from the tiniest and most insignificant beginning. What looks at best unpromising and at worst pointless is actually the miracle of growth that we take for granted.

I don't want a single seed that God has planted in my heart to stay dead in the ground. I want each seed to be watered and nurtured so it can become a tree. This is what Paul means in Philippians 3:10–11: "I want to know Christ—yes, to know the power of his resurrection and participation in his sufferings, becoming like him in his death, and so, somehow, attaining to the resurrection from the dead."

A garden contains endless possibilities for growth, beauty, color, fruitfulness, scale and use. So do our hearts. May God come and water what He has planted in you today.

Press On!

I am sure you have met burned out Christians. I know I have. Some followers of Christ have lost their first love; others are tired and apathetic. Some are critical of fellow believers and have been disappointed by the Church. Others have big problems with those in authority over them.

None of us wake up one day wanting to be in that place. But for some, that day comes. Why does this happen? I think it is because we make life too complicated, and we make it about the wrong things. We get bogged down in the details and forget the joy of our salvation (see Psalm 51).

There is much to obtain in the Christian life and much to strive toward, but we are not meant to struggle alone. In Philippians 3, Paul says we need a "righteousness that comes from God on the basis of faith" (verse 9).

Where does our righteousness come from—from ourselves, from our works, from our words or from our giving? No! It comes from God.

We can sometimes feel overwhelmed by the Bible and its many exhortations, imagining we cannot make any more progress. Paul gives a helpful answer to anyone in this position. He says, in Philippians 3:12–13, "Not that I have already obtained all this, or have already arrived at my goal, but I press on to take hold of that for which Christ Jesus took hold of me" (emphasis added).

Those two words—press on—are the key. They can be the difference between someone who backslides and someone who becomes a blessing to others. So what about you? Are you still pressing on? Are you starting out today determined to continue living your life in a way that moves you forward toward all Jesus has for you?

I pray today you would join me in that goal.

Take Hold

The more I get to know God, the more I realize I need to know of Him. He is so amazing and so hard to fathom. His understanding is way higher and way deeper than mine. His knowledge of any situation is multi-leveled, multi-faceted and takes every single thing into account. Don't you just love Him?!

It is a strange thing to be satisfied in God and yet not content—to want more of Him, to hunger after Him and to be unwilling to simply stand still. This is what Paul means in these verses we have been looking at over the last few days. He says: "Not that I have already obtained all this, or have already arrived at my goal, but I press on to take hold of that for which Christ Jesus took hold of me" (Philippians 3:12, emphasis added).

He knew he didn't have it all right. He knew there was more to come. He knew God could still work in and through and in spite of Him. He was living with that tension of being satisfied yet not content.

How about you? How do you feel about your faith? Are you growing as a Christian, or have you stayed still for some time now?

We spoke yesterday about the need to press on and keep progressing and moving forward toward all God has for us in Christ. We will never stop learning until we get to heaven. But we can journey with confidence because we know we are held. Christ Jesus has chosen to take hold of me and take hold of you. This is why we can take hold of our own calling. We do it from a place of security and safety, knowing we are walking with God.

Paul did not say, "that for which Christ Jesus took hold of us." He personalized it. Our races are individual. We each have to run our own race well.

When was the last time you took hold of all God has said and done in your life? When was the last time you held up His promises to you and thanked Him for the way He holds you?

Make today the day.

Forget What Is Behind

Many people cry when they spend time looking back over their lives, wishing things had been different. But as Christians, we do not need to dwell on what is behind in any way. In fact, God asks us to forget what is past (see Philippians 3:13).

Think of it this way, when we learn to drive, we must occasionally look in the rear view mirror, but we mustn't focus on it too much, or we will crash into what is ahead.

It is important to get the balance right in this.

I believe the best years of my life will be found in the rest of my life. I believe God will write every chapter well, and it will be better than the one before. I choose to put the past behind me and press forward. I know what is ahead is better than what is behind.

C. S. Lewis puts it this way, at the end of The Last Battle:

All their life in this world and all their adventures in Narnia had only been the cover and the title page: now at last they were beginning Chapter One of the Great Story, which no one on earth has read: which goes on forever: in which every chapter is better than the one before.

This does not mean I don't thank God for what He did back then. Or that I don't choose to learn from my mistakes. But primarily, I want to give myself to what is ahead. I don't want to live in a place of regret about anything.

Looking ahead is such a joyful thing. Do you know how much stress goes away when you have no need to rake through the past? You'll be free to win a million souls or just one. You'll be free because your life is given to Christ in God, and you are living in the present, not the past.

Forget what is behind today. Choose to leave the past where it belongs—in the past.

Strain Toward what Is Ahead

I am a dreamer. I have big dreams. Fortunately, I serve a God who does more than I can ever ask or imagine (see Ephesians 3:20). Knowing that, I move in faith toward what lies ahead.

I have huge dreams for the kids in my care and for those yet to be in our programs. We have thousands of kids in school right now. Three of our schools are really large and have 3,500 pupils. But we have 2,000 more on the waiting list.

I long to be able to serve more communities, build more schools and reach more people.

Many orphans live around us, but sometimes a child comes to us who still has a living relative of some kind, perhaps a grandma or an uncle. It is our desire to leave as many children in their own family units as possible. Our goal is only to house those who have no family to love and nurture them.

All of the children waiting for a place at school are from another faith. When they come to our schools, they are taught to read and write, but in the context of the greatest teacher of all—Jesus. They learn about the Bible, sing songs to God and learn the power of praise and worship. Suddenly they are given access to the ministry of the Holy Spirit. Many of them start to speak in tongues and receive spiritual gifts. The wonderful thing about this is that they are the best advertisements, not just for our educational work and our ministry but—so much more importantly—for the God we serve. Without using spiritual jargon, they naturally share their faith with their families and friends. They take their faith into their wider circle of influence, and others get to hear the good news of the Lord.

At IRIS we constantly desire to strain toward what is ahead. There are always more children to educate and teach. So many more people need to hear the gospel. The need is great, not just here, but everywhere. We all need to play our part.

What part will you play? What are your dreams for your future with God?

When God Rejoices

What do you think makes God joyful? What do you think makes angels dance and sing?

We find the answer in the parable of the lost sheep:

"Suppose one of you has a hundred sheep and loses one of them. Doesn't he leave the ninety-nine in the open country and go after the lost sheep until he finds it? And when he finds it, he joyfully puts it on his shoulders and goes home. Then he calls his friends and neighbors together and says, "Rejoice with me; I have found my lost sheep." I tell you that in the same way there will be more rejoicing in heaven over one sinner who repents than over ninety-nine righteous people who do not need to repent." (Luke 15:4–7)

The shepherd is joyful when he finds the sheep. He asks others to rejoice with him, and there is rejoicing in heaven. God is showing us something of His heart here.

He loves it when we are found, but He doesn't just sit and count us, content that He has everyone He needs. No, He goes out looking for the one who is still lost.

Do you know when you make God rejoice? It is not only when you turn from your sins and repent, but also when you join with Him as He seeks to save the hurting and the broken, the lost and the lonely.

God so cares about each person that He goes out in search of the one. He inconveniences Himself time and time again. He leaves behind comfort to seek in dark places.

In our ministry, sometimes we pray for thousands of people, and they all respond and become followers of Christ. But God asks us to look at them one by one by one. He doesn't see them as a sea of faces gathered in a big meeting somewhere on a dusty plain or in a stadium. He sees life after life, person after person with whom He is already intimately connected. He sees hearts turning back to Him, tuning in to Him, opening up to Him. Joy abounds in His heart when He counts every single person as safely His.

Come Closer

• Each one of us has the opportunity to grow deeper into God, but to do that we first need to die to ourselves. That can be a difficult thing to do—to lay down our desires and seek His, to allow ourselves to be made lower and less so that He might become higher and more. But there is so much joy in the discovery of that rightful place!

• In the past few days, we have looked at pressing on toward the goal He has set before us and not allowing ourselves to look back. Let's consider what that looks like practically. For example:

• What aspects of your past do you find it hard not to think about regularly? Why do you think that is?

• Who do you think reminds you of your past more, your enemy or Jesus? What does that tell you about what you keep remembering?

• Write out the amazing verse we have focused on somewhere you will see it each day: "But one thing I do: forgetting what is behind and straining towards what is ahead, I press on towards the goal to win the prize for which God has called me heavenwards in Christ Jesus" (Philippians 3:14).

Now pray with me:

Father God, I am willing to be the seed You plant, the seed that falls to the ground and dies. I am willing to be covered by Your protection and hidden as I start to grow. I am willing to be used by You in any way You choose. I lay down my rights and my life. I choose today to forget the things that hold me back, the things that pull me back into yesterday. I choose to cut any ties that make me feel unworthy of Your calling on my life and to press on toward that which You have put in my path. I joyfully give my life away for others and rejoice when I see repentance. I will keep looking for the lost until I find them, and then will go looking for more. I thank You that You are in control of my life, that my life is no longer my own but Yours. I will love those whom You send me to love, wherever You ask me to go. Amen.

The God of Healing

Sometimes when I am in a conference or speaking at an event, God crashes in. The Holy Spirit takes over, and He does His thing. I love it when He does this. It is all about Him!

Often I am in awe as people are set free from all kinds of sin and sickness. He moves among the people in waves, coming down powerfully on them with His love and His goodness.

God does not just heal the sick in Africa or India or China. He heals today in the U.K., in Canada, in America. He heals wherever the Spirit of the Lord is given freedom. He heals wherever there is faith.

One day I was preaching in the U.S., and I felt the Lord call me to stop sharing for a while as He gave me words of knowledge for those there. He spoke to me about healing people, specifically those with stress-based illnesses. He said to me, "Tell the people. Let their faith rise up. Get them to step out and believe."

One by one, I listed the things God was healing: Carpel tunnel syndrome was gone in Jesus' name. Migraine headaches were gone in Jesus' name. Insomnia was being healed right then and there. In fact, so much so that I gave the people affected permission to sleep during the rest of my talk! I told them to enter God's rest in that place and that space! The peace of God came powerfully in that time.

We can know the healing touch of God wherever we are. We don't need someone to pray for us—although that can be wonderful, too. We just need a touch from our living, healing God.

Goodbye Allergy!

I lived in Asia for twelve years, and I suffered from an enormously inconvenient problem while I was there. I had a terrible digestive disorder and food allergy. I was very allergic to MSG (Monosodium glutamate), which chefs all over the world—but especially in Asia—use to balance and blend the flavors in their food. They use it in everything—great big spoonfuls of white powder. The effects of this allergy were pretty scary. My lips would turn blue. I would vomit over and over again and then pass out. That is not a good combination. It was very dangerous for me.

Then one day God just touched me—Bam!—and healed me there and then. What a blessing that was to my life! At last, I could work and travel all over Asia with no fear of what I was eating. Praise God for His healing!

Some people who are called into ministry have real issues with food in the same way. But God will not let that stop Him and His plans for them. Sometimes at conferences, I will get a word for someone and say, "Be healed, as I was healed, of this digestive problem or that eating disorder so you can serve in India or Africa or wherever is on your heart."

Watch out! If you have said to God, "I will go when I am healed," be sure He is on your case. He has heard you and is looking for an opportunity to heal you today.

Our God is so good. If you are willing to go, He will not allow anything to hinder your destiny—not even a food allergy.

Don't Spectate

We are all human. As humans, it is natural for us to watch other people and be interested in their journey and their walk with God. It is good to walk alongside others, to stand with them and be accountable to them and aim to encourage them.

However, we need to be careful that we do not focus so much on what God is doing and saying to those around us that we forget to ask Him for fresh words for ourselves.

I don't want to spend any of the rest of my life spectating or standing around watching God at work in other ministries. I love that He does that. I praise Him for all He is doing across the world, but I do not let it distract me from my own mission in Him.

It is easy to get discouraged when we see how God blesses others. We could be in a meeting and see someone get radically healed and restored. Maybe someone else is given a fresh anointing for ministry, but we haven't felt a touch from God like that in a long time.

Should we get depressed about that? Of course not.

But sometimes we do.

If you are feeling a sense today that you need something fresh from God's table, just for you, don't wait until your prayer meeting or your church group. Don't call your pastor or your friend. Just sit in His presence today and ask Him for the ability to hear what He hears and see what He is looking at and working on in your life.

The Malnourished Bride

I travel a lot, so I see many types of people and countless problems. One of the issues I believe the Western Church suffers from the most is a painful hunger. It is a hunger they do not even know they have. I pray all the time that God would cause people to recognize their malnourishment.

God's Western Bride suffers so much with an eating disorder. In a culture of all-you-can eat buffets and high energy high calorie drinks, people are full of empty food but empty of God's food.

The Church there is literally dying of starvation. Now, I want you to hear me well on this. I love the Church. I love the Western Bride of Christ, but I see it as feeding itself on crumbs and stale bread.

I pray we would not be a people who are satisfied with eating nothing but fluff and puff! I want us to be people who eat of the living God in a way that feeds our souls and brings us life in all its fullness and abundance.

Without Him, our eyes are weak, and our hearts are too small. Our stomachs are malnourished, and our voices are not strong enough. When we feast on Jesus, we have spiritual energy to give our lives to the world in the way He did.

John 6:51 says: "I am the living bread that came down from heaven. Whoever eats this bread will live forever. This bread is my flesh, which I will give for the life of the world."

Oh God, teach us how to eat and drink of You in a way that we never have before—for Your name's sake. Amen.

Ask Father to show you where you have suffered from spiritual malnourishment. Ask Him to help you feast on Jesus so you can be His hands and feet in this world.

What Do the Dying Look Like?

If I asked a group of people to describe for me what dying people look like, they would quote me cases of children in Africa or Asia or India. They would show me distended bellies and poor sanitation. They would give me statistics and geography and science.

And they would be right. But it is also true that other people on our planet, people who don't fit those descriptions, are dying, too. They don't look poor. They are well dressed in the finest suits. They drive the nicest cars. They may be well known and venerated by those around them. But they are still dying.

They are dying because they don't know Jesus, and their god is something or someone else. They are dying because they feed their souls and bodies on food that will perish, not on things that are eternal.

In the Old Testament, during the time when God's people were in the wilderness, He gave them manna. He did not give them enough manna for a week or a month or a year. He gave them fresh food for one day only. He gave manna one day at a time for a reason. He wanted to be intimate with them, to keep in close touch with them daily. He wants the same for us.

Also, however much of the manna the people gathered, it was enough!

"The Israelites did as they were told; some gathered much, some little. And when they measured it by the omer, the one who gathered much did not have too much, and the one who gathered little did not have too little. Everyone had gathered just as much as they needed." (Exodus 16:17–18)

Whether we gather too much out of fear or not enough out of insecurity, God will bless us. He is enough for us. Even if we are spiritually starving, He is enough. He is our portion (see Lamentations 3:24), and when we feed on Him, we will never grow hungry.

Broken Bread

Recently, I was out with a beautiful friend, my daughter and my son-in-law (I call him my son-in-love). We were having dinner together in a restaurant in California.

I cannot compartmentalize my life. I am a Christian wherever I am and however I feel. I can't be on or off. I am always on. So as we were sitting in this lovely place, waiting for our dinner and having a great time catching up, the waitress brought us some amazing fresh bread. I did not think twice. I just picked up the loaf and started praying.

Out loud I said something like, "Thank You Jesus for Your body broken for us. Thank You for Your presence with us now. Thank You that Your body feeds us." Then I gave some to my daughter and her husband and my friend.

The waitress just stopped and looked at me. Then something extraordinary happened. Just very simply, the presence of God came. I hadn't preached. I hadn't gotten out my Bible. I hadn't spoken directly to her. All I had done was enact what thousands of Christians have done down the centuries in memory of what Jesus told us to do.

Suddenly the waitress started crying. Not caring about what anyone else around her was thinking or hearing, she sobbed, "Tell me how to be born again. I need to know Jesus!"

Sometimes the simplest and most straightforward actions can be the tipping point for someone to get to know Jesus. We often never know the result of our conversations with others, but occasionally God will let us be part of someone else's adventure with Him.

Join me in saying no to on-and-off Christianity. You can take your Christian life with you wherever you go, and when you do, even the simplest moments will be laden with heaven's potential.

Come Closer

• We serve a magnificent miracle-working God who is capable of anything. He can heal cancer, stop war, mend broken bones and calm raging seas. But He also stops for one person. He runs after the lost; He binds up the weary and comforts the mourning. There is nothing God cannot do. He can break into our lives in a queue, a restaurant, a conference or a desert. He is able.

• Spend some time today just being grateful for all God has done for you. Perhaps you could make a list of things He has worked for your good in your life.

• Is anything worrying you or making you feel burdened?

• Read this beautiful Scripture out loud and let the truth of it resonate in your heart and mind.

"Rejoice in the Lord always. I will say it again: rejoice! Let your gentleness be evident to all. The Lord is near. Do not be anxious about anything, but in every situation, by prayer and petition, with thanksgiving, present your requests to God. And the peace of God, which transcends all understanding, will guard your hearts and your minds in Christ Jesus." (Philippians 4:4–7)

Jesus, thank You for Your presence with us. I thank You that You are near us wherever we are, and You accept us as we are. I thank You that—no matter what I am facing today—I don't need to be anxious or upset about it, because I know You are working on my behalf. Thank You for Your peace, which covers me now and guards my heart. Amen.

Every Opportunity

Recently, while I was travelling around the U.S., I went back to the place I was raised—Laguna Beach. While there, I decided to treat myself to a massage, which is something I really love.

But when I walked into the building, I saw a plaque that really freaked me out. It said, "Reiki massage performed here." I am super careful about having anything around me that I don't consider spiritually healthy. I know Reiki practitioners believe all sorts of nonsense that is totally contrary to Scripture, so I steer clear of it.

I started to pray my head off! I asked the Lord, "God, should I stay, or should I leave? What do You want me to do?"

God said, "Heidi, I want you to stay." So I asked the Holy Spirit to shine through me, and I prayed in tongues. Until that point, no one else was in the lobby with me.

But suddenly, the massage therapist came into the lobby, where I was standing. And as she did, she started to shout and scream, "Arrrggghhh!"

"Don't worry," I said, realizing something was scaring her. "Let me introduce you to my friend, Holy Spirit. He won't hurt you." She was a spiritually sensitive lady, and she could tell someone else was in the room besides me.

For the rest of the session, this poor woman tried to massage me, but all she could do was cry huge tears onto my back. "How do I get to know Jesus?" she asked me.

So I told her.

Everywhere you go, you have an opportunity to allow Holy Spirit to shine through you. You never know what amazing things might happen.

Carrying Jesus

A while ago, while I was staying in a hotel, the maid knocked on the door to service the room. As she came in, I struck up a conversation with her.

"Hello, sweetie. Where are you from?"

"Macedonia," she replied.

Macedonia? I thought. That's perfect! I love the biblical significance of that place. In 2 Corinthians 8, we read about how generous and giving the Macedonian church was. In fact, the noun charis (grace) appears a massive ten times in chapters 8 and 9. They were a people God could use and bless to such an extent that, in 2 Corinthians 8:5, Paul described them in this way: "They exceeded our expectations: They gave themselves first of all to the Lord, and then by the will of God also to us."

It is part of my role in God to call people to go and serve the Lord in this way, so I got excited about meeting this girl. I told her why her homeland was so significant to me. I think she was a little surprised! As I began to talk to her more, I discovered she was a Muslim. I asked if I could pray for her, and she said, "Yes, please."

As I started to pray, she began to cry, not quiet tears but loud weeping and sobbing tears. When I finished praying for her, she said, "Now can you pray for my son and my uncle and my sister?" So we prayed together.

When we had finished praying, I said, "Now don't worry about the room. You are free to go. It's fine."

She hugged me, still crying with joy as she left—a new creation.

What God asks us to do is not complicated. We can carry Jesus everywhere we go.

Inner Security

I am a rascal in God. The mischievous side of me comes out once in a while. A few months ago, I was speaking at a huge convention center in Singapore. Normally, when we use a place like that, the organizers need to hire security to staff the buildings safely.

These security staff could be anyone. Normally they are not from a Christian background, which I think is a wonderful opportunity to have a little fun in God and let Him do what He wants to do.

One day as I was walking into the convention center, I saw a security guard who was a Sikh. I had forgotten my badge, so I explained who I was and asked him to let me in. But as I did so, I held on to him. I almost rocked him in the spirit, and I silently prayed over Him. All I said aloud was the name of Jesus.

Following the next session, I saw the security guard again. I asked if he had been able to come in and listen to any of the talk. He smiled and said he had. By day two, this guard and I were old friends! On day three, as I walked in and went toward the guard, he started weeping, and the presence of God fell on him. He was totally undone by God. It was a beautiful thing to see.

I like it when God does that.

The fact is, what God asks of us is simple. Often we don't have to preach or explain. We just need to love people deeply and tune in to what God is doing in them. He does the rest!

God Can Move Anywhere

I often hear people say encounters with the Lord—in the ways I have described in the last few days—just don't happen in the West. I am here to tell you that simply is not true—not at all!

If we could just see our world as God sees it, we would know there are no barriers, no impossibilities.

About Africa, people sometimes say to me, "Over there the blind eyes see. Here it's hard. People here have too much. There is no prayer. There is no faith." Lord have mercy on us for thinking like that!

We are called to be fearless lovers of God in every city, town and village on earth. If we don't speak His name, the very rocks will cry out (see Luke 19:40).

Whenever we see people who are anxious because of anything in their lives, all we need to do is radiate peace, share Jesus and be the Lord's love to our neighbor. It's so easy. It's natural. God is looking for people who are so totally yielded and recklessly devoted to Him that, in any given moment, they can just say what is on His heart.

Matthew 7:7 says, "Ask and it will be given to you; seek and you will find; knock and the door will be opened to you." Some of us are scared to ask. We are afraid to seek God. Why? We know He loves to give us good gifts, don't we?

The Scripture says, in Luke 11:13, "If you then, though you are evil, know how to give good gifts to your children, how much more will your Father in heaven give the Holy Spirit to those who ask him!"

Will you join me in asking God for new boldness today?

What Really Matters

One of my favorite places to be on earth is in a place of praise. It can be in my house on my own or at the front at a meeting. I don't mean on the stage. I mean hidden by people all around me, lost in worship. I love to go to the front because not as many people will try to get to me there. I am a small lady, and I can hide a bit. I am captivated by the place of praise. I yearn for it, and I love what God does in those spaces in my life.

Whenever I am due to preach, I need to be in a place of worship first. I kneel down and wait on God to speak to me, to make me less and to allow Him to be more.

Worship is not a time for the people organizing a meeting to discuss things. It is not a break for the preacher. It is not an opportunity for people to dash to the restroom. For me, worship is the longing of my heart.

Sometimes I will be so impacted during worship that it is like bolts of electricity flow into me. Other times, I will just be still and know He is God (see Psalm 46:10).

In that place of adoration, living a life fully given to God, we can start to hear those holy heavenly whispers. So often in worship we start to think more about things that really matter. In worship our hearts are broken, and we ask God for more of His Spirit. In worship we cry "Abba Father," and He responds.

Read and dwell on these words from Psalm 86:8–10:

"Among the gods there is none like you, Lord; no deeds can compare with yours. All the nations you have made will come and worship before you, Lord; they will bring glory to your name. For you are great and do marvelous deeds; you alone are God."

Aligning

And I will do whatever you ask in my name, so that the Father may be
glorified in the Son. You may ask me for anything
in my name, and I will do it.
John 14:13–14

When we meditate on the Word of God in the place of worship, incredible
things can happen. Look with me at the verses above. Jesus is not saying here,
"Ask Me for anything you want: a big house, a nice car, a great spouse for your
daughter"—although all those things may be part of His plan for you. What
He is saying relates to so much more than the material concerns we have.

God is interested in what we are dreaming and longing for, especially during
and after being in His presence. Because in His presence we find an abundance
of contentment. As Psalm 16:11 says, "You make known to me the path of
life; you will fill me with joy in your presence, with eternal pleasures at your
right hand."

In the place of God's manifest presence, He tells us what is on His heart. More
than this, He aligns our spirits with His Spirit. Our hearts connect, and we
hear and see what God hears and sees.

After this kind of experience of His presence, of course we have fullness of
joy. Because we understand. We see more. We get it. Our eyes are open. We
feel part of the plans of the almighty. We are submitting to His Word. We are
in tune with His almighty, miraculous, loving grace.

When we come out of this place of worship and God asks what is on our
hearts, we can answer, "The same things that are on Yours."

Do you know how to get your prayers answered 100 percent of the time?
Only pray what is on God's heart!

Come Closer

- We sometimes make our calling so complex. We complicate it. But it is quite simple. It is to be followers of Jesus, to hear what He is doing and join in!

- You might think the kinds of things I have shared in this book could never happen to you, that God could not use you like such ways. But you would be wrong.

- If you are a Christian, the Holy Spirit lives within you. He partners with you. He is not a different Holy Spirit than the one I know, than the one who lives in me. We have the same Spirit, with all the same powers and skills, living inside us. He has the same character and the same personality.

- So all you have read about is something you could be telling someone else about in your own life. Do you believe that?

- When was the last time you felt God really break in on a conversation you were having with someone, giving you an opportunity to pray and share Jesus with that person? If it was a long time ago or if you can't remember that ever happening, pray with me:

Jesus, I thank You that You came to set people free. Thank You for saving me and giving me a story to tell. Thank You that once I was lost but now I am found. Jesus, I pray boldly now for more chances to share You with others I bump into—the person who serves me coffee, the person who brings my mail, those who have a part to play in my life. God make me radically aware in those moments of what that person needs, and help me be Your mouthpiece. Help me be so aligned with You that I do not miss or waste opportunities to bring others into Your presence. Amen.

Cookies

Our children like their food, and we love to eat together. We have to have a lot of food to feed everyone. If you knew how much we needed, it might make you nervous! But I don't get anxious about it. I feel happy, because I know God always provides for me and my little ones. I get to be a little piece of the big puzzle of how He does it. I see that as a true privilege.

One day we made a big batch of cookies for the kids. They are not like western cookies; they are harder and smaller, but our kids love them, and they are a rare treat. On this day, word got out quickly that we had made them, and hundreds more children came looking for one. Juma, one of our little guys, and Dawn, a missionary, were serving the cookies. Before long, they realized they were going to run out. The kids were taking more than one and stuffing them in their pockets. There would not be enough to go around, especially as hundreds more kids were arriving.

We teach our kids to pray if they need food. That is what happened in the Book, and the Book is what we live by. So we put ourselves into the story of the Book. Accordingly, little Juma prayed for more cookies to feed the kids.

God has performed food miracles for us many times, but it is normal for Him to make more bread and chicken. This time, He worked on that cookie bag.

There were Juma and Dawn, with hundreds and hundreds of kids, and the bag of cookies did not run out. For weeks and weeks, God filled that bag over and over again!

This was not a "necessary" miracle. They didn't have to have those cookies. But God loves to bless us and give us good gifts. He also loves it when we trust Him to answer the simplest of prayers: "Help!"

What prayer do you need to trust Him with today?

Cheese and Jacuzzis

As a missionary I have sometimes struggled around wealth. I have found it hard to sit at a nice table of food and not think about the starving people I know by name. I have not enjoyed spending a night in a luxury hotel paid for by a rich church when my kids are cold and sleep on dirt. But God has taught me a few things about Himself.

One day, God spoke to me so clearly. He told me I needed to eat cheese and have hot baths when I could! He told me not to get angry when I saw those luxuries but to enjoy them as part of His favor. For years I had been given hotel rooms with baths and not used them. I had felt guilty for using hot water! I had despised others who "treated themselves" in this way, and I had fussed at God over it.

For years we had been a cheeseless family who washed using buckets, which we shared with a lot of frogs! I am used to using holes in the dirt instead of clean toilets.

But God showed me I was dishonoring those who were trying to treat me well, and therefore, I was dishonoring Him. It was a sobering but joyful realization.

I suddenly realized I was allowed to have a hot bath. I went back to my hotel room, which had a Jacuzzi bath tub. I think I had one and then got out and ran another one right away. I may have had five in one weekend!

Paul understood this when he wrote in Philippians 4:12, "I know what it is to be in need, and I know what it is to have plenty. I have learned the secret of being content in any and every situation, whether well fed or hungry, whether living in plenty or in want."

When God gives me plenty, I will enjoy it. When He gives me nothing, I will be joyful, too. In both situations, I am blessed.

Have you learned the secret of being content in every situation?

Treat Them the Way You Want to be Treated

Here is a simple, rule-of-thumb guide for behavior: Ask yourself what you want people to do for you, then grab the initiative and do it for them. Add up God's Law and Prophets and this is what you get.
Matthew 7:12, MESSAGE

Recently, I was meant to be speaking at three conferences in four days. However, all was not well at the airport. All the planes with that airline were not running. I had only had four hours of sleep the night before and was looking forward to napping on the plane. But now the planes were at a standstill. Instead, the concourse was a mess of angry, shouting people who were late for meetings, holidays, family gatherings. I was late for one of my conferences. In fact, I missed the whole thing.

Not one seat was left in the lounge area, so I spent six hours, like many others, on the floor. I was developing a fever and not feeling well. I looked at the poor ladies behind the counter. They tried to yell back at the customers for a while, but then they gave up. They just kept saying, "I don't know. I am sorry, sir. They haven't told us anything."

When it was my turn to be served, I thought, If I was this lady, what would I want right now? I know. I would like a hug. So I went around the counter and hugged her. "Sweetie, this is such a hard situation for you. I am so sorry this has happened. Let me pray for you."

She cried. I hugged a few more people serving others. They cried too. They were having such a bad day. The lady asked me, "What do you need?"

"I don't have my bag."

"Come on! Let's find your bag. We will find a way!" she said.

We didn't find my bag, but on the way I got to share more of the love of Jesus with her. I think I missed my conference for one person whom God was reaching out for that day.

When we treat others the way we'd like to be treated, Holy Spirit will give us amazing and unexpected opportunities to share His love with people.

By Your Love

Jesus wants us to carry His love into every situation, whether we are standing in a queue or sitting on an airport floor. Jesus said this is how the world will know we love Him.

"Your strong love for each other will prove to the world that you are my disciples" (John 13:35, TLB).

I get cursed by witches a lot. I could curse them back or pray in tongues or show them fear, but I don't. Do you know how I respond? I just try to hug them! They either get saved or they run really fast! Love casts out fear. If He really is greater in you, like it says in 1 John 4:4, then why are you afraid?

The Holy Spirit living in you is greater than he that is in the world. So act like you believe it!

We all have enemies, those people in our lives who wish we weren't doing what we are doing or saying what we are saying. It is our job to remind ourselves who is bigger!

But this comes with a warning: If you are living with secret sin, do not try this. You have to be clean if you are going to see people restored and healed. Get yourself forgiven and cleansed by the blood of Jesus; then try setting other people free. It is really fun!

If God can use me when I have a high fever in an airport full of crazy, cussing people, He can use you anytime, anywhere.

Keep It Simple

I have been meditating on Matthew 9:35 recently. It is one of the most incredible verses: "Jesus went through all the towns and villages, teaching in their synagogues, proclaiming the good news of the kingdom and healing every disease and sickness."

I have spent a lot of time studying complicated things to get this simple! As I read this the other day, I thought for the first time, What was Jesus longing for?

One word in the verse grabbed me—the word every. Jesus wanted to heal every disease and sickness. Or as it says in The Message version, He "healed their bruised and hurt lives."

This is radical love poured forth. But it is so simple, isn't it? God wants everyone to come to Him with every problem and situation. Not one is disqualified or forbidden from coming near.

Jesus didn't just see the people in terms of the multitude in front of Him. He saw inside them. He saw their needs. He saw their issues. He saw their stress. The next verse in Matthew 9 says: "When he saw the crowds, he had compassion on them, because they were harassed and helpless, like sheep without a shepherd" (verse 36).

We need to ask what Jesus is doing in our friends and our families. We need to know what the longing in His heart is for them. When we know that, we can ask Him what part He wants us to play in releasing His heart to them.

Word Becoming Flesh

When a man and a woman first try to attract each other's attention and go out on a date, they have to think of things to do to entertain each other. They spend money on ice skating, cinemas, meals and outings. But as they get to know each other, and especially when they have fallen in love, they no longer need to think of ways to entertain each other. Being together is all they need. They could do absolutely nothing all day, but if they are together, they are content.

I don't think many people enjoy just being with God in this way. I think many of us spend our days looking busy for God. We rush around, being in Bible studies or caring for people or loving our families. All of those are great and necessary, but they are not necessarily done from a place of being with God.

Being with God is ultimately what we need the most and what outsiders crave the most. They want to see if we know God, if we get what makes Him tick, if we dwell with Him and He dwells with us.

John's gospel makes this declaration: "The Word became flesh and blood, and moved into the neighborhood..." (John 1:14, MESSAGE).

In the NIV, this verse reads: "The Word became flesh and made his dwelling among us. We have seen his glory, the glory of the one and only Son, who came from the Father, full of grace and truth."

God made His dwelling among us. He moved in to live where we are. He did not place Himself apart from us. His plan was always to live with us and live in us.

He wants to be with you today, to enjoy your presence while you enjoy His.

Come Closer

• Sometimes in our Christian lives, we can be very nervous to ask God for "cookies." We don't want to bother Him with requests for small things that would be nice to have but aren't necessary. We think He only cares about the really important and necessary things. But we are wrong. God cares about all aspects of our lives. God is so big, and He is very capable of blessing you with the thing your heart desires. He loves it when you ask. Is there a spiritual "cookie" you want to ask God for right now?

• As we seek to treat others the way we want to be treated, we need to stop and think, What does Jesus want to do here? What would I want, if I was that person right now? Maybe you will see someone this week drop a bag or fall or struggle with a child. What can you do to help?

• What situations have you encountered this week in which you could stand in the gap for someone and be a blessing?

• In what ways could you pray differently about your everyday life to make helping others around you more of a priority?

Father God, thank You for caring about every aspect of our lives and every problem. Thank You for having compassion on the lost and seeing them like sheep without a shepherd (see Matthew 9:37). Please show me how to ask You for the things that matter to me and to seek You more for how I can love others around me. Amen.

The Cracked Basin

One day, I was travelling by boat with some of my little healing evangelists, who are ten and eleven years old, and some Norwegian mission visitors. We were going to find some unreached people and tell them the Gospel. My kids love trips like this.

I forget sometimes what adventures like this must be like for the uninitiated. The Norwegians asked, "Where are we going?"

"We will see," I said. "We will just be worshipping on this boat, and when we get there we will know."

They began shaking their heads and having conversations with each other. We started praying and praising. After some time, I knew it was time to stop. I jumped out of the boat into the water and waded to land. I left them to get in the dingy and come ashore. Again they asked a question, "How will we know where the Christians are?" This was not our first trip to this area. We had been before, and many had turned to follow Jesus. This whole area had been visited by many of our teams.

"We will just know," I said again.

Wading through the hot, dark, thick mud, I had to take off my sandals. I warned the others to take off their shoes and carry them, or they might lose them in the sludge.

We started to trek through the bush, and after we had been walking for some time, an old lady greeted us. Her language was beautiful, but I did not understand a word of her dialect. She was carrying a small plastic basin that was cracked at the top. It had water in it. I later discovered it had taken her six hours to walk to get that water. She wanted the best water. She bent down low beneath me and started to put my muddy feet in the precious bowl.

I turned to the Norwegians. "We have arrived," I said, deeply moved. "The Christians are here."

Like this beautiful woman in the bush, it is our privilege to be the love of Jesus wherever we are, using whatever we have. When we offer up the contents of our cracked basins for His service, His kingdom comes all around us.

Acts of Love

That old woman's decision to wash my feet was such a powerful act of service to me. For one thing, my feet were tired and hot. They were also truly black with mud. The humility of her love showed me Jesus was present in that place.

After that, the chiefs came out, and the multitudes came. Hundreds of people came to know Jesus, and those who already knew Him were encouraged and taught. It was a wonderful time.

What stood out to me most was that we knew we had arrived when one little woman got slow and low. She was our signpost: He is here!

Jesus showed us the way every time. He showed us the full extent of His love through service. He washed people's feet (see John 13:1–20). It was a truly humble thing for the Lord of all heaven and earth to get down and do. In Bible times, foot washing was something wives did for their husbands, children did for their parents, and disciples did for their teachers.

But this was what He chose. He chose this level of self-abasement and intimacy with us. He chose to connect with and provide for our needs, and He chose to get close to the muck and mire of our sin.

In your country, foot washing in this way may not be an act of service at all. It might seem a bit strange! But in my country, is it a very meaningful gesture.

We are all called to humble ourselves for the sake of the cross and to act the same way Jesus would act. What is He calling you to do for another today?

The Harvest

I want to pray for what Jesus prays for. As I travel around, this is the prayer I am praying more and more frequently: "Jesus what do You want me to say here? What do You need to me to do now?"

In Matthew 9:37–38, Jesus said to His disciples, "The harvest is plentiful but the workers are few. Ask the Lord of the harvest, therefore, to send out workers into his harvest field."

Clearly, there is much to do. Our world is needy. People are dying without knowledge of Jesus. The harvest of souls is plentiful. We all need to make it our priority to ask the Lord what we should do.

As I kneel before God in worship, this is what I pray for. I pray God would send out workers to His harvest in Boston, in Colorado, in The Gambia, at the UN, in Portugal, in South Africa and to the ends of the earth. This is my heart's cry. I want my life to count for something. I want to call people into fruitful intimacy with God all over the globe.

I know I am a little woman, but when my life is put in His hands, He can do so much with my little offering.

Many people have asked me how we are to be harvesters. They have told me how discouraged they get and how hard it is on the mission field. I just smile. I don't find it hard, because I am so full of the Holy Spirit that He makes it easy. He just fills me up with love, and out I go.

Do you know what Jesus did after He said these words to the disciples? He sent them out and "gave them authority to drive out impure spirits and to heal every disease and illness" (Matthew 10:1).

He knew they were part of the solution. He knows we are, too. And He sends us out with the same mandate.

Be My Witnesses

After Jesus' resurrection, He explained to His followers what He wanted them to do next.

In Acts 1:4–5, we read:

"On one occasion, while he was eating with them, he gave them this command: 'Do not leave Jerusalem, but wait for the gift my Father promised, which you have heard me speak about. For John baptized with water, but in a few days you will be baptized with the Holy Spirit.'"

The disciples did not understand exactly what He meant and asked if He was going to restore Jerusalem at that time. His answer is really interesting. Not only did Jesus say it is not for us to understand the times and dates ordained in heaven for such things, but He also clarified what we really need in order to be His witnesses and do His bidding. "But you will receive power when the Holy Spirit comes on you; and you will be my witnesses in Jerusalem, and in all Judea and Samaria, and to the ends of the earth" (Acts 1:8).

The word power here shows us what the disciples really needed. They were confused. Some were still understandably shocked and upset about the tragic end of their friend and co-worker, Judas Iscariot. Jesus' answer to their need was the sending of the comforting, powerful helper—the Holy Spirit.

Jesus told them the Spirit would come on them, not to them. In other words, He is not just a friend who visits but a spirit who dwells within you. Let the knowledge of the Holy Spirit's role as comforter and helper in your life spur you on to be His witness wherever He sends you today.

Midwives

After Jesus ascended into heaven, His disciples obeyed His command to stay in Jerusalem and wait for what He had promised them. In Acts 1:12–14, we read how they reacted to Jesus' words:

"Then the apostles returned to Jerusalem from the hill called the Mount of Olives, a Sabbath day's walk from the city. When they arrived, they went upstairs to the room where they were staying. Those present were Peter, John, James and Andrew; Philip and Thomas, Bartholomew and Matthew; James son of Alphaeus and Simon the Zealot, and Judas son of James. They all joined together constantly in prayer, along with the women and Mary the mother of Jesus, and with his brothers."

I love the way they "all joined together constantly in prayer." As they waited in that upper room, they longed together for the presence and power of God. I am sure they had no idea what to expect, but they trusted and believed He would come on them somehow, at some time.

As we press in for God, at times when we are expectant and waiting for Him to move, we are like midwives. Standing alongside God as He births something new in us and in others, our role is to support all He is doing. It takes time for a baby to be born. As all mothers will tell you, there is a period of laboring before the promised baby comes. In this time of waiting, mothers are not thinking about other things. Their minds and hearts are at one with the body's longing and yearning for the release of the life inside it.

And eventually, the presence and the power of the Holy Spirit did come upon the disciples in a physically tangible way that rocked all their senses. They heard wind. They saw and felt fire. They spoke in new languages. What a radical change must have been wrought on them in that time!

We must constantly reposition ourselves and put ourselves back into this story. We must wait on the Holy Spirit in the same way the apostles did. We must expect more of God and be midwives to what He is birthing.

Gifts

I have a very simple theology on the gifts of the Holy Spirit. It has been my experience over the last thirty years that when I pray for the Holy Spirit to make Himself manifest, He does.

Of course, He is present all the time, whether we can feel Him or see Him or not. But sometimes He makes Himself known to us in ways we cannot explain adequately on paper. He is a person, a fully God person in spiritual form. He cannot be contained. He cannot be fully described. But He is not complicated.

Whenever I ask Him to come and meet with a group of people, He is so kind. He never says no. He never says He is too busy. He will come and work miracles among the people. I ask everyone not to focus on me or on anything going on around the front. I ask them to look at what He is doing in them.

Sometimes He stretches people's faith. He calls them to new purpose. He sends holy fire on them to encourage them and strengthen them in their calling. Sometimes He heals people of deep emotional hurt, pain, discomfort and illness. There is nothing He cannot make right.

I have seen many people start to speak in a tongue when the Spirit comes on them. They all have one thing in common. They have relinquished their rights. They have handed their lives over. They have released any control.

When we allow the Spirit of the living, loving God to fill us, He will spill out all of His goodness on us. It is overwhelming to sense His presence like this. It may knock us to the floor. It may make us cry or laugh or sing or praise or jump or wail. God will not be put in a box and be told what He is allowed to do. He will come into you. But only if you let Him. He is a loving God, not a forcing God. He will not give you anything you don't really want. He will not let you have anything you will not use. He knows your heart.

Have you released control of your life today?

Come Closer

• I believe a voice is crying out deeply inside the heart of the world, asking the same thing my Norwegian brothers asked on that mission boat trip. "How will we know where the Christians are?"

• What distinguishes us from people who give to charity? What sets us apart from those who adopt children? What makes us different to the world? Jesus said they will know us by our love (see John 13:35), not by our teaching. Not by the size of our cars or the beauty of our houses or the wealth of our churches or the color of our suits. They will know us by our love.

• When that little old lady got on her knees and washed my feet, she did it unto God. That's why it was so moving. She was not venerating me. She was serving a fellow sister in Christ. She was preferring my needs above her own.

• Those of us who are indwelt by the Spirit of God have been promised something—power! We are not a weak people. We are not a poor people. We have power. This means we are strong, we are able. It means we are worthy to stand for what God has called us to stand for. It means we can accomplish all He asks of us each day.

• Think now of some Christians around you who need to know they are filled with the Spirit of God. Maybe they need filling up again today. Pray with me now for all our brothers and sisters across the world, especially those who are suffering for the sake of Christ.

Lord, You came as a servant. You made Yourself nothing and emptied Yourself for me. Help me to see others who need my service. Help me to find ways to bless and encourage Your people. May I work for You in a way that is constantly refueled and refilled. Help me not to serve You from a place of spiritual emptiness, but from a place of emptying. Bless all Your family across the world today. May those who are standing for Your truth be honored and know Your great mercies and peace. Amen.

Transformation

I am no stranger to the enemies of God. Plenty of times we have had rocks thrown at us. We have even been attacked with machetes, and some of us have been sent to jail for what we believe. But it has not discouraged us. We know we have the power of the Holy Spirit working in and through us.

A huge transformation happened in the apostles after the Holy Spirit came. When Jesus was on trial, Peter was so afraid He couldn't even own up to being His friend.

"A servant-girl saw him seated there in the firelight. She looked closely at him and said, 'This man was with him.' But he denied it. 'Woman, I don't know him,' he said. A little later someone else saw him and said, 'You also are one of them.' 'Man, I am not!' Peter replied. About an hour later another asserted, 'Certainly this fellow was with him, for he is a Galilean.' Peter replied, 'Man, I don't know what you're talking about!' Just as he was speaking, the cock crowed. The Lord turned and looked straight at Peter. Then Peter remembered the word the Lord had spoken to him: 'Before the cock crows today, you will disown me three times.' And he went outside and wept bitterly." (Luke 22:56–62)

Peter didn't have any ability to witness. He couldn't stand up for Jesus, and he was terrified about what others said to him and what was going to happen to his beloved friend.

But when the Holy Spirit fell on him, everything changed! In Acts 2:14, "Peter stood up with the Eleven, raised his voice and addressed the crowd.." The man who couldn't witness started preaching! The result of his message was that "about three thousand were added to their number" (Acts 2:41).

What an amazing transformation!

Like Peter, you have the power of the Holy Spirit working in you. Perhaps you have lacked boldness in certain areas of your life. Ask Holy Spirit to come and fill you afresh and transform you, like Peter, with great boldness for the Gospel.

Divine Protection

Often when I am preaching I sense the enemy crouching around trying to distract people or make them anxious. He will do anything to stop people from committing themselves to Jesus.

But the power of prayer is so strong, and at the very name of Jesus, demons have no choice but to flee. Ephesians 6:10–12 reminds us how we can protect ourselves against the enemy's attacks and devices.

"Finally, be strong in the Lord and in his mighty power. Put on the full armor of God, so that you can take your stand against the devil's schemes. For our struggle is not against flesh and blood, but against the rulers, against the authorities, against the powers of this dark world and against the spiritual forces of evil in the heavenly realms."

It may look as though people are against us, but the enemy is behind their attacks. It may look as though authorities have it in for us, but behind their actions are the forces of darkness.

When David fought Goliath, he didn't come at him with a sword or a spear or someone else's ill-fitting armor. David said, "The Lord doesn't save by using a sword or a spear. And everyone who is here will know it. The battle belongs to the Lord" (see 1 Samuel 17:47).

As we step out in the power of God, we need to remind ourselves that the battle belongs to the Lord, and He has already won. But we must not be unwise and face the battle without the protection He has provided.

Consider It Pure Joy

In the Church, we don't talk enough about heavenly rewards. We don't like the thought of some people getting a better or a worse deal. But heavenly rewards are mentioned in the Bible, so we'd better know what it says.

"Then Jesus said to his disciples, 'Whoever wants to be my disciple must deny themselves and take up their cross and follow me. For whoever wants to save their life will lose it, but whoever loses their life for me will find it. What good will it be for someone to gain the whole world, yet forfeit their soul? Or what can anyone give in exchange for their soul? For the Son of Man is going to come in his Father's glory with his angels, and then he will reward each person according to what they have done.'" (Matthew 16:24–27)

The Church teaches a lot about staying out of trouble, but actually we need to get into trouble! Why? Because Jesus will reward each one of us for what we have done.

I am not talking about deliberately offending someone or being rude to a fellow believer. I am talking about things we actually get rewarded for— overcoming, enduring to the end, destroying the work of the devil, showing the world what we think of God.

Taking it easy, allowing life to just go along, with everything safe and fine, is actually the best way for us to short-change ourselves. We don't get rewarded for that kind of living.

I really understand James when he said, "Consider it pure joy, my brothers and sisters, whenever you face trials of many kinds, because you know that the testing of your faith produces perseverance" (James 1:2–3). That is what I want—perseverance under fire, not boredom on a sofa!

Paul explains it further in 2 Corinthians 12:10: "...I delight in weaknesses, in insults, in hardships, in persecutions, in difficulties. For when I am weak, then I am strong."

When we rely on God in this way, no matter what we are facing, not only are we rewarded in eternity, but we also get to spend our earthly lives maturing and becoming more like Jesus.

Shoulder to Shoulder

In 1980, we began IRIS Global as a holistic ministry by taking small evangelistic street drama teams to Asia on short-term mission trips. Our emphasis was the creative presentation of the Gospel, and our ministry grew greatly. But we were so impacted by the condition of the poor that we changed direction drastically. We began to "stop for the one" and show the love of God by first addressing the temporal needs of the broken and humble—"the least of these" (Matthew 25:45). We focused on the bottom of society rather than the top. Because of our stance on this and other issues, we are often accused of being all sorts of things we are not.

We do not court controversy. But sometimes it comes our way. I think this is because neither one of us fits the mold of a "typical missionary."

But we are orthodox, center-of-the-road, Bible believing Christians. We believe in the need for repentance, faith in Jesus and the power of the cross. We stand shoulder to shoulder with the great company of witnesses down the centuries. We have not invented anything new or come up with some brand of teaching that is contrary to Scripture. We stand within the Body of Christ with respect for our fellow believers in the Lord. We are not a wacky, weird, out-there group of followers. We are just a bunch of people seeking to serve God and lay down our lives for Him.

The most important thing to us is not what people think of us but who God says we are. We don't dismiss the comments of those in the Body of Christ, but neither do we rely on them to be either right or wrong.

What we set out to start thirty years ago has flourished and grown under the guidance and leadership of our Holy God, and we are so grateful for His calling and joyful in our service of Him.

Won't you join us, shoulder to shoulder, in laying down our lives with reckless devotion to our King?

Creative Communication

Heidi and I have always sought to communicate the Gospel well. Over the years we have told people about Jesus in many ways—dance, song, theater presentations and even talking, when that has seemed best. Reaching God's world with the Good News requires creativity, because He made so many different sorts of people.

Sometimes our work has been to help translate parts of the Bible alongside others, like the Wycliffe translators. These men and women are champions of the faith who think nothing of spending twenty years in a tribe somewhere—watching and observing the language, learning it, developing a coded system of sounds and an alphabet and then going about the laborious but wonderful task of translating parts or, in some cases, all of the Bible.

In 1991, I was privileged to work among a people group in South West China, near Tibet. These wonderful people had never before had their language written down. Nothing had ever been printed in their mother tongue. Can you imagine that? Not one word of their history or their stories was recorded anywhere except in their collective memories.

Working closely with them and with an ingenious linguist named Robert Morrison, I invented an alphabet for them. It wasn't easy, because their language has many more sounds than English. It wasn't just a case of finding 26 letters and turning them into symbols. It was much more complex. We had to invent letters that stood for sounds and then teach the people how to read them. Can you imagine their joy when they read their own words and their own language for the first time?

We were so blessed to have Robert working with us. God has made him so fast at his work that he could translate more of the Bible in six months than some linguists could in twenty years. He was given such a skill in this area.

God calls us to be those who reach out to those around us—sometimes in ways that look impossible or improbable. Often, He will send us people who will stand with us to accomplish what is on His heart.

Who has God sent to you today to help you as you serve the Lord?

Smugglers

Heidi and I are no strangers to dangerous situations and close calls. God has gotten us out of some tight spots and allowed us to do some amazing things with Him and for Him. In the days when no Bibles were allowed in China, God sent us in. Guess what we had in our suitcases. That's right—a lot of Bibles!

We took a Chinese plane, and each of us had a case filled to the brim with heavy Bibles, with a light layer of clothes on top to form some kind of disguise. We walked slowly carrying the massive weight of those cases through the airport. Our lack of speed meant we were the last people into the customs house. Every single passenger on our plane was already there. Every single case was opened and officials were inspecting every single sock, toothbrush and all the other items that had once been neatly packed but now looked a total mess. I glanced at Heidi and she looked back, alarmed.

Inwardly we both prayed very short and very desperate prayers. Some of our most profound prayers have just been one word—Jesus! He knows what we need!

One guard looked at me, "Put your suitcase up here," he bellowed. "I want to check it." In my head I was saying the word God! over and over again. In those days, we locked our luggage. Most suitcases had a little key.

So I started to fumble around in my pockets for my keys. I pretended I had a whole bunch of stuff in my pockets. I looked at the guard. He was getting cross and fidgety. He wanted to go home. He was tired. I kept up the pretense a little longer.

"Forget it!" he shouted, "Just go!"

For some reason we will never know, Heidi's suitcase just shot through the scanning machine, and the Bibles went unnoticed. We ended up with the only two cases unopened in the whole plane.

Isn't that so like our God?

He likes to work miracles for you, too. What miracles do you need Him to perform in your life today? What obstacles are trying to block your work for Him? Cry out with that simple and powerful prayer—Jesus!

Come Closer

• A huge transformation always occurs when the Holy Spirit is given free rein to do what He likes in us and through us. Sometimes He will answer the craziest prayers, provide impossible ways out, offer miracles or turn our attitudes around.

• As you spend time getting lower and slower before God, drink in the presence of the Holy Spirit wherever you are and however you are feeling. He is with you. Take some time to stop your mind from whirring and your heart from wondering about the many things you have been busy with today. Make a note of anything you need to remember later, but then stop.

• Maybe you are struggling to be still because your life feels chaotic and in some kind of turmoil. One of the main distractions to prayer is a lack of quiet and stillness, both inside and outside a person. An old Latin quotation taken from an inscription found in a pub in Pitlochry, Scotland, says: Venit ad nos ut ad eum veniemus. It translates best as: "He came to us that we might come to him."

• Do your best to do that now. Just come. Be still before Him now and offer yourself as you are, with all your thoughts and feelings, your successes and failures. Hold nothing back. Give yourself with reckless devotion.

Whom to Bless?

As we walked down the road in China, our heavy suitcases full to bursting with Bibles—illegal Bibles—we wondered what to do next. Whom should we give them to? Some people had prayed twenty years for such a treasured possession. We didn't want to get it wrong and give it to someone who would not appreciate it. So we asked Holy Spirit to lead us to the right people and the right places. He did not let us down. He never has.

He led us to person after person who had been praying in secret for so long. Some cried. Others almost did back flips for joy. There were tears and laughter and screams of excitement. God was answering their prayers.

We reached one place where we knew we had to take the Bibles. But it was heavily guarded. We asked the Lord to send us a local Chinese Christian who could smuggle the Bibles in. God heard us and connected us with a wonderfully humble man. When we told him what we wanted to do, he wept because he had been in prison many times for smuggling the Good News and declaring Jesus. Through his tears of joy, he said something I have never forgotten: "I am just not worthy of such a great task!" He got the Bibles through.

We did not know, at the time, that twenty years earlier a prophet of God had visited that town and told the people, "God is going to bring the Bible in your language to this place." Nobody believed him. He was laughed at, dismissed and ridiculed. But God had spoken the truth. That night the people danced. They danced around fires for weeks, praising God for fulfilling His word. We met an entirely different category of Christians on that trip. God had been readying His people for revival.

None of us can make revival happen. But God has called each of us—like the humble Chinese believer who knew he was not worthy of such a great task—to share the love of Jesus. As we do, He will lead us to the ones who are hungry for the Good News. As we faithfully listen and obey, He will bring the increase.

Start As You Mean to Go On

As a younger couple, we were told how we ought to go about becoming people God could use. People told us to start off as assistant pastors somewhere small, to run a nice youth group and learn the ropes of leadership. They told us to try to influence a small town first and then move up to a bigger one. They told us to think about feasibility studies and personal fundraising.

Something about all of that seemed so unexciting for me. I did not want to be any of that. That was not what was burning in my heart. I wanted something much simpler. I wanted revival. We both did. We weren't interested in normal procedures and human-made routes to a so-called "successful" ministry.

We were so sold out on God we just wanted Him to use us to do something miraculous and exciting. We decided we needed teams to help us. We had no experience in training others, so we learned on the job. The next six months of our lives were the most hair-raising, unbelievable time. We lived every day with our hearts in our mouth, with our faith being tested off the charts. We didn't know how we were going to feed anyone on our team, where we were going to preach, where we would sleep. Absolutely everything we experienced was totally miraculous. It had to be. God was in control, and we were not.

Matthew 10 tells us the conversation Jesus had with the twelve before He sent them out. One of the verses speaks this incredible truth: "What I tell you in the dark, speak in the daylight; what is whispered in your ear, proclaim from the roofs" (verse 27).

We saw God provide for us day after day. We started how we were meant to continue. Some thirty years later, God still has this kind of relationship with us. If we need something, we ask. Then it comes. It may not come in the way we think or in the timing we had in mind. But it will come.

He will do the same for you if you will lean on Him and give Him full control of your life.

The Presence

It's nearly impossible to go to a Billy Graham crusade and not get saved. The Spirit is so strong and the power is so great. You can't leave without feeling it. Those meetings are soaked in the majesty of God.

Heidi and I are wired in this same way. We would starve on a diet of basic doctrinal evangelism without the manifest presence of the Holy Spirit. We have a built in non-negotiable hunger for God. Don't get me wrong. We love Scripture, and we need the Word of God every single day, but the Lord speaks to us in our ears, too (see Matthew 10:27).

My dad told us that in our first six months in Indonesia we saw more miracles than he had seen in twenty years. Why was that? Was it because God liked us more or favored us more or because we trusted Him more? No. It was because of the presence of the Holy Spirit.

By nature I have always gravitated to the white-hot center. I am not a mediocre kind of guy. I don't want to hurt people, but my views are pretty set on this. I feel called to feed the hungriest of the hungry, not just physically but spiritually, too.

When I heard about the Indonesian revival and the incredible miracles happening there, I wanted to get there as fast as I could. I wanted to see people raised from the dead. I wanted to be in the presence of deep, abounding faith. I was fed up with being surrounded by doubt and apathy so thick you could cut it with a knife.

So we left America with the unheeded advice of many well-meaning people in our ears and thirty dollars in our pockets. We were so excited. The enemy had tried so hard to keep us back and stop us from going, but God had won.

Wherever we have gone, we have known the presence of God. We have waited on Him. We have pressed in for more, and we have sought Him first. Without Him we would be nothing. The same is true for you. In whatever you do, be sure to seek His presence first, to always live with reckless devotion to Him.

Ice Cream God

When we started out, we called ourselves Rainbow Productions. We were a street drama company—a completely broke one. We couldn't afford our own transportation, so getting anywhere was always a big adventure.

I remember being squeezed into tiny seats on a 24-hour bus trip, our knees in our chins, with all our suitcases piled high in the aisle. One time we encountered a 200-mile-long traffic jam. The driver was asleep on the hood of the bus. The smoky air and heat swirled through the little van. On those sorts of days, we had to keep smiling and remembering why we were doing it.

All the trips involved bouncing through dry river beds. We would sit on unforgiving wooden benches in the back, bouncing up and down with every pothole; our ribs and bottoms were bruised for weeks afterward. One day, after a long trip, we had a stopover in an industrial smoke-filled slum town for nine hours. As we got out into the hot, broken down bus stop, which was nothing more than an office with dirty windows, my sister let out a sigh. Trying to be funny and lighten the mood, she said, "God, give us some ice cream."

We had brought a beggar with us on the trip. He had told us he needed to go where we were going, so we let him tag along. At this moment he piped up, "I have an old friend who runs the biggest ice cream factory in this area. I will call him."

Moments later, ice cream trucks appeared. Not only that, but we were driven to the businessman's home. He happened to be an extremely wealthy businessman who owned a large mansion replete with a swimming pool. We spent nine hours enjoying his hospitality and sampling the most delicious ice creams his company sold—including mango, pineapple and other exotic flavors. Nine hours later, we were back in the bus depot waiting for our trip, rested, sunned and stuffed full of ice cream.

We discovered the power of God that day in a fresh way. He heard the longings of our hearts, just like we heard the longings of His. He hears the longings of your heart, too.

Seek Me and Find Me

One of the key Bible passages for us, in whatever we have been doing, is Jeremiah 29:11–13:

"For I know the plans I have for you," declares the Lord, "plans to prosper you and not to harm you, plans to give you hope and a future. Then you will call on me and come and pray to me, and I will listen to you. You will seek me and find me when you seek me with all your heart."

I love those words, and I speak them often to other people. They are a comfort and an encouragement in my walk with God. I love that it says I can call on Him, and I love that He promises to listen to me and help me seek Him and find Him.

Sadly, this belief in God's voice is not universal in the Church. Some people actually strongly contest the idea that God speaks today, that He wants to be found in this way and that He likes to hear our prayers.

What does it mean to find God? What does it mean to seek after Him with all your heart?

If we don't do this, what are we left with—a missionary calling, a ministry project, some attainable goals, some decisions for Christ, mental assent to important doctrines? I am not decrying any of these things. They are important. But they are not the reason why we are alive.

I have wonderful friends from other church backgrounds who object to my newsletters. They don't like our encounters with and revelations from God. They do not consider it "sound" or normal Christian experience. For them Christianity is not about feelings but facts. It is about getting the job done, preaching the truth, convincing people into the Kingdom. It is about doing the work of an evangelist but not expecting anything more.

I can't live that way. I need more. I need to seek God daily, expecting to hear from Him. And I do.

He loves to speak to each one of us, personally. He loves to speak to you. What is He saying to you today?

Finding God

Every day we learn more. God teaches us so many precious lessons as we serve Him in what we do. The things we believe are not unique to us. People have been doing what we do for thousands of years. But of course, each of us has a slightly different take on how we seek to carry out the Great Commission.

I am fascinated with the many ways people present the Gospel. Whenever I travel, I try to spend some time watching local Christian TV to see how people speak about Jesus. I find it amazing what a breadth of experience, wisdom and thought exists.

There can be dangers though. It is possible to be so captivated with our experiences of God, the manifestations, miracles and phenomena—the effects of His presence—that we actually miss God altogether. Great saints of God have faced this problem, too. Some were so intent on getting close to God, on finding union with Him, that they did not want to see visions, in case they were a distraction to their faith. They didn't want to see with their physical eyes in case it detracted from what they saw with the eyes of faith.

It is a little like reading a great book and then seeing the film afterward. Your own ideas are colored by what you see. Early mystics and men and women of faith did not want that kind of distraction.

It is possible to idolize miracles and manifestations over the person of Jesus. And, of course, the exact opposite is possible, too, when people decry any outward sign of God.

The verse we looked at yesterday, Jeremiah 29:13, says, "You will find me." That is the most exciting thing to me. It is not about bringing heaven to earth, feeding orphans, seeing nations transformed or establishing justice. All these are worthy and wonderful, but they are not the same as finding God.

My most exciting mission on earth is not to be a missionary in Mozambique but to find Jesus—not the things He does but the person He is.

What excites you? What is your mission?

Come Closer

"Seek me and live. Don't fool around at those shrines of Bethel. Don't waste time taking trips to Gilgal, and don't bother going down to Beer-sheba. Gilgal is here today and gone tomorrow and Bethel is all show, no substance. So seek GOD and live! You don't want to end up with nothing to show for your life but a pile of ashes, a house burned to the ground. For God will send just such a fire, and the firefighters will show up too late." (Amos 5:4–6, MESSAGE)

• These are sobering words. Let's focus on a few of them. God says, "Seek me and live." What does that mean to you? When I read those words, I think about what it means to seek and find God with all my heart. I think about the mandate of Jesus when He spoke in John 10:10, "...I came so they can have real and eternal life, more and better life than they ever dreamed of" (MESSAGE).

• Ask yourself honestly if your life is a better life than you thought possible. Is it more exciting, more wonderful, more abundant, more fulfilling, more challenging, more incredible than you ever dreamed it would be? Or is it safe, ordinary, dull and far from it? Jesus came not to give us rules and regulations but to give us life and life to the full.

Pray with me now:

Jesus, Thank You for taking me on this adventure through my life. There are so many blank pages ahead. Help me to fill them with exciting and satisfying service of You. Help me to be one who seeks You and finds You. Help me not to seek Your hand as much as I seek Your face. Forgive me for the times I have asked You for blessings and miracles instead of simply for the gift of Your presence. I thank You that this is all I need. You are my portion (see Psalm 16:5). Amen.

Jealous

I am learning that God is a jealous God. This is a problem for some of us. We see jealousy in a negative, as a sin. But we need to remember that the root of God's jealousy is not sin at all. At the heart of God's jealousy is love. God knows what is best for us, and it hurts Him when we choose another over Him.

Deuteronomy 4:24 says: "For the Lord your God is a consuming fire, a jealous God."

God wants to consume anything that keeps us from loving Him first. When I first realized this, I complained to Him, saying, "God, isn't there anything or anyone you are not jealous of?"

"No," He said.

That was it. He wants to be the focus of our lives. This is not because He is selfish or unkind but because He is loving and wants us to understand His intentions for us.

Human jealousy is often rooted in envy. A person might be jealous of someone because of some kind of skill or ability that person has. But God is not jealous of us in this way, of course. He doesn't envy us our skills and our talents. He is not jealous of our prowess or our beauty. His jealousy for us is a pure and wonderful thing.

God is possessive of the worship and service that belong to Him—and rightly so. He knows the mess idolatry gets people into. He doesn't want that for me, and He doesn't want it for you. He designed you to love Him first. I guess the question is, Do you?

Affection for Jesus

I have found out that no amount of ministry success, miracles, healings, offerings and even prayers of salvation can take the place of affection for Jesus. All these things are fantastic; without them we are nothing more than a dead branch. We love fruit like this, but it has to come from a place of loving affection.

Sometimes I watch evangelists preach. They talk about the amazing schedules they have, the effects of their healings, the money they are offered or the favor on their ministry. They talk about the Bible or speak about encounters they have with people. But it is possible to do all that without even mentioning Jesus. And some of them manage it.

I don't think you can have one without the other. I want to see all those things happening too, but they have to flow from a heart that is totally in love with Jesus. I don't want to be so excited about all the things Jesus can do. I want to be excited about Jesus Himself.

Consider the story in Luke 2:43–44, where Mary and Joseph take Jesus to Jerusalem for Passover. "After the festival was over, while his parents were returning home, the boy Jesus stayed behind in Jerusalem, but they were unaware of it. Thinking he was in their company, they travelled on for a day..."

Sometimes we can leave Jesus out of our travelling. We can walk ahead and think He is in our company. But He is not. We can leave Him out of our services, our preaching and even our worship. That is a frightening thought, but it is true.

We all need to have a daily encounter with Him. We need to examine our hearts and test our thinking. More than this, we need to spend time in the presence of Jesus.

Jesus—the Image of God

Imagine how hard it would be to relate to an invisible spirit or to follow God without the model of Christ. Imagine the Bible without any of His stories. Imagine the Word of God without the Gospel. Imagine the story of love without the cross. Imagine trying to understand heaven without the resurrection. It would all be so hard.

The truth is, we need Jesus to understand God. We need Jesus to have faith. God chose to manifest Himself fully in Jesus. Jesus is fully God, yet in a form we can fully identify with. Jesus came so we might have a perfect companion—in the image of the invisible God.

The most common request I get via email comes from people who want a more intimate relationship with Him. So many people tell me their churches don't teach them how to love Jesus more, but instead how to be the best "them" they can be. Much of the Church is obsessed with prosperity, influence, ambition. I have a hard time seeing that in Jesus.

He made Himself nothing. He emptied Himself and took the position of a lowly servant. It is up to Him whether or not I have influence or affluence. He can use me as He likes, because He is sovereign and in charge. It is my not ambition to be more successful. He is my ambition.

The Church does not talk about Jesus enough. People don't want a romance with Jesus; they want a God who helps them do. They want to pay the rent and get a job and do good deeds. But Jesus can be all things. He can be tough and strong and at the same time wonderfully affectionate and gentle.

"He is the image of the invisible God, the firstborn of all creation. For by Him all things were created, both in the heavens and on earth, visible and invisible, whether thrones or dominions or rulers or authorities—all things have been created through Him and for Him. He is before all things, and in Him all things hold together." (Colossians 1:15–17)

Won't you join me today in making Jesus your sole ambition, in pursuing Him with reckless devotion? Knowing Him is the best part.

Supernatural Normality

For some people, supernatural occurrences are rare—or non-existent. They hear about miracles. They may read about miracles, but they would not expect to witness a miracle in a million years.

Heidi and I are not those kind of people. Manifestations and visitations of God are not rare in our experience. In fact, they are daily happenings that keep us on track.

Heidi came to God in such a supernatural way, at the age of sixteen, that she sees supernatural experiences as "normal." Some people we know are so used to visions and miracles that they almost take them for granted as part and parcel of their faith.

This is what we have learned. To the extent that we open ourselves up to God and totally trust and depend on Him, God will arrive and miracles will occur. Are we blasé about this? No. Do we expect God to do things in this way? Yes.

I have been careful to say that all the manifestations and blessing and honor in this life do not mean a thing if God isn't central. But when He is in His rightful place, He can do amazing and wonderful things.

We live on miracles. We don't just enjoy them once in a while. We don't just believe they happen. We live them. We don't just need them from time to time. We don't need them to fill in for us, in case our plans don't work out. We start off with them. They are our Plan A. We utterly depend on them. We know we cannot function without them.

What about you? Is your life a string of miracles, or is it empty of the supernatural? Why could this be?

Lack of Faith

Not everyone we have worked with has our stance on miracles. In fact, for many Christians it is a very contentious and controversial issue.

Years ago, we started off as missionaries in Bali in Indonesia. At that time, it was such a strong Hindu area that Christian missionaries were summarily beheaded, killed or sent home. The government was incredibly anxious about any kind of Christian presence, and the few Christians who remained were bullied and ostracized. Demons were everywhere.

Among three million people, only two missionaries existed. When we arrived, we doubled that number. It was a wild and crazy time. Many powerful witchdoctors practiced supernatural dark arts. We were cursed so many times we lost count. Demons manifested in front of us, appearing to us looking like some of the masks the tribal people wore.

The problem was, the two other missionaries did not believe in miracles. They saw all the demon possession, the dark supernatural forces at work, but they did not believe they could counter any of it with the power of God. We could not believe it. We were on the same team but not working in the same way.

Once God is the most exciting thing in our lives, He loves to do exciting things with us and for us. We saw a large number of people set free from demon possession during our time there. God also did plenty of miracles. We would not have survived for one day if He had not.

I always find it sobering to read in Matthew 13:58 of a time when Jesus was not able to perform miracles. "And he did not do many miracles there because of their lack of faith."

If we believe God can perform amazing deeds, our belief somehow activates Him. He loves to operate in an atmosphere of expectancy and faith. How expectant are you for a miracle today?

Fresh Revelation

I love new things. In fact, I am so grateful God's mercies are new every morning. I need Him to be like that for me. He doesn't give us old mercy. He doesn't give us old revelation. It is always new and fresh and pure.

As Lamentations 3:22–24 says, "God's loyal love couldn't have run out, his merciful love couldn't have dried up. They're created new every morning. How great your faithfulness! I'm sticking with God (I say it over and over). He's all I've got left" (MESSAGE).

In the New International Version, this passage says, "Because of the LORD's great love we are not consumed, for his compassions never fail. They are new every morning; great is your faithfulness" (Lamentations 3:22–23).

Aren't you glad you have a God like that?

I love to wake up in the morning and think, What is exciting about You today, Lord? What new things do you have for me to learn? What fresh ideas are you going to give me? I always start with Him.

That is what keeps me going. I would die if I had to repeat yesterday. I want to find God to a greater degree today than I did yesterday. I know He will reveal Himself to me in new ways that I couldn't have imagined last year or last month. Why? Because His Word tells me so. His compassions are new every morning. I have a fresh supply when I wake up each day. That is why life is so amazing.

When I ask most people what they live for, they say the saddest things. They talk about being the best politician or soccer player, or they mention how they want to get a 2 percent market share increase over the next ninety days. What is all of that for? It is so temporary. It is not looking at life from eternity's perspective.

I need so much more than that.

I need Jesus at the very center of my being; then, when I get some of those peripheral things, they will mean so much more. The same will be true for you. Make Him your purpose, and He will make your heart and life full.

Come Closer

• Some of us look for Jesus a little bit, but then we give up. Some of us don't even realize we have left Him behind. Like Mary and Joseph, we are happily chatting away to other people on the journey, totally unthinking about where He is. I don't want to leave Jesus behind in any of my decisions. I don't want to leave Him behind when I worship or preach or minister or pray. I need Him to be there in the center.

• I need Him to be jealous for my heart and jealous for my affections. I need Him to tell me if my balance is off or if someone or something else is vying too hard for my attention and pulling me away from Him. Consider what He might be saying to you about this.

• If you long to see more miracles in your own life, remember that what attracts God to us more than anything is our faith. Ask God to give you an uncompromising and growing faith that expects Him to move supernaturally. Don't give up praying just because you don't see an answer in the next day or so. Sometimes we must push in hard in prayer before God will answer. At other times, God will answer us straight away. He is in charge of the timings of all things and will do what is best for us and to bring Him glory.

• It is wonderful to know God's compassions are new every day. Maybe this week you have felt in need of those daily blessings because of something you are going through. Perhaps this week has led you to feel in need of time reorganizing your priorities and putting Jesus back in the center of your world again.

• Think for a minute about the character of Jesus and what you love about Him. Perhaps take some time now to formulate your own prayer, thanking Him for who He is.

Believe It

Matthew 6:25–26 has been an incredible passage for our ministry, a benchmark.

"Therefore I tell you, do not worry about your life, what you will eat or drink; or about your body, what you will wear. Is not life more than food, and the body more than clothes? Look at the birds of the air; they do not sow or reap or store away in barns, and yet your heavenly Father feeds them. Are you not much more valuable than they?"

Can they be true? Can we live by them? we wondered. What would life look like if we actually believed what the Bible says here?

Jesus addressed His listeners' biggest fears with encouragement to seek God for everything they needed. He reminded His followers, "Your heavenly father knows what you need" (see Matthew 6:32).

My own father found those words so difficult. My grandfather had been a revivalist, but my dad was an old school missionary. He was always telling us we had to be practical, that missionary work was about discipline and coping with disappointment. He wanted us to be realistic.

He was in a constant war with Heidi and me. When he got really mad with us, he would say, "You remind me more of your grandfather than anyone else I know!" I took that as a compliment.

My dad did many great things. People used to take his Bible classes twice because they were fun and had incredible depth of knowledge. But he was ultra conservative in matters of faith. Dad would get so upset with us. He did not want us to take the Sermon on the Mount as literal truth. He wanted us to see the meaning in the words and live by the themes of them—as he had done. But we wanted the fullness. We saw such holiness, beauty, passion and excitement in those words.

So we decided we were not going to be missionaries unless the Sermon on the Mount was totally true. That's how we started out.

What about you? Do you believe the Sermon on the Mount can be totally true in your life? Ask Holy Spirit to help you trust Him with your needs more today.

Specific Words

Years ago, while Heidi was on a trip to Mexico, God told her she would marry a man named Rolland Baker. He even told her the day I would ask her. God was very specific with her. He also told her we would go to Indonesia as missionaries. We relied on those words. They were everything to us in our early days.

We had to do everything by faith. At our wedding we didn't ask for presents. All we wanted was money for our airfare. On our wedding night, we added up the money we had been given. It was exactly enough for two one-way tickets to Indonesia.

We were not going to get up in front of people, moaning about being poor and acting like we had no provision. We knew God is our provider. We believed in the Sermon on the Mount.

God didn't tell us to go to others for finances. He told us to go to Him first and trust Him to give all we needed. This has been our experience. We have trusted God, not when we have run out of things but from the very start.

Matthew 6:28–30 tells us more about how God provides for His people:

And why do you worry about clothes? See how the flowers of the field grow. They do not labor or spin. Yet I tell you that not even Solomon in all his splendor was dressed like one of these. If that is how God clothes the grass of the field, which is here today and tomorrow is thrown into the fire, will he not much more clothe you—you of little faith?

When we first went to Indonesia, our church had promised us $1,000 a month. Unfortunately, a crisis in the church leadership arose, and we never got a dollar. A few months later, we called to see if any money had been put in our bank account, and it hadn't. God wanted to prove to us that He was all we needed.

He is all you need, too. Trust Him today with all your needs. Trust Him enough to go when He says go, no matter what. He will come through for you.

Living on God's Words

Matthew 4 tells us the amazing story of the devil tempting Jesus in the desert. "The tempter came to him and said, 'If you are the Son of God, tell these stones to become bread.' Jesus answered, 'It is written: "Man shall not live on bread alone, but on every word that comes from the mouth of God"'" (Matthew 4:3–4).

We really fed on God's words in our early days in Indonesia. We were so starving hungry to hear from Him. We had nothing but the joy of the Lord. We both lost a great deal of weight. My wedding ring actually fell off because my hands got so thin. Food was really scarce, and we didn't have any money. Occasionally a lady in a village would take pity on us and give us a can of noodles, and we would break an egg into it. That would be our only food for a week. We have never been hungrier.

One day God sent us an amazing present in the form of a guy from New Zealand who offered to buy us dinner. It was not just any meal but a big juicy steak for each of us. If you haven't eaten a solid meal in weeks, this is the most incredible gift. It was wonderful and such a boost for us.

Those were not easy times, but we decided we would rather die than give up. It took a lot of faith for us to learn how to take care of ourselves, then our kids, then a small team, and eventually a church.

God had to teach us the principle of trusting Him for everything, and He let us learn how to handle the little He gave us. Luke 16:10 says, "Whoever can be trusted with very little can also be trusted with much..."

God taught us many lessons in those years, lessons we have always tried to put into practice. What little things is God trusting you with at this moment?

Others Joining In

In the early days of IRIS, we did not think about having churches at all. Our ministry was primarily focused on helping and educating children. But adults started to hear about what we were doing with the children, and they wanted to be part of the movement.

We have always wanted to use whoever God has sent us.

We told the adults to start praying for those in need. They prayed for all sorts of people, for the sick and the lame, the deaf and the blind. They prayed for dead people, and the dead were raised. They started to see miracles and the power of the Holy Spirit at work, just like we had.

Faith working through love like this is the most powerful combination. We can't have one without the other.

We have not advertised for people to come and join us. We did not beg people to come and see what we are doing. God just sent them.

Financially we have had so many miracles. We have put millions of dollars into Mozambique without asking anyone for a dime. I find that so incredibly exciting. We don't have a TV ministry. We don't have to implore supporters to give to us. We just have to believe the Scripture is true. Scripture tells us we do not have to beg. We are not desperate for human help. We have a mighty all-powerful God to rely on.

The same is true for you. You don't have to tell people what you need. You don't have to plead with them to spare you some money. You don't have to ask people to come and join your ministry. They will just come when you are open to God and seek Him first.

Imitation

Let the message of Christ dwell among you richly as you teach and
admonish one another with all wisdom through psalms, hymns, and songs
from the Spirit, singing to God with gratitude in your hearts. And whatever
you do, whether in word or deed, do it all in the name of the Lord Jesus,
giving thanks to God the Father through him.
Colossians 3:16–17

We often speak about what God is doing in our midst. We love to tell stories
and boast in Jesus—in the manifestations, the miracles, the healing and the
provision. But we don't feel we need to persuade people to come and spend
time with us. We travel around the world and bring the wealth of faith from
the poor to the rich. Our people in Mozambique have very little financially,
but they are so wealthy in the Kingdom.

So many others in our field specialize in one kind of ministry over another.
Some are farming or agricultural specialists who teach people to farm the
land. Others work in education and training. Others focus on medication,
immunization or healing. We are so grateful for all those people and all they
do.

But we have realized God does not want us to imitate others or to specialize
in just one area. We are a holistic ministry. We need God for every sort
of outreach opportunity He sends us. He has used us to bring emotional
healing, physical provision and training; to build churches, schools, Bible
schools, ministry schools and more.

We are not specialists at healing crusades. People need food and water, too.
We are not specialists at schools or farming, because people need church,
too. We don't just teach Bible school, because people need the whole package.
God is a holistic God. He wants to give us everything we need, and He wants
us to be that for others.

You are not a cookie cutter Christian, either. God doesn't want you to look
and sound and act like anyone else. He wants you to imitate Christ in your
own unique way (see 1 Corinthians 11:1, NKJV). Who has He called you to
be?

No Room

Our expectation that the miraculous power of God is normal and natural in everyday life creates a lot of opposition for us. I get emails all the time from people who think we are wacky nut jobs. Many complain it is not wise or fair of us to preach what we preach.

Many people in Christian ministry spend their whole lives making contingency plans. Most missions are planned around the premise, "If God does nothing, what are we going to do?" They spend so long working out how they are going to network to find the right people or organize to get their funds in place. Everything is set up and predictable, leaving absolutely no room for surprises, for the Holy Spirit to move.

I love when things are effective. I married a woman who is a real go-getter. I don't know anyone who can get more done than Heidi. She is amazing, but she does it all from a place of being sold out to God, being recklessly devoted to Him. That is where her effectiveness lies.

Proverbs 19:21 says it well: "We humans keep brainstorming options and plans, but God's purpose prevails" (MESSAGE). Let us not be so organized that we push God out of our lives.

I want to challenge you today to leave room for God to move. Don't be so planned and organized and regular that there is no space for Him to surprise you.

Come Closer

• Here is an amazing prayer to say to Jesus today: I would like You to have the most exciting day because of me.

• I want Jesus to be glad He made me. Do you ever feel the same? I know I am the apple of His eye. I know He loves me and longs to see me be all I can be. More than that, I know He wrote His Word to be my guide, and He loves it when I take Him at His Word. He loves it when we live by Scripture.

• I want to set my heart on Him afresh, to remind myself of all He is to me and all He has done for me. I want to praise Him for every miracle, every kindness, every amount of grace He has ever shown me. I want to thank Him for every word from the Bible that has blessed me and challenged me, for every nugget of truth it contains.

• The longest Psalm in the Bible is Psalm 119. It is full of incredible wisdom. It begins in Hebrew with the words Ashrei temimei derech, which translate as "happy are those whose way is perfect." In what ways has God shown you His love for you through His perfect Word?

"Because I love your commands more than gold, more than pure gold, and because I consider all your precepts right, I hate every wrong path. Your statutes are wonderful; therefore I obey them. The unfolding of your words gives light; it gives understanding to the simple." (Psalm 119:127–130)

Father, often my understanding of things is so simple. I am so one-dimensional, God. Please show me how to live, not using my own wisdom but Yours. Help me not to organize and plan my life so much that I leave You out. Please teach me to trust in Your Word in a deeper, more radical way and not to use Your Word as a last resort. Amen.

Being a Child

Imagine being like a little child again and believing everything you hear. There is something so wonderful about that trusting, open-hearted naïveté that God loves.

The more I have grown up, the more I realize that maturity in Christ is all about "growing down." It is about becoming a child again. Not being childish but being child-like in our ways and our thinking.

For years, Psalm 131 has been my favorite psalm. I love the thoughts expressed here: "My heart is not proud, Lord, my eyes are not haughty; I do not concern myself with great matters or things too wonderful for me. But I have calmed and quieted myself, I am like a weaned child with its mother; like a weaned child I am content" (Psalm 131:1–2).

The whole psalm has only three verses, but I could preach for my whole life on it. I like it in all versions. I love where it says, "I am like a weaned child with its mother." In The Message it reads, "I've kept my feet on the ground, I've cultivated a quiet heart. Like a baby content in its mother's arms, my soul is a baby content" (verse 2).

Can you remember curling up with your mother and not worrying about anything? Have you ever experienced that sense that everything is well with the world and you don't have to do anything to be loved? That is such an amazing feeling.

Jesus was clear about how He saw children. In Matthew 18:2–4, we read:

"He called a little child to him, and placed the child among them. And he said: 'Truly I tell you, unless you change and become like little children, you will never enter the kingdom of heaven. Therefore, whoever takes the lowly position of this child is the greatest in the kingdom of heaven.'"

Being like a child in this way is actually the perfect picture of what it means to be a strong, responsible, mature adult Christian. It means having so much faith in Daddy that we can rest and be content.

We are not meant to grow up, but down. Have you experienced this in your life? In what way is Daddy God inviting you to "grow down" today?

God Can Tell

Some people sound really holy when they say they don't look for anything external, or they don't express themselves outwardly. I have heard some people say those who draw attention to themselves during worship are actually resisting the Holy Spirit. But my experience is different. I think it is awesome to be so totally in love with God that you cannot help moving your body in strange ways or making incredible noises. Love is sometimes involuntary. I think dancing like David danced, with all his might before the Lord, is a sign of true humility—not attention-seeking (see 2 Samuel 6:14). That kind of attitude truly honors God.

Remember why David was dancing. He was dancing out of awe. He had just seen God kill a man for his lack of respect in carrying the Ark (see 2 Samuel 6). David was not thinking about what his wife Michal might think. He did not mind that she despised him. He was only concerned about God's view of him. That is a good way to think.

Some people are worried about the flesh. They think their motives become mixed up, and they feel uncomfortable. They tie themselves in knots trying to work out why they did something. "I think that reaction may have been 62 percent flesh." God does not look at us like that. He looks at our hearts (see 1 Samuel 16:7). When we sing and dance, we are using our flesh in a voluntary way to praise and worship God. He likes that.

God can tell if you are really loving Him. People sometimes can't. Do not worry about what other people will think of your reaction to Him. He likes it when we give heart-felt responses.

Before God is the only place we can be truly free. We can't be free at the office or the supermarket. Some people may break out a little in the shower. But other than that, church should be the most unrestrained place you go to in the world. It should be where you can show God just how you feel about Him in any way He gives you.

Revival Indicators

God is an upside down God. His ways are above our ways, and His understanding is at a different level from our own (see Isaiah 55:9). Whenever we think we know what to do or how He might work in a situation, He shows us something completely different, something we were not expecting.

Humanly speaking, we want to impact as many people as possible, and we want to make the biggest difference we can make. So we might think we need to impact the most influential people in society. When we started out, we were told we needed to concentrate on big cities and crowded countries. We were advised to host leadership meetings and seminars with the "movers and shakers." We were told to invite business people and the rich and the famous, to be where the most people would gather. We were told such actions would cause a "trickle down" effect in our ministry. We were told not to waste time on the little people.

Many mission strategies run along those lines. Huge missionary journeys have begun with research to define where the most needs are and where the most people live. Organizations have planned and ploughed their resources into targeting the areas that research has given them to follow.

I got a hold of some of that research, and I found out the best way to waste your time would be to start something in Pemba, Mozambique. According to research, nothing should happen there. Instead, we have found it to be the most responsive group we have seen anywhere in the world. God has done immeasurably more than we could have dreamed or imagined there.

God doesn't start revivals based on statistics, percentages or data. He starts moves of His presence when His people fast and pray and call upon Him. As Psalm 91:15 says, "He will call upon me, and I will answer Him; I will be with him in trouble, I will deliver him and honor him."

Don't rely on human wisdom to decide where you should go or what you should do to serve the Lord. Listen to Him. He may take you somewhere unlikely, but when He is with you, the unlikely becomes likely.

Don't Despise Small

Do not despise these small beginnings, for the LORD rejoices to see the
work begin...
Zechariah 4:10, NLT

We started off doing dance, drama and theater before huge audiences. We
were involved in large public meetings in Hong Kong, Indonesia and Asia.
Thousands of people came to the shows. It was big stuff.

But then I heard about a revival in Mexico. It broke out in the most beautiful
way and had the gospels written all over it. What happened was so simple. A
Jesuit Catholic priest who was full of the spirit of God invited some beggars
from the local city dump to a special Thanksgiving dinner. That was all. It
doesn't sound that complicated, does it?

But a revival broke out. All kinds of miracles started to happen. Soon the
leaders of the city and other pastors got involved, and an incredible move of
God happened in that place. It got everyone's attention. Including ours.

That revival did not start with approaching the mayor and the politicians and
all the churches. It did not even start with prayer meetings or with getting
the educated and the influential together. Something of heaven came down
when the lowest and the least were invited to a feast.

Luke 14:12–14 says:

"...When you give a luncheon or dinner, do not invite your friends, your
brothers or sisters, your relatives, or your rich neighbors; if you do, they may
invite you back and so you will be repaid. But when you give a banquet,
invite the poor, the crippled, the lame, the blind, and you will be blessed.
Although they cannot repay you, you will be repaid at the resurrection of the
righteous."

God releases His power when we stop for one person, when we care for
those around us. Through the story of the Mexican revival, He began to
teach us about the heart of our mission. What about you? What are the small
beginnings in your life with God? Be sure to cherish them.

The Still Small Voice

One day we were in Hawaii, on the way to Asia, and we found ourselves at a little church where we met a Filipino lady who pleaded with us to go preach in her country. She was incredibly insistent.

"We don't have a ticket. We don't have any visas for the team," we replied, simply.

"I will tell my brother there about you, and he will look after you," she said. "Please go to the Philippines!"

Something about that lady caught my spirit, so I went to the Filipino embassy in the city. Incredibly, they gave us all visas that day with no trouble at all. The whole team was simply granted entry. It was truly remarkable. Our travel agent was also able to change our itinerary at no extra cost. It seemed clear God wanted us to go to the Philippines.

We had no money for anything, not even a hotel or food. We had nothing. We arrived in Manila trusting God was going to do something.

The lady had not told us who her brother was. As it turned out, he was a famous pilot with a flight demonstration team in the military. As we got off the plane, we were suddenly met by many people and told we were to be the guests of honor at a meeting for all military base personnel that evening. Of the 5,000 people there that evening, 2,500 came to the Lord.

The commander of the unit then gave us the use of his private jet so we could go and minister to all of the military people in that area. It was an incredible time.

Imagine if we had not listened to that little lady. Imagine if we had ignored her plea to go to her country. So much opportunity would have been lost.

What opportunities is God whispering to you today?

Where God Changed Us

We then visited a place in the south of the Philippines—an beautiful but poor island called Negros. The government there was corrupt, and unemployment and poverty were widespread. The people were desperate and diseased, and the streets were full of orphans and naked babies. It was hugely distressing.

We were staying with a very rich man. He had a large house with ornate iron gates that shut out the poverty and kept in the wealth. It was hard for us when those gates closed. The children would hold out their hands to us and cry for food. The man who hosted us was very angry with them. He told us not to believe their stories. He said their parents sent them out onto the streets to beg and lie about themselves, that they were not orphans at all.

One of the girls on our team gave a little girl one of her dresses. This made our host incredibly cross. He told us we were letting ourselves be taken advantage of, that these people would grab anything we gave them.

But we saw a different story. When we taught the children in a little Sunday school, they were dressed in rags. They were coughing up blood because of an outbreak of Tuberculosis. Their faces were not the faces of liars, putting on a show, but of children in desperate need of love and help and someone to care for them.

We had seen poor people before, but this was on another level. It was in our faces now, and the Holy Spirit was at work in us. Overnight, we ditched our large evangelistic meetings. They came to a complete stop.

We ended up back in Hong Kong with beggars in a back street. We came to a total stop for individual people. We were hungry for revival. We wanted more revival than we had ever seen. But we knew we were not going to find it in big meetings anymore. It had to start with the beggars on the rubbish dumps, the orphans, the poor and the forgotten.

God calls all of us to stop for the one, to pour out His love on the poor. What part is He calling you to play?

Come Closer

• I am so glad I serve a God who does not shut the iron gates on the poor. I am so glad I serve a King who invites the neediest, the most broken and the most hurt to His table. I am so glad I hold hands with a man who died that I might live.

• Heidi and I cannot stand by and watch little children dressed in nothing lying in the mud. We cannot sit in rich houses, drinking expensive tea when people outside have no clean water and are riddled with disease. God means more to us than that. He gave me so much love for these children. It was overwhelming. And it didn't just impact me. Heidi, too, was filled with a new compassion for those who were lost, lonely, little and forgotten.

• What about you? How do these kinds of stories impact your heart? What do they make you feel?

• I have met so many people who feel helpless because the problem is so huge. But even if we take one orphan off the streets, we have made a huge difference.

• What will your response be today to the still small voice of God who says, "Whom shall I send? And who will go for us?" (Isaiah 6:8). Spend time praying now, and ask God what He wants you to do differently.

The Least

If we want to understand what love looks and sounds like, we have to look at God.

God has more compassion than we can possibly understand. He shows his grace to the least of these (see Matthew 25:31–46). He doesn't start with the champions, the influencers, the revered and important. He starts with the nobodies. That gives me so much hope. I love that God starts at the bottom.

My grandfather spent five years in China as a missionary, doing everything "correctly" (in the way he had been told), and only one person got saved.

The second time he went to China, he had been filled with the Holy Spirit. He arrived not knowing what to do, but he was at peace. His wife started taking in beggar children and giving them baths and clean clothes. Their friends said they were wasting their time. But God poured out His Spirit on that house and on those children, and miracles started happening.

I learned from that. God's love chooses the ones nobody else wants. God does everything in a way that is diametrically opposed to the way the world would do it. He is pure love. The world is tainted by greed, competition, unholiness, unrighteousness, impurity, fear, malice and many other terrible things. But God is not affected by those sins. He can see what we can't see. He looks at the heart.

Some of the people whom God considers worthy of His love—like those beggars on the dump in Mexico—are ones we might pass by and even deliberately avoid. But these are the ones who attract God. These people make Him want to move in and help. His compassion is so strong.

Psalm 103:8 says, "The LORD is compassionate and gracious, slow to anger, abounding in love." Verse 13 adds, "As a father has compassion on his children, so the LORD has compassion on those who fear him..."

Ask God to open your eyes and heart to the poor around you and around the world. Ask Him to help you see them with His eyes so you can love and pursue them the way He does.

Sheep and Goats

While Heidi and I lived in Hong Kong, it was the fourth richest city in the world. But the community we lived in was not among the wealthy. It was so cramped and full of people living on top of one another. In fact, our apartment complex alone had over 60,000 people in it. We could have had the biggest church in Asia without ever leaving home.

It was so cramped I couldn't even go for a jog. I simply had to run up and down thirty flights of stairs. People gave us cars while we were living there, and we gave them back. In that part of the city, there was nowhere to park a bike, let alone a car. It was overcrowded and oppressive. But we could have spent our whole lives in one alley ministering to the thousands in the slums behind some glittering hotel. The needs were very great.

We had started a little church there that was open 24/7. It was called the Home of Loving Believers, and that is what we set out to be. Lonely, broken people came to our church at all hours of the day and night. We had huge woks of Chinese noodles on the stoves. Prayer teams and counselors were available for people to talk with, and we were open all the time. This was church. People came in off the streets all day with all kinds of problems, and God moved mightily in that cramped place.

In everything we did, we aimed to be what Jesus taught in Matthew 25, where He summarized everything He had taught His disciples for three years. He told them that when they fed someone, they were feeding Him.

We gave people water in Jesus' name. We held the hands of the dying in Jesus' name. We fed the hungry in Jesus' name. We tried to radically live out the Bible. We went lower still. We could have said, "There is no room here" and made that our excuse for not starting something. But wherever there are people, God has plans.

Today I encourage you to ask Him about His plans for the people around you, for the places that seem too inconvenient. He has a plan.

Take Your Inheritance

Matthew 25 is a scary chapter in the Bible. It does not make for comfortable reading. What makes you a sheep and not a goat? It is about meeting people's basic needs.

The most loving, power-packed, amazing thing you can do for people who are thirsty is to give them water—to treat them how you would want them to treat you. That is the pure love of God in action. That is what starts revivals.

"I was hungry and you fed me. I was in prison and you visited me. You loved me in a way that I could feel, appreciate and receive." This is the kind of love God wants us to show. Why? Because we are showing that love to God Himself. "Truly I tell you, whatever you did for one of the least of these brothers and sisters of mine, you did for me" (Matthew 25:40).

Jesus is clear that the sheep go on the right and goats go on the left. A divine reckoning happens based on what we have done to the least of these. If we see someone who needs a drink and we turn that person down, we are saying no, not just to that person but to Jesus, too. That is a dangerous decision with eternal consequences.

Recently, we did an outreach where we dug a new well in a village. Before that, they had to walk once a week to a distant, muddy water hole for new water. It would not have helped them if we had arrived and preached about all the glories of heaven and then said, "Sorry we can't help you get clean water." No, we had to give them a drink as well.

We shouldn't pass by, walk by, cross over or move away when we see the unsavory, unlovely and needy. We should be the first to talk to them and try to meet their needs in some way. This is the sobering difference between those to whom Jesus says "Take your inheritance," and those to whom He says, "Depart from me."

Ask God today what you can do for the least of these.

Jesus' Correction

Jesus steers us constantly toward the lowest of the low and the least of these. This does not make sense to the world. In fact, it looks foolish, like a big waste of time and resources. But if we refuse people something as simple as food in their stomachs or water in their cups—and look for someone more worthy of our dollars and our time—we have said that to Jesus, too. We have said no to part of Him.

Jesus gave us the parable in Matthew 25 to correct us. It gives us heaven's perspective. We can't look to business management schools for growth models instead of looking to Jesus. We can't emulate executive leadership styles; otherwise, we will end up looking like corporations. Christians are meant to be as different from that as possible. We need to start where nobody else is. We need to start where nobody else does. We have to start with the most helpless and least influential people. This is where Jesus starts.

Years ago, when we were asking Jesus where we should go, I got a copy of Time Magazine and read about a horrendous civil war in east Africa. The war in Mozambique had lasted decades and killed many more people than were killed in Iraq, Bosnia, Vietnam or any other modern war. The country was run by cruel communists. Christians were summarily persecuted, and every Christian family had someone in jail. Red Cross trucks were blown up on sight. The average age in the army at the end of the war was twelve. But before the U.N. arrived to inspect the country at the end of the war, the government rounded up all the boy soldiers and machine-gunned them into a pit. It was the poorest most desperate place on the planet.

Hardly any public buildings still stood. There were only bomb craters. People were on government rations. Street kids were eating dead rats in the gutters.

My instant reaction, after reading the article, was, "Let's go there!" And so we did.

What place of need is God putting on your heart today? What can you do for the lowest and least?

Ninety-nine Percent

"Then Jesus told them this parable: 'Suppose one of you has a hundred sheep and loses one of them. Doesn't he leave the ninety-nine in the open country and go after the lost sheep until he finds it? And when he finds it, he joyfully puts it on his shoulders and goes home. Then he calls his friends and neighbors together and says, "Rejoice with me; I have found my lost sheep." I tell you that in the same way there will be more rejoicing in heaven over one sinner who repents than over ninety-nine righteous people who do not need to repent.'"
Luke 15:3–7

We went to a place on the planet that was statistically the most unlikely area for revival. This place, Pemba, is at the center of our hearts, and we have seen how close it is to God's heart, too.

Doing everything in an upside down way, loving the unlovely and caring for those who are forgotten, is such a Jesus thing to do. We read in Luke 15 that the shepherd left the 99 sheep to go out and find the one lost sheep.

This is why we are in Pemba. This is why we are in a sparsely populated part of the world, not a big city or a large town. We are looking for the one.

Jesus' heart to leave the 99 is hard for many people to understand. They don't like the thought of the Good Shepherd going out to look for "the one." That is not good math. It is not sensible. It does not make sense in the world's eyes. It does not even make sense for many missionary societies and churches. It is not a good use of people's resources and gifts. Ninety-nine percent seems like a good ratio. One percent is not a good ratio. It is a low success rate.

But God does not see people that way, does He? Ninety-nine percent of people is not enough for God. He wants the one, too.

Because it is not enough for God, we have made it not enough for us, either. Join us—and Jesus—in seeking out the lost ones in the least likely places all over the world.

Disorganized for Jesus

We do not make any effort to publicize anything we do. In fact, we try to do the opposite. We don't hide what we do, but we don't beg people for money or work to get publicity. We don't need people to know what we are doing. Heaven is well aware of us.

It is strange that, without us saying anything, people have begun to notice what we are about. But it wasn't always the case. Do you know that no one would pay any attention to us if God wasn't in the midst of everything? He is what makes our ministry work, not us. It is not because we have great theology or wonderful teaching or healing gifts or any of that. It is all because of Him.

At the outset, we weren't trying to have pastors or churches. We were just working with orphans, street children, beggars and outcasts. Do you know what happened? The adults around us got jealous that the street kids were being saved and having dreams and visions. They watched as our kids started to preach, cast out demons and see people set free from years of sickness, spiritual and emotional oppression, fear and grief. The dead were being raised. God was mighty in our midst. The pastors and leaders wanted in on it. They demanded that we open a Bible school and teach them what we know. It wasn't our idea. It was theirs. We gave them our first ever building for their students.

We thought we would just have a small orphanage somewhere. We didn't expect a people movement to grow; we didn't expect God to send people of the same heart from all over the world.

We arrived here years ago with no support, no financial back up plan, nothing. Now, somehow, we have put more money into Mozambique than any other nongovernmental organization. Millions of dollars every year go into the national economy through IRIS. I don't know where it comes from. It is God's doing. Not ours. We do not and cannot take any credit for what He has made possible.

What in your life would be impossible without God? Ask Him what other impossibilities He wants to do through you.

Come Closer

• We joke about being disorganized, but I think it is one of the things that makes what we do so "of God." He gets all the glory, because so much of what happens is in spite of and not because of us. He gets all the glory, because He gives us every good idea we have. He gets all the glory, because He brings something out of nothing and specializes in doing the impossible. He gets all the glory, because we are not so organized and planned and set up that we don't need Him. Without Him, we are nothing, and we know it.

• Consider these questions: How is your life strategy? What is it based on? What are your goals? Who set them for you?

• Are your goals based on learning, sound doctrine, other people's advice, your hopes and your experience? If so, you may need to look again at all we have talked about over the last week. Sometimes the wisdom of man is nothing but foolishness to God and vice versa. His ways are higher than our ways.

• Perhaps your ways are too normal, too expected. Perhaps they are based on a theology of disappointment rather than one of majesty. Perhaps they are focusing on the wrong side of the percentages. Check your heart today and ask the Lord to search it.

• Read with me this amazing verse: "And you, my son Solomon, acknowledge the God of your father, and serve him with wholehearted devotion and with a willing mind, for the LORD searches every heart and understands every desire and every thought..." (1 Chronicles 28:9).

Sweet Partnership

We are not lone rangers. We loving working with and helping people from different parts of the worldwide Church. We have not sought these relationships for our own sakes. God has given them to us over time.

For us, one aspect of partnership is blessing the pastors and missionaries God sends our way. Often they invite us to speak at seminars and leadership schools. Such opportunities are costly for us; they mean time away from the kids in Pemba and often from each other. But they are opportunities from God. We get to pass on what we've learned about "going lower" in order to do more in the Kingdom. We get to teach the upside down theology we have adopted at IRIS.

God does not want us to work totally alone. He sends us out to work in teams so we can effectively reach more people. Jesus sent out the twelve, He sent out the 72 and He sends us out. And we are always on a team with the Holy Spirit, even if we appear to be alone.

God does not need us on His team. He could accomplish everything on His own, but amazingly, He loves to partner with us. As Acts 17:24–27 says:

The God who made the world and everything in it is the Lord of heaven and earth and does not live in temples built by human hands. And he is not served by human hands, as if he needed anything. Rather, he himself gives everyone life and breath and everything else. From one man he made all the nations, that they should inhabit the whole earth; and he marked out their appointed times in history and the boundaries of their lands. God did this so that they would seek him and perhaps reach out for him and find him, though he is not far from any one of us.

It is always important to consider your motivation for serving on a team. Do you want to serve to make a name for yourself? Do you want to build the biggest thing in order to boast to everyone how great your ministry is? Or are you willing to partner with others to see the Kingdom come?

A Theology of Suffering

Did you read today's title and think about skipping it? Think about reading tomorrow's instead? I am going to be writing about suffering tomorrow, too. The topic of suffering is a hard one to grasp, but trust me, no theology is sweeter or more wonderful when you grasp even the tiniest morsel of it.

What I am writing about here is highly controversial. Not everyone in the Church likes this doctrine. To be honest, I didn't like it myself for a long, long time. I didn't like the idea of denying myself and dying daily. In theological circles, one group of Jesus' teachings is called "The Hard Sayings." These include teachings like "give up all you have," "leave your family behind," "take up your cross" and "if you try to keep your life, you will lose it." For a long time, I didn't like sermons on those subjects. I wanted to hear about protection, favor, blessing, shields and heaven on earth. I wanted overweight angels on my side to make sure I didn't have to suffer anything.

But hidden in suffering is value so deep and wonderful. It is something many in the West have not experienced. Like I used to, they think the coffee machine not working is persecution.

You don't hear a lot of sermons preached on the hard verses. But let me tell you, they are essential to a holistic understanding of faith, the Gospel, life, eternity and just about everything that matters. You may think that is a sweeping statement, but I base it on a list of Scriptures as long as your arm. The Bible is rich with verses about suffering, but these have not become our bumper stickers and our memory verses. We chose to remember verses like "The one who is in you is greater..." (1 John 4:4) instead.

To be on track with God, we must have a balanced understanding of His Word. Are you willing to accept something from His Word that you may not like? Ask Him to help you be open to His truth, even if it offends your theology.

Lack of Love

Suffering for righteousness' sake is the road to joy. There is no short cut. But what is suffering? I have come to understand it like this: Put very simply, suffering is learning to love. If you don't want to suffer, you don't really want to love.

What do I mean? A lack of love is marked by putting yourself first, not wishing to be inconvenienced, protecting yourself and trying to make sure you don't get hurt. We might call it "looking after number one."

We all have a severe lack of love because we are imperfect people. We get tired. We get angry. We get easily offended. But learning to love the way Jesus loved us is about putting down our rights. It is about suffering. I have realized you cannot demonstrate the love of God if you are not willing to suffer. That is radical my friends.

It is not just about loving those who love you. Anyone can do that. In fact, the Bible says even unbelievers can do that. Suffering is more than that. It can even bring out the best in you.

Matthew 5:43–47 says:

"You're familiar with the old written law, 'Love your friend,' and its unwritten companion, 'Hate your enemy.' I'm challenging that. I'm telling you to love your enemies. Let them bring out the best in you, not the worst. When someone gives you a hard time, respond with the energies of prayer, for then you are working out of your true selves, your God-created selves. This is what God does. He gives his best—the sun to warm and the rain to nourish—to everyone, regardless: the good and bad, the nice and nasty. If all you do is love the lovable, do you expect a bonus? Anybody can do that. If you simply say hello to those who greet you, do you expect a medal? Any run-of-the-mill sinner does that." (MESSAGE)

When was the last time you allowed someone or something difficult to bring out the best in you?

The Fact of Suffering

People get very confused about suffering. They think, because Jesus prayed, "Your kingdom come" in the Lord's Prayer (Matthew 6:10), everything we do must be in fulfillment of that. We want earth to be "as it is in heaven," and we think this gives us the right to not have a hard time here on earth. I am learning to question this understanding. The more I read and dwell on Scripture, the more I find a need for and a value in our suffering for Christ.

Let us look at the million dollar question: Is it ever God's will for something tough to happen to you? Or does He always want you to be protected from hardship?

My theology and my experience tell me God loves me. They also tell me He allows me to go through sometimes horrific and hard times in my walk with Him. If we examine not just the question—Is it ever God's will to allow suffering?—but also ask the question—What is God's will for us?—this will help us.

Was it God's will for Jesus to die on the cross? Yes, it was.

Was Jesus suffering at that point? Yes, He was.

Was God still in control? Yes, He was.

Consider these questions. What are God's purposes? What are His methods? How does He accomplish His purposes in history? We can answer these in part by saying His methods are not ours. He does not need to follow human-made ways of thinking. His understanding is higher, greater, wider, wiser, stronger, deeper, accurate, holy, everlasting, pure and right. Sometimes God allows us to suffer to make us more than we were before.

How does this understanding of suffering fit with the testimony of Scripture? Can you see how it has been true in your own life?

The Reward of Suffering

I have heard people ask, "How could it be God's will for anyone to suffer at the hands of Satan?" I have heard people say that if the early Church had prayed harder for Stephen he would not have been stoned.

I have heard others question why some disciples were let out of prison and others weren't. They suggest it was all about the power of prayer at that time or the believers' faith or something else.

But what if suffering is part of God's will for us? What if by suffering we become more like Jesus? What if God designed suffering as a way to mature us?

Let me ask you this question, "Why is Jesus glorified now in heaven? Why is He so honored? Why is He the worthy Lamb of God? It is because He endured evil opposition without sin. He was tested to the maximum and proven worthy. He was tested and found to be without sin.

We don't get a reward in heaven for having an easy time of things. We don't get a better resurrection by playing it safe and hanging out with our buddies. We have millions of years to relax without any persecution. How would you like to be worthy of millions of years of blessing?

Matthew 16:24–27 says,

"Then Jesus said to his disciples, 'Whoever wants to be my disciple must deny themselves and take up their cross and follow me. For whoever wants to save their life will lose it, but whoever loses their life for me will find it. What good will it be for someone to gain the whole world, yet forfeit their soul? Or what can anyone give in exchange for their soul? For the Son of Man is going to come in his Father's glory with his angels, and then he will reward each person according to what they have done.'"

God will reward us, not according to what we thought about doing or wished we had done but according to what we actually did. Do you want a reward in heaven? Then it is time to question what you allow yourself to go through on earth.

The Scriptures of Suffering

Any quick search of Scripture reveals a whole gamut of teaching about this subject. You don't have to look far in the New Testament before you find suffering being spoken of by Jesus and by those leading the early Church.

I want you to spend some time today researching for yourself some of these precious words from God. I want you to do this so you understand, not because I have told you, but because you have seen for yourself what God thinks about this issue. If you start to realize what is on God's heart in this area, you will view hardship in a new way.

I will start you off with Philippians 3:10–11, which says, "I want to know Christ—yes, to know the power of his resurrection and participation in his sufferings, becoming like him in his death, and so, somehow, attaining to the resurrection from the dead."

This alone is an incredible truth. We can know power, the power that raised Christ from the dead and left behind an empty tomb, when we participate in His suffering.

Here are some other verses for you to study:

- Colossians 1:24—rejoicing in suffering
- Acts 9:16—Paul being told how much he will suffer for the name of Jesus
- Romans 5:3—suffering produces perseverance
- Philippians 1:29—suffering for Christ
- 2 Thessalonians 1:5—being counted worthy by suffering
- 2 Timothy 1:8—not being ashamed and joining with others who suffer
- 1 Peter 1:6—suffering produces the genuineness of faith and results in honor
- 1 Peter 4:12— do not be surprised by suffering as though it is strange; rejoice

There are so many more to find, too. Make it your business to search them out and deepen your understanding.

God has hidden many precious truths in suffering that He wants us to discover. When we understand His will in this area, we will never be depressed or disappointed again. We will rejoice when things are hard for us.

Come Closer

• One of the passages I asked you to look up yesterday is 1 Peter 4:12–14. It says:

Dear friends, do not be surprised at the fiery ordeal that has come on you to test you, as though something strange were happening to you. But rejoice inasmuch as you participate in the sufferings of Christ, so that you may be overjoyed when his glory is revealed. If you are insulted because of the name of Christ, you are blessed, for the Spirit of glory and of God rests on you.

• Have you experienced suffering for your faith? What form did that take? With that experience in mind, how do these verses encourage you? Go back over them and underline the parts that speak most to you.

Let us pray together:

Father God, I thank You that You are so wise. You are so much wiser than I am. Thank You for planning my life to be a life that teaches me and blesses others. Forgive me for the times when I have grouched my way through the day because I have been angry with Your methods or unsure of Your presence. I thank You that there is value in suffering for Your name and that You plan a great reward for those who are willing to lay down their lives and take up their cross for You. Teach me how to do that more and more in the places You have sent me to. Amen.

Discipline

No one enjoys being disciplined. But when God disciplines us, He does it for our good.

Hebrews 12:11 says, "No discipline seems pleasant at the time, but painful. Later on, however, it produces a harvest of righteousness and peace for those who have been trained by it."

Many of us want the harvest of righteousness, and we all want peace, but we are not always keen on the methods God uses to get us there.

I have heard so much preaching lately that does not mention God's punishment, discipline or judgment. Everybody wants to speak about loving people, the blessings of being a Christian, joy, freedom, mercy, forgiveness and the goodness of God. We are afraid to make anyone feel uncomfortable. We speak like sports coaches shouting, "You are the head and not the tail! You can do all things! Be the best at everything! You are an overcomer!"

That is all true. But it is only half the story. It is not all the Bible says. We are warned not to make light of the Lord's discipline because by it we understand more of His love. Hebrews 12:5–6 says:

And have you completely forgotten this word of encouragement that addresses you as a father addresses his son? It says, "My son, do not make light of the Lord's discipline, and do not lose heart when he rebukes you, because the Lord disciplines the one he loves, and he chastens everyone he accepts as his son."

God wants us to understand who we are in relation to Him. We are His beloved children. What sort of loving parents never correct their child? It is precisely because He loves us and accepts us as His children that we are disciplined by Him.

Perhaps you are going through a time of correction from God right now. If you are, try to remember that it is a mark of His love and affection for you.

Learning to Be Selfless

Some people believe, because Jesus died and suffered, we don't have to. But that is not what the Bible says. Jesus died to save us from our sins, not our suffering.

The Christian life isn't about how blessed you can get on earth and how honored you can be this side of heaven. It is sometimes about standing up to the enemy and being found faithful in hard times.

If we look at someone as incredible as the apostle Paul, it is clear he suffered much for the sake of Christ. He was naked, imprisoned, shipwrecked, lonely, ill, cold, hungry and despised. Ephesians 3:7–8 tells us how he saw himself: "I became a servant of this gospel by the gift of God's grace given me through the working of his power. Although I am less than the least of all the Lord's people, this grace was given me: to preach to the Gentiles the boundless riches of Christ."

We hear no complaint in his voice. He doesn't list his trials and tribulations. He calls himself less than the least of all the Lord's people, but his understanding of his duty was to preach to the Gentiles the "boundless riches of Christ." Paul understood his place, and he knew the privilege of his calling.

You might ask, "How am I meant to suffer? Am I meant to be like Paul?" Some people are called to suffer more than others. Not everybody will be heavily persecuted. God is not always looking for actual martyrs (although there are more of them at this time than in any other in history). He is searching for faithfulness in how we handle every day little things. Even in our conversations, tensions and disagreements, during every time when someone disappoints us or we feel hurt and misunderstood, we are learning to suffer. In these situations, we are learning to be selfless. This is basic Christianity.

Rejoice if you are facing these situations in your life now. They are training you for God's richer purposes.

Our First African Orphanage

After we first arrived in Mozambique, we waited to see what God would do. We just wanted a little building where we could take in some orphans. So many fathers had been killed in the civil war, and mothers had lost their lives from unexploded landmines in the fields. Before we arrived, I assumed children's centers would already exist on a large scale, and we would become a really minor player. But that was not the case at all.

There were virtually no children's centers. A few tiny ones existed here and there. But nothing was organized. And needs were everywhere. One day, without me speaking to anyone, someone came up to me and asked, "Hey do you want an orphanage?"

He took me out to see a derelict ex-government building in the middle of nowhere. This facility had once been a center that was well built by the Portuguese. It had workshops, bakeries, dormitories, kitchens and ovens. In its day, it had been well equipped, but after thirty years of war, it had been almost entirely trashed. Rats were rushing in and out of the pipes, the roofs were all caved in, the doors had been removed for firewood, and the overflowing septic tanks stank. A few children hung around with parasite-swollen bellies. Bandits and gangs, still at large, were shooting each other at will. The place was full of demons, too, choking people and keeping them in fear.

The man would brought me there said, "Do you want it?"

Heidi hadn't come with me on that particular visit. It was up to me. I looked around again at the grouchy kids—all screaming, yelling and kicking. I gazed at the power lines sagging down to the ground and sparking dangerously. I looked at the tormented people in desperate need.

"This is the most perfect test of the Gospel I have ever seen," I said, smiling. "We will take it."

If we had been afraid of suffering, that was the last place we would have gone. We had a long road ahead of us, but in the end, the suffering yielded glorious fruit.

What would you do today if you weren't afraid of the possibility of suffering?

The Beginning

The eight kids we started out with were soon saved, and before long they went out preaching and healing others. Soon more came, and it wasn't long before some South African church groups started coming to visit us. Very slowly, we started getting food and rebuilding things. We planted the garden and began to repair what we could, when we had the money.

Heidi is no electrician, but she would go to hardware stores over the border and ask for advice and come back with 300 switches, fuse boxes and all kinds of wiring. It was crazy.

We also faced huge opposition. Every morning we woke up to AK-47 fire from bandits. The local witchdoctors would curse us with their drums right outside, shouting and singing, "Mama Ida! Mama Ida!" and pouring out filthy curses on us.

Soon the government Department of Education heard about what we were doing. Many atheists were among them, and they kept coming to inspect us. One day they told us we were not allowed to pray on site and that no religion would be tolerated. They banned us from passing out medicines and praying for the sick. They thought they would break us, but they were mistaken.

The children all marched out and said they would rather sleep under the trees than not be able to pray. So the government confiscated everything. They kept it all. They took over fifty buildings and everything we had in them. They made everybody homeless, and they put a contract out on Heidi's life. It was so wrong and unrighteous.

All our hard work went to waste. The buildings all fell apart again. Those were awful, dark days. Our enemies seemed to be very powerful indeed. But God had plenty more in store for us.

Have you ever faced dark days? Understanding the value of suffering for the Gospel can give us the strength we need to persevere.

Forgiveness

South African TV reporters heard of our story and wanted us to retaliate. They wanted us to make it public and fight the injustice. It was tempting. But it was not what God wanted us to do.

That is exactly how the world would respond. We felt a real challenge to react differently. We decided to operate in forgiveness and turn the other cheek. We wanted to prove who we were and what kind of God we served.

Eventually, through the gifts and grace of God, we got more land with enough room for the kids we had been given to look after. We used ex-South African army tents to sleep and work in. The government still tried to make life impossibly hard for us, and they refused to give us a license for a school. They were always trying to shut us down and constantly denied our visas. We kept learning more about loving our enemies.

Today, our school is not only licensed, but our students have the highest exam scores in the area. The police round up all the difficult kids and bring them to us. They love IRIS now. Some of the top government officials have been saved. During the floods of 2001, we sat in the Chief of Staff's office as he sobbed, saying, "Our people don't need more NGOs, we need the love of God!"

We never would have gotten that response if we had retaliated when we were thrown out. But because we had turned the other cheek and allowed God to work on our behalf, we now receive great favor. In suffering there is a value that we often don't know about at the time. Only later does it become apparent. Have you ever experienced this in your life?

Loving Your Enemies

In 1 Peter 2:19, it says, "For it is commendable if someone bears up under the pain of unjust suffering because they are conscious of God."

Being "conscious of God" in this way means putting Him first, even when that feels difficult.

Perhaps you read the stories of the last few days and thought, How can I relate to this? I am never going to experience those kinds of heavy persecutions and opposition. You might be right. But all of us face opposition for what we believe.

It might be in what people say to you or in how you are treated at work. Maybe the next time you talk to someone who doesn't agree with you, you can think and act differently toward that person. Instead of flying off the handle and trying to prove you are right, maybe you can stay calm and turn the other cheek.

Luke 6:27–30 explains more about this kind of radical response to people:

"But to you who are listening I say: love your enemies, do good to those who hate you, bless those who curse you, pray for those who ill-treat you. If someone slaps you on one cheek, turn to them the other also. If someone takes your coat, do not withhold your shirt from them. Give to everyone who asks you, and if anyone takes what belongs to you, do not demand it back."

These verses are not an optional extra. They do not apply only to Christians suffering in the persecuted churches across the world. We can all treat those who dislike us more lovingly. Loving our enemies and suffering at their hands is part of the Gospel. We cannot choose to leave this part of our faith out. Otherwise, we will miss out on untold blessings.

Ask God how you can more intentionally love your enemies and those who persecute you today.

Come Closer

• Seven hundred years before Jesus, Isaiah described exactly what His experience on earth would be: "He was despised and rejected by mankind, a man of suffering, and familiar with pain. Like one from whom people hide their faces he was despised, and we held him in low esteem" (Isaiah 53:3).

• How accurate that word turned out to be. In John 1:11 we see the fulfillment of that prophecy. "He came to that which belonged to Him [to His own—His domain, creation, things, world], and they who were His own did not receive Him and did not welcome Him" (AMP).

• Jesus is a man who was acquainted with grief. He bore His own sorrows, as well as the undeserved weight of our sins and pain. No one has ever suffered more—both physically and spiritually— than Jesus. God calls us to bear up under the pain of undeserved suffering in order to be like His Son. No one is pretending that is easy. It is the opposite of our natural reactions and human understanding.

Pray this prayer:

Father, I am sorry I struggle to make myself nothing when others come against me. I pray for those today who are facing hardships and imprisonment or even death for the sake of the name of Jesus. I pray for those now who are trying to work against oppression in peaceful and godly ways. I ask You to strengthen weak knees and give indescribable joy to those who are hounded for speaking out the truth. Amen.

The Joy of the Lord

Hebrews 12:1–3 says:

"...And let us run with perseverance the race marked out for us, fixing our eyes on Jesus, the pioneer and perfecter of faith. For the joy that was set before him he endured the cross, scorning its shame, and sat down at the right hand of the throne of God. Consider him who endured such opposition from sinners, so that you will not grow weary and lose heart."

Jesus was motivated by an incredible force when He was suffering on the cross. If we read the above passage, we see this force was joy. If he needed joy to endure what God had asked Him to do, the likelihood is we will need it, too.

So what is the path to that kind of joy? The Bible is very clear on this in 1 Thessalonians 1:6: "You became imitators of us and of the Lord, for you welcomed the message in the midst of severe suffering with the joy given by the Holy Spirit."

Countless Christians over numerous ages have gone through severe suffering and discovered a new level of joy through it and in the midst of it. The joy does not happen when the suffering is over. It is not relief, akin to respite. It is joy "in the midst," while suffering is still taking place. This is what makes it so supernatural.

Without the suffering, you don't get that kind of joy. The more you suffer, the more you are fast-tracked to joy. We have found this to be so true in our lives. Sometimes, in the worst times of persecution, we have sensed the most joy and experienced the sweetest communion with Jesus and with each other.

We are truly motivated by joy. It is a driving force in our lives. There is a reason that the Bible declares in Nehemiah 8:10, "...the joy of the Lord is your strength." It is true. We have found it to be so.

Have you experienced the joy of the Lord as your strength?

In the Midst

I used to think most of the Christian walk was about "toughing it out"—enduring suffering, living with disappointment and struggling through hardship. But I have realized something very precious, especially in the last year, as God has been teaching me and training me.

James 1:2–4 says, "Consider it pure joy, my brothers and sisters, whenever you face trials of many kinds, because you know that the testing of your faith produces perseverance. Let perseverance finish its work so that you may be mature and complete, not lacking anything."

Suffering has purpose. Understanding this changes how we feel about undergoing it.
Having joy because of trials in this way bears so much fruit. It actually leads us to a place where we are truly mature in Christ and lack nothing. Joy fills in the gaps.

In 2 Corinthians 8:2, Paul writes, "In the midst of a very severe trial, their overflowing joy and their extreme poverty welled up in rich generosity." Joy doesn't change circumstances, but it does change our attitude toward what we face.

Joy is a fruit of the Spirit. It is part of the Holy Spirit's character (see Galatians 5:22). He loves to bring "...the oil of joy instead of mourning, and a garment of praise instead of a spirit of despair..." (Isaiah 61:3).

What about you? Are you a carrier of joy or misery? How would people describe you? Would they say you lighten the atmosphere around you, or do you add to the heaviness? Being joyful is not the same as being happy. Happiness depends on outward things, but joy wells up from within.

All of us can feel relief and contentment when we have come through a hard time. We can rejoice and praise God for how He has brought us out of it. But the challenge is, how joyful are we in the midst of it?

Everyday Joy

I could not do what I do without the joy of the Lord. Heidi is the same. We could not operate with a small amount of joy. We are quite greedy in regard to the amount we need. And God always supplies us with the levels we require and so much more. There is an avalanche of Scripture pointing us to our need for joy and the source of all our joy.

We have been heavily and widely criticized for our involvement in and support of the Toronto Blessing, which had, as one of its hallmark manifestations, what some have termed "holy laughter." There was much controversy in the Church about this particular sign. A lot of people found it uncomfortable and sought to question its authenticity as a mark of God's presence.

We understand nothing is more irritating to joyless people than joy. It is annoying for the unhappy to see happiness where it makes no sense. Those who laughed were criticized for cheapening the Holy Spirit or demeaning the power of God. Some of the biggest and most famous preachers threw their weight behind the opposition crying, "God is nothing to laugh about!"

I disagree. I think if you can't be joyful about grace, eternal life, total forgiveness, mercy, peace, joy, life in all its fullness, then you can't laugh about anything. There is so much to be happy about when we know, love and serve Jesus.

I also think a sign of an accurate manifestation of God is the longevity of the impact. I was not filled with the Spirit on one day in 1994 and never again. The Holy Spirit has filled me and Heidi with the same joy ever since. That's twenty years worth of joy. Not twenty minutes.

Our joy motivates us to love like Jesus loved. Our joy gives us energy to go out into the world and make disciples. Our joy gives us protection against depression, oppression, illness, fear, apathy and listlessness. I value my joy and guard it more than anyone else I know.

If you can show the joy of the Lord while suffering, the world takes notice. So does heaven.

So, are you a joyful person?

Not Ashamed

For I am not ashamed of the gospel, because it is the power of God that
brings salvation to everyone who believes...
Romans 1:16

At times in my ministry, I have felt really out of control. I haven't always
understood what God was doing. But I am not embarrassed or ashamed of
anything He does. I am not going to put on a severe face when I talk about
the Lord to please someone who tells me I need to be more reverent. I don't
set out to offend people, of course. But some people can be horrified by
Christians acting a little less than sober in church.

We cannot please everybody, and we are not meant to. I find that so liberating.
Our master is not another person. Our Master is God. As long as He is
pleased with how we are living and what we are offering, we are all good.

For every email I get complaining about how someone showed a sign of
manifestation that was somehow distracting and unhelpful, I get ten from
people who are extremely interested when they see someone showing signs
of God's presence.

They can't help but say, "Wow! God is in the room. Tell me more." They are
hungry. They are thirsty.

Don't let people decide what your meetings should look like or what should
happen in them. Don't let people define how you worship God and how you
pray. Let God do what He wants to do in you.

God doesn't need a PR agent to tell Him how to come across, how to make
Himself look better and protect His reputation. But sometimes we treat
Him as though this is what He needs. We question what we will put on our
Facebook and think about how what we share about Him is coming across.
That is good, as long as we are not ashamed.

The Gospel is power. As Romans 1:16 says, it is the "power of God that brings
salvation." God will work His way in His time. We just need to join in.

Running a Mission School

People often ask Heidi and me for nuggets of wisdom on how to run missions. They expect to receive training in practical things that will enable them to go out onto the field.

Some expect to be taught how to repair Land Rovers or set up satellite Internet dishes or solder mic cables when the sound goes down. All of those things matter, of course, but we don't major on them first.

We spend a great deal of time talking about who people are and what their personal devotional lives with God are like. We talk about joy, about being in love with the Lord and about being filled with Holy Spirit.

We ask people, "Why would anybody want to be converted under your ministry?" We have to understand that the average person out there— whatever and wherever they are—doesn't wake up one morning longing to be a "convert." They don't want to add to your statistics on your church growth projection chart. They don't care who you are. They don't care if you're a famous preacher. They don't care how many followers you have on Twitter. They don't care about your reputation. They don't want to be argued with, manipulated, used or persuaded. They don't want to be a testimony on your website. They don't care about your ambitions at all. They don't know why you are there.

Because of this, we need to ask, What is it that people really want?

Time and time again, we have found that people want to be loved and cared for. They want someone to commit to friendship with them. They don't want the kind of friendship that says, "I will only care for you if you come to my church or are part of my Bible study group." They want friendship that says, "I want you to be part of my life."

Are you willing to be that kind of person?

Loving People In

Before I became a missionary, I had a job in the U.S. I had a Mormon friend there, and I also had a Mormon boss. I could hardly do my work because my boss was so busy trying to convert me. I wanted to tell him to leave me alone so I could just get on with my job, but he was totally insistent. One time, I hinted that maybe Joseph Smith had done something wrong. His neck veins bulged, and he got so upset. The four letter words he used on me were incredible. It was a prime example of how not to witness. Poor man.

I tried a few things on him, too. I took him to a meeting where a man who was an expert in cults was speaking against Mormonism. My boss' response afterward was, "If that man is going to heaven, I don't want to be there!" We had a stalemate.

How do you witness to people who are so set in their ways and their beliefs? We may be so fervent and eager to share the Gospel that we do it in all the wrong ways. I ended up turning my boss off to Christianity even more. I kept trying to win the argument, not the man.

The thing is, people have to want what we have. They have to see something in our lives and see it missing from their own. If they can't see anything attractive and real and lasting in you, they will run a mile or stay where they are. They will even try to convert you.

One of the earliest lessons we learned in Indonesia—which was at that time 90 percent Muslim—was this. If you see someone holding a valuable silver bowl, you don't throw mud on it. You show them your gold bowl.

We are not called to make people feel bad about what they have. It is all they know, and it will take time for them to see the truth. We are called to make them feel good about what we have.

Do you do this? Does your life show people there is something golden about your relationship with God?

Come Closer

- Some of Heidi's earliest visions of Jesus were some of the most significant for our ministry. She has suffered over the years with bouts of chronic fatigue syndrome and multiple sclerosis. During one of the times when she was very ill, she had a vision of Jesus. He offered her a drink. But it was not a cup of comfort, ease and rest. He said to her, "Heidi, this is a cup of suffering and joy. Will you drink it?"

- Heidi told Jesus she would. We have been drinking from that cup ever since. Why? That is what He offered us. He didn't offer us a year's vacation for good service or a cup of influence in the world. He offered us suffering and joy.

- What do you think that cup has meant to us? How do you think it has helped us continue? That precious drink has kept us from becoming bland and boring. It has kept our hearts soft and our eyes focused. It has kept us humble and low.

- You might read that and think, I really hope Jesus doesn't give me that cup, too. It's not what I want at all! You would not be alone. I don't think any of us would naturally choose the hard road in life. But somehow God gives us the grace, time and time again, to spend ourselves on behalf of the poor.

Pray today that God would show you what this means for you.

"...If you do away with the yoke of oppression, with the pointing finger and malicious talk, and if you spend yourselves on behalf of the hungry and satisfy the needs of the oppressed, then your light will rise in the darkness, and your night will become like the noonday." (Isaiah 58:9–10)

Stop Arguing

When wanting to reach out to someone who is not a Christian, it is not wise to say, "My way is better. Your way is bad." That is not going to win anyone for Christ.

With my Mormon boss at work, a long time went by before anything happened. I wasn't getting anywhere. So I tried a totally different tactic. I stopped trying to fight and argue with him. At college, I had been used to comparing and analyzing things. I had made arguing my case a mental exercise. But I began to realize that even the best argument in the world couldn't make someone want what I had. I stopped doing that. I started sharing what meant a lot to me instead.

I told him the story of the thief on the cross in Luke 23:41–43:

"[The criminal said,] 'We are punished justly, for we are getting what our deeds deserve. But this man has done nothing wrong.' Then he said, 'Jesus, remember me when you come into your kingdom.' Jesus answered him, 'Truly I tell you, today you will be with me in paradise.'"

I shared how this man didn't have the chance to do one good thing for Jesus. My boss told me Mormons don't believe Jesus meant paradise as in "proper" heaven, but as some kind of lesser heaven. Again, I wasn't getting anywhere.

After months and months, one day out of nowhere, my boss said, "Rolland, I want you to come home with me and spend time with me and my wife. I want what you have."

Finally. God had been working on the inside of this man's heart without any help (or hindrance) from me. He got saved and then became a really key leader in Ex-Mormons for Jesus. He is amazing.

People have to want what you have. It doesn't do any good to preach and scream and argue and reason with them. They may need some time to come to their own conclusions. What can you do to live in a way that causes people to want what you have?

Immanuel

What are people looking for? I think it is this: They want to see if God is with us.

If people can tell God is with you, it will get their attention. If they can see He is walking around with you, living your life with you, it will be so intriguing to them. This is why I cannot and would not ever cover up the manifestations of God's presence in our midst.

To people who have put God in a severely limited box, this kind of thing is annoying, but those with no preconceptions find it exciting. Often, we only have to give them a taste of His love and what it feels like to be known by God, and that is enough to build their hunger for more.

We have learned in Mozambique that you could build a beautiful church in a big town and put in a great sound system, and it would just stand empty. People are not interested in going to church here. But if we go to a village and God starts healing people and reaching into their lives, people will come. They will walk barefoot for a week. They will cross rivers and ravines and encounter hunger and danger if they hear Jesus is there. That is all they want to know. They don't care about us and our ministry. They don't want to know why we are there. They just want to know if God is with us.

During the floods in 2001, we found that people's spiritual hunger was higher than their physical hunger. Yes, they needed bread and food, but what they wanted more was to know God was there. They wanted somebody to lead them to reality, to God and to salvation. They wanted someone to give them life. If people see you have this, they will automatically want it, too.

Paul explained this well when he wrote, "Do everything without grumbling or arguing, so that you may become blameless and pure, 'children of God without fault in a warped and crooked generation.' Then you will shine among them like stars in the sky as you hold firmly to the word of life..." (Philippians 2:14–16).

Dwell

Psalm 91:1–5 says,

"Whoever dwells in the shelter of the Most High will rest in the shadow of the Almighty. I will say of the LORD, 'He is my refuge and my fortress, my God, in whom I trust.' Surely he will save you from the fowler's snare and from the deadly pestilence. He will cover you with his feathers, and under his wings you will find refuge; his faithfulness will be your shield and rampart. You will not fear the terror of night, nor the arrow that flies by day.'"

One of our friends is a staunch Muslim. His family has lived in Mozambique for five generations. When it comes to unburdening his heart, for some reason he has chosen us. He is a deep thinker, and he loves to talk about democracy, freedom, religion, politics and all kinds of things I enjoy discussing, too. He calls when he is sick. He calls at midnight. He calls me all the time. He is a Muslim, but he is stuck with a Christian missionary as a close friend.

One night we were talking around the dinner table. He was really uptight and stressed. He told me he wanted to move to somewhere nice, that he was fed up with Africa. Then he asked, "What's wrong with you? Why are you so peaceful? Aren't you afraid? Don't you feel your life is in danger here?"

I smiled. "No, I am not afraid," I said. "I dwell in safety."

One night soon afterward, he called me. "Rolland, would you come over to my house and just talk to me? I need a spiritual counselor."

He wanted what I had. He wanted to dwell in safety and feel secure.

Simply being a person who carries peace is so incredibly influential. If we are not stressed and anxious, it is such a witness to others. They may be infuriated by it, but they will question it. "What makes that person so happy? Why is that person so peaceful?"

Above all, people want security. If we show them we dwell in that place with God, they will naturally ask for more.

Are you a peace carrier? Ask God how you can make this more of a reality in your life.

Dwelling in Safety

What does it mean to dwell in safety? The Scriptures are full of passages using this word. Psalm 4:8 says, "In peace I will lie down and sleep, for you alone, LORD, make me dwell in safety."

As David was writing this, he was on the run from Saul, hiding in a cave. He was surrounded by Saul's warriors. You would think he would have been anxious or frustrated and angry about his situation. But this verse shows us how at peace he was. He knew God and God alone allowed him to dwell in safety.

In the Amplified version of this verse, we read the extra words "for You, Lord, alone make me dwell in safety and confident trust" (emphasis added).

We receive daily death threats on our cell phones, but we both lie down and sleep. Why? Because we know who is in charge of us, and we know He is not leaving us alone. All around us can be chaos and disorder, but we can dwell in safety and in peace.

Our peace isn't dependant on us understanding anything. It doesn't mean we have to solve all our problems. It doesn't mean we know what we are doing all the time. It means we can dwell with someone who does.

Proverbs 1:33 says, "But whoever listens to me will dwell safely, and will be secure, without fear of evil" (NKJV). That is just priceless. Especially when you have enemies like ours.

In whom do you place your confident trust? Is your faith allowing you to dwell in safety right now?

Dwelling in God

I believe there are better ways to have peace than to use guns to protect yourself. I can't blame people for wanting to protect their families in this way, but I know another way of doing it.

When my grandfather was a missionary, he lived in a wild and crazy bandit town in China. The outlaws would set fire to houses and steal from anybody. But they could not burn down my grandfather's orphanage. It wasn't because they did not try. They threw fire bombs over the walls. They tried to set light to the roof. The house just would not burn. This did not make sense. It was an old, dry, wooden Chinese house, like every other around it. But it would never burn. Not even a little. Word got out to the bandits. "We can steal from anywhere we want. But we can't steal from the orphanage. Jesus lives there. We can't burn it down. Jesus lives there."

My grandfather never had anything stolen from that house, even though the town was knee deep in thieves and robbers. Why? I think it was because he knew who protected him.

Think about Psalm 27:4: "One thing I ask from the LORD, this only do I seek: that I may dwell in the house of the LORD all the days of my life, to gaze on the beauty of the LORD and to seek him in his temple."

If you could ask the Lord for one thing, what would it be? Would it be the same thing David was asking for in this psalm?

We need to develop such a presence of God in our lives that people can sense Him with us and in us. When God is over us in this way, even our property is soaked in His power. It will not even burn when set alight.

We can dwell in safety when we dwell in God.

Longing

When people see God is with us and for us, they want to know how they can get to that place, too. They don't just want what we have; they want to live where we live. I have encountered countless people over the years who have asked, "Can I live there, too? Can I be in that place where God dwells?"

And of course, the answer is yes. We only need to whet people's appetite for God. We don't need to try to convert, fix or change them. That is not our role.

Our job is to pitch a tent in God. To dwell in Him. That's a whole lot more profound than having a to-do list. Nobody wants that. If people can tell you are living securely in God, it will be attractive to them.

Psalm 61:4–5 says, "I long to dwell in your tent forever and take refuge in the shelter of your wings. For you, God, have heard my vows; you have given me the heritage of those who fear your name." David, the warrior and giant slayer, was not asking God to enable Him to capture cities or gain power. He was saying the one thing he wanted was to take refuge in God.

What about you? Are you secure? Are you living in the shelter of God's wings? What is the longing of your heart?

Do you carry that longing around with you with such a passion that it is obvious to everyone around you?

God Dwelling in Us

Conversations will not last long if you have nothing anyone is interested in hearing. Opportunities to witness will be short if you open your mouth and don't say what God tells you to say. If you show up in a village somewhere to preach, you will find out in a hurry whether the people there are interested in listening to you or not.

So much of what we say isn't what we say at all. It is the way we say it. It is the authority we speak it from and the experience behind our words that counts. People do not want to hear about rules and lists. They want stories and testimonies. They want to see the difference that knowing God makes in us.

As in the Old Testament, the writers of the New Testament also used the word dwell. What is so wonderful is that in this part of the Bible, God explores for us not only the concept of us dwelling and living with Him, but also that of Him abiding in us.

In 2 Corinthians 6:16, Paul, referring back to the Old Testament, says, "...For we are the temple of the living God. As God has said: 'I will live with them and walk among them, and I will be their God, and they will be my people.'"

God's great ambition is to dwell among us. It is significant that God does not talk about the great plans He has for us here. He does not mention miracles and wonders and manifestations. He talks about belonging. "They will be Mine, and I will be theirs." There is something so comforting about this promise. We don't have to do anything impressive to belong to God. He is not interested in us because of what we can rush around and achieve for Him. He just wants to hang out with us.

Are you allowing God to dwell in you? What difference has His indwelling made in your life?

Come Closer

• We have been talking about dwelling in safety, dwelling with God and dwelling in peace. This doesn't sound like a great strategy to reach the lost. It is not some impressive missionary outreach plan with power points and lists and goals. It is not some hard-won theological advance gained through years of study. It is the opposite of having to try hard and strain and be tense and uptight.

• Psalm 26:8 says, "LORD, I love the house where you live, the place where your glory dwells." I don't know about you, but I love any place where God's glory dwells. That place, whether it is a slum in Calcutta or a condo on a beach somewhere, will be wonderful. God's presence makes all the difference.

• People can sense God's presence in and with us. They can sense it in our homes, and they can feel it when they pass by us. Something about us sets us apart. It is not how good we are at being Christians but how good we are at dwelling and resting in God.

Join me in this short prayer:

Father God, thank You for Your presence. I thank You that it is all I need. I love dwelling with You, God. Teach me how to dwell more closely and more intimately with You. Help me not to be afraid or fearful of what is around me, but to rest in You. Thank You for Your glory, Lord. I thank You that Your glory can rest on me and on the place where I live. May Your glory attract others my way, Father, and may I help them find peace in You. Amen.

Final Words

Sometimes I am asked where I have most enjoyed living. People ask if I prefer Mozambique, China, Indonesia or the U.S. I honestly answer, "None of the above." I like to live in Jesus. He is my home. He is wherever I am, and I am wherever He is. We don't need anything else but Him. He strengthens us in our inner beings. As Paul writes in his letter to the church in Ephesus:

For this reason I kneel before the Father, from whom every family in heaven and on earth derives its name. I pray that out of his glorious riches he may strengthen you with power through his Spirit in your inner being, so that Christ may dwell in your hearts through faith. . . .
Ephesians 3:14–17

Christ dwells in our hearts through faith. That is one of the most amazing truths of the Bible. Revelation 21:3 adds to our understanding even more: "And I heard a loud voice from the throne saying, 'Look! God's dwelling-place is now among the people, and he will dwell with them. They will be his people, and God himself will be with them and be their God.'"

I cannot think of a more profound and wonderful fact than this: God is with us wherever we go. He made His dwelling place among us.

Where are you dwelling today? Where is your heart living? Have you allowed God full access to your life? Is He truly dwelling among you?

I hope you have enjoyed journeying with us through this devotional. We are so grateful for your partnership in the Gospel. We hope our words and testimonies have blessed you, challenged you and given you hope as you "lean in" with reckless devotion to all God has for you.

And now, a final prayer for you from the pen of the great apostle Paul:

"...And I pray that you, being rooted and established in love, may have power, together with all the Lord's holy people, to grasp how wide and long and high and deep is the love of Christ, and to know this love that surpasses knowledge—that you may be filled to the measure of all the fullness of God." (Ephesians 3:17–19)

About IRIS

Iris Ministries is a Christian organization committed to expressing a living and tangible response to those commandments that Jesus called greatest: "Love the Lord your God with all your heart and with all your soul and with all your mind and with all your strength," and, "Love your neighbor as yourself." It is our conviction that the Spirit of God has asked us to make this love concrete in the world, incarnate in our thoughts, our bodies, our lives, and our every action. Iris Ministries exists to participate in bringing the Kingdom of God to earth in all its aspects, but most especially through our particular calling to serve the very poor: the destitute, the lost, the broken and the forgotten.

We have been sent to places where "love" must every day mean bread for the hungry, water for the thirsty and healing for the sick. It must mean family for the orphan, freedom for the captives and peace for the war-torn. We want always to make our love real in these ways, for as long as the poor are with us. Our ministry is built around the application of the Gospel to some of the most desperate economic and spiritual circumstances on earth, with all the boldness of which we, in Christ, are capable.

As we seek to display God's heart in the outpouring of this love, we have found that we are also constantly blessed by a great many treasures uncovered in the hearts of those we are sent to serve. We believe it is also an important part of our calling to share these treasures with the whole body of Christ. It is our hope, therefore, that every one of our trials, our testimonies and our victories may in turn become life and encouragement for the entire Church – *"until we all reach unity in the faith and in the knowledge of the Son of God."* While our primary efforts are focused on the poorest of the poor, we remain constantly aware that we are enabled to make those efforts through the astonishing faith and generosity of men and women from all walks of life and all corners of the globe. As God has provided for us in this way, so we believe that together we receive our greatest reward, as members of a single people – one body, one bride.

On the national level we are committed to working with indigenous leaders, with the aim of facilitating a strong, empowered citizen leadership that can ultimately take the reigns of Iris's main in-country activities. In our home nation of Mozambique these include the building of schools, children's centers, homes and churches; extensive feeding programs; evangelism and healing; well-drilling; medical care; training programs for local and international ministers; conference hosting and local pastoral care. In Mozambique, without exception, we are also committed to offering a home to every child we find who does not have a family. As our organizational capacity has grown we have been privileged to extend many of these activities to other nations, a growing list which currently includes Brazil, the Democratic Republic of Congo, India, Indonesia, Israel, Kenya, Madagascar, Malawi, Nepal, Sierra Leone, South Africa, South Korea, Sudan, and Tanzania.

Iris Ministries has worked with a broad spectrum of churches with varying theological backgrounds. We believe in the present power and desire of the Holy Spirit to guide, to teach, to inspire prophecy, to give gifts of all kinds and to work signs, wonders and miracles. We are committed to remaining sensitive, flexible and obedient to the day-to-day leading of the Holy Spirit, from the least of our organizational decisions to the greatest. We are closely affiliated with Bethel Church in Redding, California and belong to the Revival Alliance and Partners in Harvest network of churches.

About Heidi and Rolland Baker

Heidi Baker was born and raised in Laguna Beach, California. At sixteen she was led to the Lord by a Navajo preacher while working at a Choctaw reservation with the American Field Service. Her experience of conversion was a radical one; a few months later she was taken into an open vision for several hours, in which the Lord spoke with her and told her that she would be a minister and a missionary to Africa, Asia and England. When she returned to Laguna Beach she began to minister at every opportunity, leading short-term mission teams and enrolling in Southern California College (now Vanguard University) in preparation for going overseas.

Rolland Baker was born in Kunming, in China's Yunnan province, the son of American missionaries. Raised until the age of eighteen in China and Taiwan, he is a third-generation missionary on both his father's and mother's side. From childhood he was enormously influenced by his grandfather, Harold A. Baker, who had written *Visions Beyond the Veil*, an account of the extended visions of heaven and hell that his rescued Chinese children had received at the Adullam orphanage in southwest China during the early 1930s. Later, he was also greatly influenced by Mel Tari's account of revival in Indonesia, as told in the book *Like a Mighty Wind*. After coming to the United States to attend university, he had a strong desire to pursue a ministry in which the same kind of supernatural signs and wonders could flow freely. He met Heidi in a small charismatic church in Southern California, while she was attending Southern California College. Six months later they were married, united in their desire and calling to seek an extreme outpouring of the Holy Spirit among the desperate, the poor and the lost in the unevangelized world.

Rolland and Heidi founded Iris Ministries together in 1980, at first leading dance-drama outreaches in the Philippines, Taiwan, Indonesia and Hong Kong. They were ordained as ministers in 1985 upon completion of B.A. and M.A. degrees in Biblical Studies and Church Leadership. They then moved to Indonesia and eventually to Hong Kong, planting churches and working predominantly in the poorest slums with drug addicts, gang members, street sleepers and the very elderly.

In 1992, after more than a decade of living and ministering in Southeast Asia, they moved to England to begin doctoral studies in Systematic Theology at the University of London. While studying they served as head pastors of the Believer's Centre church and continued to minister extensively among the homeless. Heidi Baker completed her PhD. in 1995. Later that year Rolland and Heidi relocated to Mozambique, along with their children, Crystalyn and Elisha.

Rolland and Heidi remained in Mozambique's capital city of Maputo for nearly a decade, establishing several permanent children's centers and a network of churches. In 2004 they moved to the northern coastal city of Pemba, where they currently reside. In addition to serving as the directors of Iris Ministries, Rolland and Heidi now itinerate worldwide, speaking at events and outreaches hosted by a wide variety of Christian denominations. While at home they teach regularly at the Harvest Missions School, as well as leading frequent outreaches by truck, boat and plane through Mozambique's remote bush country, ministering to the Mozambican church and preaching the Gospel to the remaining unreached villages of the north.

CONTACT IRIS:

Iris Global
P.O. Box 493995
Redding, CA 96049-3995, USA
tel: +1-530-255-2077
email: irisredding@irisglobal.org
www.irisglobal.org